Development and the Politics of Administrative Reform

Westview Replica Editions

The concept of Westview Replica Editions is a response to the continuing crisis in academic and informational publishing. Library budgets for books have been severely curtailed. Ever larger portions of general library budgets are being diverted from the purchase of books and used for data banks, computers, micromedia, and other methods of information retrieval. Interlibrary loan structures further reduce the edition sizes required to satisfy the needs of the scholarly community. Economic pressures on the university presses and the few private scholarly publishing companies have severely limited the capacity of the industry to properly serve the academic and research communities. As a result, many manuscripts dealing with important subjects, often representing the highest level of scholarship, are no longer economically viable publishing projects--or, if accepted for publication, are typically subject to lead times ranging from one to three years.

Westview Replica Editions are our practical solution to the problem. We accept a manuscript in camera-ready form, typed according to our specifications, and move it immediately into the production process. As always, the selection criteria include the importance of the subject, the work's contribution to scholarship, and its insight, originality of thought, and excellence of exposition. The responsibility for editing and proofreading lies with the author or sponsoring institution. We prepare chapter headings and display pages, file for copyright, and obtain Library of Congress Cataloging in Publication Data. A detailed manual contains simple instructions for preparing the final typescript, and our editorial staff is always available to answer questions.

The end result is a book printed on acid-free paper and bound in sturdy library-quality soft covers. We manufacture these books ourselves using equipment that does not require a lengthy make-ready process and that allows us to publish first editions of 300 to 600 copies and to reprint even smaller quantities as needed. Thus, we can produce Replica Editions quickly and can keep even very specialized books in print as long as there is a demand for them.

About the Book and Author

Development and the Politics of Administrative Reform:
Lessons from Latin America
Linn A. Hammergren

This book addresses the problems of administrative reform in Third World countries by examining recent reform efforts in Peru, Colombia, and Venezuela. Dr. Hammergren discusses the politics of administrative change and the interaction of the political and technical dimensions of reform in the three countries. The failure of many reform programs, she suggests, can be traced to their conception primarily in technical terms; the neglect of the political dimension encourages a division between the interests dominating the technical, planning stages and the groups needed for implementation. In the case of Third World programs, this division is further aggravated by the impact of external actors on the power base and orientation of national reform planners. While international support helped establish reform programs in the three countries studied, it also dissuaded planners from building ties with other national groups and from broadening and intensifying their political bases.

Dr. Hammergren explores the sources of program content in the case studies and the notion of reform success or failure and examines alternative strategies for designing reform programs. Her emphasis is on identifying political, programmatic, and organizational variables that can be manipulated to enhance program implementation and effectiveness.

Dr. Hammergren teaches in the development studies program at the Agency for International Development in Rosslyn, Virginia.

Development and the Politics of Administrative Reform
Lessons from Latin America

Linn A. Hammergren

Westview Press / Boulder, Colorado

A Westview Replica Edition

Copyright © 1983 by Westview Press, Inc.

Published in 1983 in the United States of America by
    Westview Press, Inc.
    5500 Central Avenue
    Boulder, Colorado 80301
    Frederick A. Praeger, President and Publisher

Library of Congress Cataloging in Publication Data
Hammergren, Linn.
    Development and the politics of administrative
reform.
    (A Westview replica edition)
    1. Latin America--Executive departments--Reorganiza-
tion--Case studies. 2. Administrative agencies--Latin
America--Reorganization--Case studies. I. Title.
JL960.H35 1983   351.007'3'098   83-6739
ISBN 0-86531-956-1

TO MY PARENTS

Contents

ix

xii

Acknowledgments

This book is the product of seven years of work, several changes of venue, and many more of opinion. As a result, it and I have incurred numerous debts of gratitude along the way. Financial and related support for the field research came from two summer research grants (1976 and 1978) from the Vanderbilt Center for Latin American Studies and a Fulbright-Hays Fellowship for Lecturing and Research (1978). Marcia Koth de Paredes of the Fulbright office in Lima deserves special thanks for her help during the field research and her patience in awaiting the results.

Equally important, if largely nonmaterial support for the broader effort of putting this all together was provided by colleagues and staff at Vanderbilt University and within the Development Studies Program of USAID. Among the individuals there and elsewhere who deserve particular thanks for giving encouragement and advice (although they remain blameless as regards content) are Barbara Weinstein, Margaret Sarles, Fred Hayward, Raj Menon, David Dunlop, Robert Bond, Gene Bigler, Richard Price, and Phil Tiegerman

There is one other group who deserve particular thanks as without them this work truly could not have been done. These are the many public officials, scholars, and other individuals in Peru, Colombia, and Venezuela who devoted so much of their time to answering my questions, arranging interviews, and providing material on the topic. The list is too long and varied to begin citing here. I would like to single out one of them, Juan I. Jimenez Nieto, whose considerable investment of his own time at the beginning of this project may have provided enough impetus to get it over the rough spots encountered later. Neither he nor any of the others are responsible for my interpretation of the information provided. They did, however, furnish the essence of this study as well as many of the pleasant memories connected with it.

Finally, I am grateful to the several individuals who have shared in typing the many versions of the final product. Those with a major role include Betty McKee and Mildred Tyler of Vanderbilt, Judy Alexander of the Development Studies Program/AID, and Sherry McVeigh.

Linn A. Hammergren

Part I

Introduction

1
Contemporary Administrative Reforms: The Experts and the Politicians

"Power is for the politicians... All I
want is to be an expert."
--Karl-Otto Pohl, President, Bundesbank[1]

Over the past few decades widespread dissatisfaction with the performance of public bureaucracies, cutting across national, socioeconomic, and ideological boundaries, has made the need for administrative reform a universal political theme. The same period has witnessed a growing cynicism about the success of reform efforts. Despite the persistence of the problems addressed by reform, a consensus has seemingly emerged among theorists, practitioners, and the public in general that reform is unlikely to produce the desired improvements. This skepticism has not prevented governments from attempting periodic reforms of their bureaucracies, but even when the public applauds these efforts it does not appear to hold great expectations for their success. Meanwhile, theorists and practitioners in public administration and management increasingly have preferred to avoid the term as well as the specific strategies most closely associated with it.

The rejection of the concept of administrative reform is nowhere more complete than in the field of development administration. This contrasts sharply with the situation two or three decades earlier when the wholesale restructuring of Third World administrative systems was a key element of development doctrine. By the late 1960s such comprehensive reforms were being dismissed as overly ambitious, simplistic, and misguided. Foreign donors drastically cut back the administrative components of their assistance programs[2] and it was several years before they gave administrative problems the direct attention they had in the past.

1

Although attempts to improve administrative performance still figure in the development programs of many Third World nations and in current assistance strategy, present activities are on a smaller scale, are characterized by a less unified thrust, and emphasize techniques conceived as alternatives to reform.

This book reexamines these developments in the context of the experience of three Latin American nations: Colombia, Peru, and Venezuela. Its most general purpose is to use that experience to explore the basic issues and problems of development administration and to draw some practical lessons about making and implementing policy to improve administrative performance. While sharing the view that the earlier fascination with reform was unrealistic, it argues that the subsequent reaction has been equally short sighted. This reaction may have less to do with the real failure of real programs than with a wider skepticism about our ability to redirect and accelerate socioeconomic processes. Whatever the merits of that skepticism, the immediate problem is not that the emphasis on reform is worth reviving, but that we have learned so little from its failure. Without an understanding of how and why programs failed, a new generation of policies runs the risk of repeating the same mistakes under different names.

The reaction against reform was accompanied by remarkably little effort to collect and compare data on national programs. There is consequently a good deal that is not generally known about their evolution and outcome, much of which could be used in designing new strategies and approaches to the underlying problems. The lessons come at several levels. First, even where programs failed in the most general sense, some parts did work better than others. There are a number of practical conclusions to be drawn about ways to improve aspects of administrative performance and induce change. Second, taken as a whole, the programs reveal important insights into policy making for administrative development in a national and international setting and especially about the identification and definition of administrative problems. These perspectives suggest the need to evaluate reform and other change strategies as more than single-dimensional, technical (or political) exercises. It is only with a more sophisticated approach to the policy process that we will be able to interpret past failures and avoid their repetition. Finally, the experience raises several points about the interaction of foreign and domestic inputs in the evolution of development programs. This suggests a different interpretation of the cultural explanation for program failures. It also reveals some

important constraints on the long range impact of
administrative and other types of development policy.

In dismissing reform, its critics have left no
shortage of reasons as to why it failed. One obvious
question is which, if any, of them is accurate. A more
significant issue is why anyone had much faith in reform in the first place. The answer requires a shift
in emphasis from identifying correct policy to understanding how policy is made. In exploring administrative change policy, development administration has usually operated in the former area. However, the lack
of attention to the policy process contributed to many
of the problems of the reform programs examined here;
more emphasis on how policy was made might have eliminated several obstacles to its implementation while
simultaneously improving its quality.

The remainder of the present chapter provides some
further background on the theory and practice of administrative reform and introduces a model of administrative reform politics. The second chapter explores the
complications added by a Third World setting and the
participation of international actors. It also examines a series of common explanations for the failure of
reform in developmental contexts. The next four chapters present the case studies. The final chapter returns to the lessons and broader implications for development administration and specifically for current
efforts at management or administrative development.

SOME WORKING DEFINITIONS

Definitions present a special problem in development administration. Standard usage, even of key
terms, is a rarity. Too many concepts chase too few
words, and the resulting multiple meanings are at the
very least a source of confusion. Later sections explore some of the theoretical and practical repercussions. For the moment a few working definitions are
provided for the sake of clarity.

There are four key terms: development administration, administrative reform, administrative change, and
administrative development. The first of these, development administration, is used to designate the subdiscipline which studies public administration in a
particular group of countries -- the Third World, late
industrializers, or less developed countries (LDCs).
In this sense, it clearly covers more than reform or
other kinds of administrative change; it also includes
the study of more permanent behavior and characteristics. The term has at least two other usages which
should be acknowledged although they are not followed
here. Like public administration, development administration refers to the practice of administration in

its respective area.[3] More recently, it has been adopted to describe what is referred to below as administrative development policy, or policies and activities
aimed at improving administrative performance.

The other three terms refer to different aspects
of the same basic process. This is <u>administrative</u>
<u>change</u>, the <u>spontaneous or induced transformation of</u>
<u>administrative structures or procedures</u>. While the
primary concern here is with induced change, it should
be remembered that much change and many improvements
are either the unintended by-products of other programs
or the result of unplanned events or trends. Demographic changes, for example, may have substantial impact
on the administrative system by altering the composi-
tion of the pool of would-be employees. Planned or unplanned changes in other subsystems may have unforeseen
consequences for the administrative sector. Thus, the
political changes brought by the 1968 coup in Peru (and
especially the closure of the Congress and the eclipse
of the political parties) transformed at one blow many
of the linkages between the public bureaucracy and the
rest of the political system, requiring substantial
behavioral adaptations on the part of administrators.
A recent suggestion[4] that reform may not be responsible
for many improvements in the performance of Western
bureaucracies in effect implies that they are the result of such accidental or spontaneous developments.

Where change is not accidental but is induced for
the purpose of improving administrative performance, it
has most often been referred to as <u>administrative re-</u>
<u>form</u>. Reform's declining popularity in development
studies and the effort to find alternative ways to produce improvements create the need for a more general
term to encompass both reform and other change policies. Although it too has shortcomings (and like development administration, a number of other meanings)
the term used here is <u>administrative development</u> or
<u>administrative development policy.</u>

This leaves a definition of reform: <u>planned or at</u>
<u>least premeditated, systematic change in administrative</u>
<u>structures or processes aimed at effecting a general</u>
<u>improvement in administrative output or related charac-</u>
<u>teristics</u>. This definition is an invention. It draws
from the available definitions[5] of reform but is also
the product of efforts to identify common strands in
the uses of the term. Because they vary most, it leaves
open ended the nature of the initial changes and of the
intended improvements. It does not equate reform with
efforts to build Westernized bureaucracies. It does
suggest that reform is a relatively comprehensive, coordinated approach to change and one which assumes a
knowledge of the causal links between the internal
state of the administrative system and its output.

Reform's goal is general improvement rather than the solution of a number of discrete, program-specific problems. How well this definition holds up in the case of actual reforms and how well it serves to distinguish them from other approaches to change are questions addressed in later chapters.

DEVELOPMENT ADMINISTRATION AND ADMINISTRATIVE REFORM: A NOTE ON THE LITERATURE

Because the emphasis here is on administrative reform as one approach to improving administrative performance, the relevant literature is not limited to that on reform. Nor, despite the Third World orientation, is it limited to development administration. While the greatest amount of relevant material comes out of that subdiscipline, some important contributions are drawn from mainstream public administration, comparative administration, and organization theory. While the discussion thus draws from many sources it is chronologically divided into two parts, marking a major change in the treatment of reform during the period covered.

This change is most apparent in development administration. In the earlier literature (roughly 1950 to 1970) reform was the only change policy and was also a principal theme. An abrupt shift, beginning in the late 1960s radically altered this situation. Following a few years in which what little was written on reform programs aimed at questioning and criticizing them, the emphasis is now on outlining alternatives to reform and devising new approaches to improving administrative performance.

In the nondevelopmental literature where reform and administrative change were not central themes, neither one has suffered a comparable decline. At least in recent decades, the attachment to reform was not so enthusiastic and the expectations surrounding it not so high as in development theory. It thus continues to be a minor topic in public administration. The present tendency is to define its scope and aims still more narrowly and to limit the focus of research and analysis accordingly.[6] There are other changes in the treatment of related issues which have affected current trends in development administration. One of these is the emergence of the "new public administration"[7] and the series of literatures on alternatives to classical bureaucracy. Thus, while taken as a whole newer trends in these disciplines have influenced development administration's revised approach to administrative change, their treatment of reform has become less relevant and is generally ignored.

Earlier Discussions of Administrative Reform

For all that was written on administrative reform, administrative development, and administrative change in the two decades from 1950 to 1970 the treatment of these issues is remarkably narrow. Most of the literature and especially that dealing with development, is prescriptive in outlook and focuses on describing common problems and their solutions.[8] The less frequent efforts at a more empirical approach to administrative change[9] usually go to the other extreme, examining broad historical tendencies, but ignoring the mechanics and details of policy making and program design. Both types of literature and, in fact, much of what was written on administrative change, share a bias toward Westernized bureaucracies in general, the Weberian model and the rules of classical management theory. They often unself-consciously equate improvement or reform with approximations of these models, ignoring the possibility that change might take other directions. In their extreme development, they move toward a universal prescriptive model of reform, applicable to all political systems. In the broadly historical works, this may take the form of an anticipated convergence of bureaucratic structures in advanced societies.

With few exceptions, the political side of change and reform gets scant attention. The historical treatments do recognize a place for politics, but only in the grand sense of the clash of social forces. One important exception which lies outside the mainstream of works on reform (and outside the development tradition) is the series of studies on the politics of administrative reorganization and other strategies for rationalizing public bureaucracies.[10] Much of this work is based on more recent experience in the United States at the federal, state, and local levels. Among other lessons, it emphasizes that reorganization and for that matter organization are political acts and that at any point in time administrative structure is the product of the political interests and pressures that have worked to produce it. This political interpretation of administrative organization has affected more general thinking about all types of induced administrative change. It has, for example, reinforced an awareness that reform proposals will be evaluated and manipulated by groups within and outside of the bureaucracy in terms of impact on their own interests.[11] The approach also suggests that individual reform proposals arise directly from the pressures of special interests, although it usually leaves open the possibility of reforms with less biased origins and impacts.

At a different level of analysis but still incorporating some of the same perspectives are a number of

historical studies of specific reform movements focusing on the political forces producing them. The nine-
teenth century transformations of administrative systems throughout the West are interpreted as the product
of new demands and the emergence of new political classes and forces.[12] In a similar fashion, changing administrative styles and structures in a number of Third
World countries have been analyzed in terms of broader
socioeconomic changes and the new demands and pressures
emerging with them.[13] These studies constitute an alternative to the prescriptive and macrohistorical approaches. They are still too broadly focused and too
unconcerned with actual policy making to be of much
help in understanding specific reform programs as opposed to evolutionary, long term change. They frequently share the prevailing bias toward the Weberian
model and the tendency to equate it with improved performance and higher levels of output. As in the general historical approaches, this perspective often
implies an expectation of improvement and an eventual
convergence in structural characteristics by all national systems. Taken to an extreme, these interpre-
tive histories make reform policies seem superfluous.
Even in more moderate forms, they are of little help in
explaining short term efforts to produce specific
changes or in understanding other aspects of reform
policy making.

Development administration provides still a third
approach to fill some of the gaps. The works included
here also mark the beginnings of the disillusionment
with reform. They appear as attempts to evaluate reform programs in a number of Third World countries,
with an eye to proposing improvements.[14] These studies
usually focus on the obstacles to reform -- identifying
such factors as vested interests, poor program design,
and cultural incompatibilities. Unfortunately, many of
the earlier examples still demonstrate an unconscious
ethnocentrism about administrative structures and procedures. They also suffer from a common weakness of
case studies, providing near exhaustive explanations of
what went wrong with a particular reform, but suggesting little in the way of comparative generalizations.
Some more recent examples surmount both limitations by
identifying ethnocentrism itself as a key problem and
arguing that the Western, Weberian biases of most reforms may not be suitable to Third World administrative
systems and indeed may not produce improvements at
all.[15] Where such programs are implemented, the argument goes, the resulting imitation Western bureaucracies create new problems because of their incompati-
bility with their surroundings or because the individual reform measures simply do not improve performance.

While such revisionist criticisms raised important questions about the relationship between administrative reform and other political goals and values, and while they suggested the need for a reexamination of our assumptions about reform, they provided no alternative. Intentionally or not, their major impact was to discourage interest in the entire topic, as witnessed by the phenomenal decline in related research from the early 1970s on. Although writers in this tradition suggested that really effective reforms would have to arise from the social and political systems to which they were applied, they rarely went further in developing this idea. Furthermore, while rejecting the models recommended by earlier reformers, the revisionists often shared their belief in the rationale underlying reform -- the notion that it was possible to produce general improvements in organizational output through the planned transformation of internal structures and procedures. Thus they were not questioning the method -- the reform strategy -- but rather the specific, culturally determined causal linkages and the type of improvements sought.

New Approaches to Administrative Development

The earlier perspective on reform with its emphasis on the prescriptive and macrohistorical as opposed to empirical and policy specific was typical of development theory as a whole during this period. The subsequent reaction, arising both in the perceived failure of reform programs and in the charges of ethnocentrism, was typical of later trends. The reaction was reinforced by changes within the discipline of public administration, and in particular, the loss of faith in the principles of classical management theory. Reform and related themes received little attention for several years and virtually disappeared from development administration.

Toward the end of the 1970s some new trends began to appear. While not couched in terms of reform, they built on the earlier criticisms, attempting to deal with the implied need for new kinds of administrative systems and organizations relevant to the needs of specific societies and cultures. They also built on slightly earlier trends in public administration, management and organization theory which emphasized alternatives to or at least variations on classical models (e.g., contingency theory) and new techniques for improving organizational performance (e.g., organizational development).[16] Somewhat paradoxically works from these disciplines specifically devoted to reform were less influential because of the narrower focus of the programs they examined.

There was still another intermediate group of influential studies. They were more speculative efforts,[17] in some cases lying outside any particular discipline. While often not written by development theorists they had some impact on the latter because of their efforts to devise models of new administrative styles based on non-Weberian principles or to derive such models from specific real organizations which seem to represent innovative approaches.

Finally there is the larger set of writings directed specifically at Third World programs.[18] These have collectively taken the title of development administration although there is clearly an effort to distinguish them from the earlier works produced under that name. These current efforts borrow selectively from the more general theories of management and the administrative sciences as well as from sociology, psychology, political science and anthropology to develop strategies for introducing change into Third World organizations. The resulting approach or approaches are of particular interest because they have replaced reform as the preferred solution to Third World administrative problems. They are predominantly operational in thrust although often accompanied by empirical research. Unlike reform they are bottom up rather than top down strategies whose guiding assumption is that improved performance is most effectively achieved when attached to specific substantive problems and directed at individual organizations or programs.

The new approach differs from reform in its denial of the utility of seeking general improvements in performance through general changes in structures and procedures. It also differs in its implicit models and values. In both areas the influence of the new public administration and related approaches to management and organizations is evident. Perhaps the most important and generalizable differences in this regard are the rejection of the notion of a single correct solution to problems and the emphasis on wide participation in planning and implementation of change. The two are related in that participation by a number of interested groups -- clients, bureaucrats, and others -- becomes a means of defining the problem to be solved and of designing acceptable solutions. It also should guarantee more cooperation with the decisions finally reached. At least at the organization or agency level, the expert is no longer operating in isolation, imposing reforms from above. Instead he or she is responsible for facilitating a broadly based process of investigation, analysis, training and implementation. The extent and nature of the participation varies considerably but the notion of involving groups targeted for change is a constant.

Despite these differences the new approaches do show some similarities to the reform policies they replace. Aside from a common interest in improving administrative performance, the most important of these is the persisting tendency to see this task as essentially an issue of technical problem solving, directed, if not controlled, by experts. The technical emphasis has shifted slightly, from knowing what change should be made, to knowing how to find a solution, but the expert's role remains. This similarity described in the abstract may seem unnecessarily subtle, but it leads to a second shared trait, a continued exclusion of the political component[19] and of the relationship of administrative change policy to the rest of the political system. Whatever improvements it represents, the approach's continued fascination with finding a better answer still diverts attention from some basic questions about how and for whom that answer is being sought.

REFORM AS TECHNICAL POLICY MAKING

A reexamination of the literature on administrative reform reveals that most writers have approached it either as a political issue (that is, one that is resolved through conflict-of-interest politics) or a technical one (to be resolved through expert knowledge and thus with one correct answer for each situation). In practice and in policy making, administrative reform is treated as both simultaneously. The key to understanding the evolution of reform programs lies not in examining either the technical or political aspects of the process in isolation, but in exploring them individually and in interaction.
The quasi-technical, quasi-political status of administrative reform or for that matter all administrative development policies, is not unique. In contemporary politics, the involvement of technical experts in policy making has become an increasingly common phenomenon. There are some additional characteristics of administrative reform as both a technical and political issue which make it somewhat unusual. Still some general points about the "politics of expertise"[20] are of help in understanding the reform process.
We begin with the notion that the politics of expertise involves the addition of a technical dimension to the policy process (or alternatively the politicization of a technical issue) and the incorporation of experts whose technical knowledge is their chief resource. This amounts to more than the simple addition of another set of actors to a one-dimensional political conflict. The experts' resource base is

specialized in the manner and location of its application. Their knowledge gives them an enhanced and in fact unique role in one stage of policy making (i.e, planning) but it does not help them much in other stages. The experts are not powerless, but their power is generally limited to the ability to define a problem and form alternative solutions. Their knowledge alone is of less help in getting those solutions accepted and of little use at all in their implementation.

The second point is that "politics" is not limited to the political arena. It is also part of technical policy making, but under different rules and with different stakes. Here the major conflicts usually precede the actual planning of policy. They focus on the status of the experts, the validity of their expertise, its applicability to the problem, and the boundaries of the area within which they may legitimately operate. The participants are the members of one expertise or of two or more competing ones. Their immediate goal, and a precondition for further input to the process, is to legitimize themselves in each others eyes, and more importantly, in the eyes of those who will make the final decisions, and who in effect they are serving.

Most narrowly defined, these latter actors are the decision makers or politicians, although in some sense all of society is the relevant audience. However they are defined, their recognition is essential to the existence of the technical sphere and the experts' position within it. This recognition hinges on their own judgment as well as the experts' effectiveness in making their case. It is also a product of cultural and philosophical traditions beyond the immediate control of either group.[21] At times the conflict over expert status may involve nonexpert members of the political arena attempting to strengthen or attack the credentials of one set of experts. The case studies provide examples of all these types of conflicts. More important than the conflict itself is the general observation that the technical dimension of the policy process while in one sense independent of the political arena is also a product of the latter. Its precise boundaries and the status and identity of the experts operating within it are all determined by political actors, and form, along with the technical plans themselves, one of the two major links between the arenas.

The third point is that in the nontechnical stages of policy making and especially during the passage and implementation of programs, a different set of resources comes into play. These are the more familiar and more varied political resources like authority, control over elements essential to this or other programs, or popular support. As the experts are unlikely to hold these resources, the dominant actors also

change as do the rules of the game and recommended
tactics. Given all these differences, the "political"
fate of the experts' proposals is hardly guaranteed and
may range from acceptance to rejection to simple neglect. Reactions in the political arena may also cause
proposals to be substantially modified, either through
a second phase of technical readjustment or as a result
of overt compromises. The distinctions between these
stages and their neat chronological ordering have of
course been exaggerated here. There is usually a good
deal more crossover than this simple description suggests. The critical point is that within the minds of
the actors a distinction does remain between the technical and political phases of the process and among the
resources and decision making rules appropriate to
each.
        Finally, there is a fourth point which is partic-
ularly relevant in the case of all types of administrative development policy. As issues develop a technical
as well as a political dimension, there is a potential
division between the interests dominating the planning
stage of a program and those needed to implement it.
This is the result of new perspectives, objectives and
values being added -- those of the experts or the political actors (depending on who one sees as owning the
issue). If the division develops and no adjustments
are made, the chances of a program being implemented
and having its anticipated impact are considerably
lessened. Later chapters examine the ways in which
this division may be avoided or aggravated and the
extent to which policy makers can manipulate it.

POLICY MAKING FOR ADMINISTRATIVE REFORM

        To understand how these four points and the poli-
tics of expertise in general affect reform policy we
turn to a model of the policy making process based on
the identity and roles of the major participants. For
simplicity's sake the model is defined in terms of reform, but it is applicable to all administrative policy. Three principal groups are involved: the political leaders (actors holding political power, but not
necessarily the "rulers" alone), bureaucrats (who carry
out the programs) and the reform experts. Because
these groups have been identified by functional role,
there is the possibility of some overlap among them.
This is particularly true where politicians or bureaucrats are called in to plan reforms in place of more
specialized experts. The result will be viewed as a
hybrid situation; the planners retain some of the
perspectives of their original position as well as
adopting some more appropriate to their new role. It
should be noted that membership in a single functional

group does not necessarily mean an identity of interests on reform, although it does presume that actors
will have similar kinds of interests or stakes in reform. This point is further discussed below; for the
moment it is sufficient to recognize that some of the
most serious conflicts over specific reform proposals
may occur among members of the same group.[22]

There is a fourth possible participant group composed of the public or segments of it. Because its
role is generally a lesser and largely reactive one it
is not included as a direct participant. The public as
a whole or in part may constantly be drawn into the
reform process in any one of a number of secondary
roles, for example as an audience whose support the
others may seek or in a more limited fashion in promoting or reacting to specific programs. Although the
public is often portrayed as the beneficiary of
reforms, the impact of those reforms on the public or
even on select groups within it is generally less
intense and less direct[23] than it is on one of the
three major groups, the bureaucrats. The latter,
intended or not, are usually the most direct targets of
reform programs and it is among their ranks that the
most direct costs and benefits are distributed. This
means that the bureaucrats, because they also implement
the proposals, play two roles, and in so doing give
rise to one of the essential conflicts in reform policy
making. The chief consequence is the aggravation of
the normal mistrust between planners and implementers.[24] The problem is not that bureaucrats are necessarily adverse to change -- they may in fact have recommendations of their own for reform. However, their
vested interest and their desire to control the changes
decrease the chances of cooperation between them and
the experts at the planning stage and so pose further
obstacles to implementation. While the relationship
between expert planners and bureaucratic implementers
is not an easy one in any policy area, it thus becomes
a particular problem in administrative reform.

There is a second major problem arising out of the
interaction among major participants, this time stemming from the centrality of reform policy to their
interests. While in most policy areas it can be assumed that these three or perhaps four major groups
will be equally interested in getting something done
about a problem although not necessarily in doing the
same thing, in the case of administrative reform the
levels of interest are not comparable. Administrative
change is a roundabout way of meeting a number of more
substantive goals (e.g., improved program output) and
the three groups thus have different stakes in the
reform process. The indirect connection of these goals
frequently serves as a justification for the broadest

types of reform, but for actors with specific substantive interests the types of change involved are not
necessarily the most logical or most obvious ways of
meeting their objectives.

Although all three groups of participants are
involved in the reform process, administrative change
is not equally central to their objectives and strategies. The political leaders, with a position outside
the bureaucracy and no intrinsic interest in administrative change, are most likely to utilize reform in a
strictly instrumental fashion for the attainment of
specific ends. These ends may vary enormously, ranging
from increases in power to an improved image, or to the
better performance of certain programs. The type of
changes likely to achieve them varies similarly meaning
that members of this group favor the widest variety of
reform types. The politicians for example are the only
ones of the three likely to initiate highly symbolic
programs. However, their instrumental outlook combined
with the alternatives open to them pose some limitations. Programs which do not produce results rapidly
or at least appear to be moving will be abandoned
easily, especially if their backers have other interests to pursue or other means to pursue them. Programs
initiated by political leaders are also likely to be
less complex and broader reaching than those proposed
by the other two groups given the latter's greater
familiarity with administrative details.

Participants within the bureaucracy are no less
instrumental in their outlook although their alternatives are considerably more limited. Because of
their insider's perspective they are more likely to
propose substantive reforms of one of two types. The
first is linked to substantive program implementation
and is usually promoted by small groups of higher or
mid-level bureaucrats who have simply found a shorter
way for getting things done. A variation on this theme
involves the group of insiders who are also interested
in redefining and redesigning program output. The second type tends to affect working conditions or status
for all or at least larger groups of bureaucratic
employees -- in essence a personnel reform. In both
cases, although the administrative medium is the
natural target of change, the end pursued is very
specific and is usually separate from the change
itself.

Finally, turning to the reform experts, we find a
group with a less purely instrumental interest in
reform. Reform for them becomes an end as well as a
means; the categories often seem reversed. For this
reason, and because it allows them the most room to
operate, the experts tend to favor broadly focused,
substantive programs (true even when applied within a

single agency). Although these programs most enhance
their role, they are by their nature extremely difficult to implement. Thus even when the reform experts
are pursuing objectives compatible with those of the
other two groups, their preference is for programs that
are more complex and ambitious and which thus require
more support. (This seems likely to hold even in the
case of project level, "problem-led" change, a point to
be readdressed later.)

SUMMARY

        Administrative reform, a central element of devel-
opment strategies twenty years ago is today in so much
disrepute that it has all but disappeared from the vocabulary of development theory. Still the problems
addressed by reform remain, and, more recently, have
become the targets of a new group of nonreform strategies. This raises several questions: first, as to what
the reform strategy actually was and to what extent it
differs from its would-be successors, and second, as to
why and in what sense reform failed and what can be
learned from that failure. It has been argued that the
answers to such questions lie at least in part in a
better understanding of the reform policy process, a
topic almost entirely ignored by both the old and new
approaches. A central part of that process is the fact
that reform and all administrative change policies are
designed by technical experts, but depend for their implementation on administrators and politicians. This
quasi-technical, quasi-political status is a characteristic of many types of policies, but it poses greater
problems in administrative reform because of the participants' different perspectives on the stakes involved. In the next chapter it will be argued that the
differences are still further aggravated in the case of
Latin American and Third World reforms in general as a
result of their origins.

NOTES

1. Quoted in <u>Newsweek</u> (April 21, 1980), p.70.
2. The United States Agency for International Development provides one example. During the 1950s and early 1960s when the agency followed a strategy of exporting U.S. administrative expertise, this was channeled through the Office of Public Administration. The latter was abolished in the early 1960s and by the end of the decade most of AID's field technicians in public administration had also disappeared. Despite a renewed emphasis on administrative development from the mid 1970s on (although increasingly under the title of management development) by late 1980 AID had only eight full time management specialists in its entire Washington and overseas staff. U.S. AID, "Management Strategy Paper" (unpublished draft, June 1981), pp. 19-20.
3. Earlier definitions of <u>development administration</u> more often focused on the applied rather than theoretical aspects and so come closer to this definition. See for example, Weidner's "the process of guiding an organization toward the achievement of progressive political, economic, and social objectives that are authoritatively determined in one manner or another," or Esman's "...the role of governmental administration in inducing, guiding, and managing the interrelated process of nation building, economic growth, and societal change." The ideological baggage accompanying such definitions and their inherent circularity argued against their adoption here and indeed may make any use of the term development administration undesirable. The term has been preserved here, shorn of some of its ideology if not all of its circularity because it still conveys an emphasis on themes other than those stressed by conventional public administration. See Edward Weidner, "Development Administration: A New Focus for Research, " in Ferrel Heady and Sybil L. Stokes (eds.), <u>Papers in Comparative Public Administration</u> (Ann Arbor: Institute of Public Administration, University of Michigan, 1962), p. 98; and Milton J. Esman, <u>Administration and Development in Malaysia: Institution Building in a Plural Society</u> (Ithaca: Cornell University Press, 1972), p. 1. For one of the most comprehensive discussions of the topic see Richard Gable, "Development Administration: Background, Terms, Concepts, Theories, and a New Approach (Development Studies Program, U.S. Agency for International Development, unpublished manuscript, 1975).
4. See Victor A. Thompson, "Administrative Objectives for Development Administration," <u>Administrative Science Quarterly</u> (June 1964), pp. 91-108.

5. Definitions of reform are remarkably scarce in the literature. Most authors apparently assume an implicit agreement on what it includes. This agreement has changed over time. Recent changes include an effort to eliminate its ethnocentricity. Still, more "objective" definitions like Gerald Caiden's "artificial inducement of administrative transformation against resistance" leave something to be desired in their apparent inclusion of much that would not normally be regarded as reform. Other definitions worth noting include Montgomery's "political process that... adjust(s) the relationship between a bureaucracy and other elements in a society, or within the bureaucracy itself, in order to change the behavior of the public service... Both the purposes of reform and the evils to which it is addressed vary with their political circumstances;" and Robert Backoff's reinterpretation of Caiden's statement to include a "moral purpose" or intent to "improve the status quo." See Gerald Caiden, Administrative Reform (Chicago: Aldine, 1969), p.8; John Montgomery, "Sources of Bureaucratic Reform: A Typology of Purpose and Politics," in Ralph Braibanti (ed.), Political and Administrative Development (Durham: Duke University Press, 1969); Robert Backoff, "Operationalizing Administrative Reform for Improved Governmental Performance," Administration and Society (May 1974); p. 74. Many writers simply continue to equate reform with the usual "reform programs" (merit systems, reorganizations, etc.). See for example Fred W. Riggs, "The Structure of Government and Administrative Reform" in Braibanti, op. cit., pp. 220-324; and Roderick T. Groves, "The Colombian National Front and Administrative Reform," Administration and Society (November 1979), pp. 316-36.

6. The tendency has been to focus less on what reform should be and more on an analysis of the implementation and outcome of specific reform programs. The 1978 United States Civil Service Reform is one example as are any number of institutional and programmatic reforms at the national, state and local level. Comparable studies have been done of programs in other industrialized nations, once again with the emphasis on policy analysis rather than advocacy. For an overview of some recent approaches, see Gerald Caiden (ed.) "Symposium on 'Public Policy and Administrative Reform,'" Policy Studies Journal (Special Issue, 1981) and Peter Szanton, (ed.) Federal Reorganization: What Have we learned? (Chatham, New Jesey: Chatham House Press, 1981).

7. See for example Frank Marini (ed.), Toward a New Public Administration: The Minnowbrook Perspective (New York: Chandler, 1974); Orin F. White, Jr., "The

Dialectical Organization: An Alternative to Bureau-
cracy," Public Administration Review (January/February
1969); Frederick C. Mosher, "The Public Service in the
Temporary Society," Public Administration Review
(January/February 1971); Dwight Waldo, "Developments in
Public Administration," The Annals of the American
Academy of Political and Social Science (November
1972); Dwight Waldo (ed.), Public Administration in a
Time of Turbulence (Scranton, Penn: Chandler, 1971).
    8. Two types of literature are important here:
first, purely prescriptive works concerned for the most
part with how to reform the administration, and second,
more theoretical writings, many of them influenced by
some of the same premises about what was needed to
improve the bureaucracy. The first group includes
works intended as guides for the practitioner many of
them drawing on classics like H. Gulick and L. Urwick,
Papers on the Science of Administration (New York: New
York Institute of Public Administration, 1937). Examples include United Nations Technical Assistance
Administration, Standards and Techniques of Public
Administration with Special Reference to Technical
Assistance for Underdeveloped Countries (New York:
1951) and United Nations, Department of Economic and
Social Affairs, A Handbook of Public Administration
(New York: 1961) as well as others with a more theo-
retical and speculative component, for example John C.
Honey, Toward Strategies for Public Administration
Development in Latin America (Syracuse: Syracuse
University Press, 1968); and Martin Kriesberg (ed.),
Public Administration in Developing Countries
(Washington: The Brookings Institution, 1965). The
second group which is both more theoretical and more
empirical in its foundations and orientations is best
represented by the products of the Comparative Administration Group. The works included, although certainly
not the worst offenders in terms of ethnocentricity
(and often remarkably sensitive to the kinds of criticisms that would be voiced later), have come to take
much of the blame for that trait, largely because of
their visibility and greater influence. See for example, Ralph Braibanti, op. cit.; and Fred W. Riggs,
Frontiers of Development Administration (Durham: Duke
University Press, 1970). For two critical surveys of
the CAG's accomplishments see Warren Ilchman, Comparative Public Administration and "Conventional
Wisdom" (Sage Professional Papers in Comparative
Politics (II, 01-120) Beverly Hills, Sage, 1971) and
B.B. Schaffer, "Comparison, Administration and
Development," Political Studies (XIX, September 1971),
pp 327-37.
    9. A good part of the development and comparative
administration literature focusing on the relationship

between administrative and other kinds of change fits
here. Examples include Joseph LaPalombara (ed.),
Bureaucracy and Political Development (Princeton,
Princeton University Press, 1963); Fred W. Riggs,
Administration in Developing Countries (Boston:
Houghton Mifflin, 1964) and Nimrod Raphaeli, (ed.)
Readings in Comparative Administration (Boston: Allyn
and Bacon, 1967). The comparative administration literature overlaps the former to a considerable extent,
but also includes works on administrative change and
reform in the industrialized countries.

        10. Perhaps the best known of these is Harold
Seidman, Politics Position and Power. (New York:
Oxford University Press, 1970). Later works in this
tradition include Peri E. Arnold, "Reorganization and
Politics: A Reflection on the Adequacy of Administra-
tive Theory," Public Administration Review (May/June
1979), pp. 205-11; David S. Brown, "'Reforming' the
Bureaucracy: Some Suggestions for the New President,"
Public Administration Review (March/April 1977), pp.
163-69, and Willis D. Hawley, "Even the Best Laid
Plans... Lessons in the Politics and Administration of
Reorganization from the Carter Efforts." (Unpublished
draft, 1980).

        11. The self-serving roots of many reform pro-
posals were not lost on others writing on the topic.
However, this perspective is most apparent in the case
study format, as a means of explaining the details of
decision making. Studies viewing reform in a more general fashion are less prone to feature it. One exception, and an interesting attempt to build a political
theory of reform is found in John D. Montgomery,
"Sources of Bureaucratic Reform" in Braibanti For
other discussions of the political roots of reform, or
"induced change" see Gerald E. Caiden, Administrative
Reform and the classic study of pre-modern bureaucracies, S.N. Eisenstadt, The Political Systems of
Empires (New York: Free Press, 1963).

        12. See for example, John R. Gillis, The Prussian
Bureaucracy in Crisis, 1840-1860 (Stanford: Stanford
University Press, 1971); H. Rosenberg, Bureaucracy,
Aristocracy, and Autocracy: The Prussian Experience
(Cambridge: Harvard University Press, 1958); Brian
Chapman, The Profession of Government (London: Allen
and Unwin, 1959); J. D. Kingsley, Representative
Bureaucracy (Yellow Springs, Ohio: Antioch Press,
1944); E. N. Gladden, A History of Public Administra-
tion, (London: Frank Cass, 1972), articles in Michael
T. Dalby, (ed.), Bureaucracy in Historical Perspective
(London: Scott, Foresman and Co., 1971), and Caiden,
op. cit.

        13. See sources listed in note 9 above. See also
M. Berger, Bureaucracy and Society in Egypt (Princeton

University Press, 1957); R. O. Tilman, Bureaucratic
Transition in Malaya (Durham: Duke University Press,
1964); Fred W. Riggs, Thailand (Honolulu: East-West
Center, 1966); William J. Siffin, The Thai Bureaucracy
(Honolulu: East-West Center, 1966); Ralph Braibanti
and Joseph Spengler (eds.), Administrative and Economic
Development in India (Durham: Duke University Press,
1963); James F. Petras, Political and Social Forces in
Chilean Development, Chapter 8 (Berkeley: University
of California Press, 1970); C. E. Grimes and Charles
Simmons, "Bureaucracy and Political Control in Mexico:
Public Administration Review, (January/ February 1969),
pp. 72-79; Charles Denton, "Bureaucracy in an Immobil-
ist Society: The Case of Costa Rica," Administrative
Science Quarterly (September, 1969), pp. 418-425; Peter
Smith, Labyrinths of Power (Princeton: Princeton
University Press, 1979); and W. Hardy Wickwar, The
Modernization of Administration in the Near East
(Beirut, Khayats, 1962).
    14. See for example Roderick T. Groves, "The
Colombian National Front and Administrative Reform,"
Groves, "The Venezuelan Administrative Reform Movement,
1958-1963" in Clarence E. Thurber and Lawrence S.
Graham (eds.), Development Administration in Latin
America (Durham: Duke University Press, 1973); Gilbert
B. Siegel, "Brazil: Diffusion and Centralization of
Power" in Thurber and Graham; Lawrence S. Graham, Civil
Service Reform in Brazil (Austin: University of Texas
Press, 1968); selected articles in A. F. Leemans (ed.),
The Management of Change in Government (The Hague:
Martinus Nijhoff, 1976), Braibanti's introductory arti-
cle in Braibanti and Spengler, op. cit., provides an
interesting view of Indian civil service reform and
modernization. Braibanti considers the program a suc-
cess and suggests that the reason lies in the ICS's
ability to transform itself without much foreign inter-
ference. See Braibanti, "Reflections on Bureaucratic
Reform in India," Braibanti and Spengler, pp. 1-68.
For a view of the problems of introducing national
planning with some relevance for the administrative
reform dilemma, see Gary Wynia, Politics and Planners
(Madison: University of Wisconsin Press, 1972).
    15. See for example Norma de Candido, "Further
Thoughts on the Failure of Technical Assistance in
Public Administration Abroad," Journal of Comparative
Administration (February 1971), pp. 379-400; Peter
Savage, "Optimism and Pessimism in Comparative Adminis-
tration," Public Administration Review (July/August
1976), pp. 415-23; William J. Siffin, "Two Decades of
Public Administration Research in Developing Coun-
tries," Public Administration Review (January/ February
1976), pp. 61-71; Victor A. Thompson, op. cit., Irving
Swerdlow and Marcus Ingle (eds.) Public Administration

Training for the Less Developed Countries (Syracuse: The Maxwell School, 1973).

16. In addition to the works mentioned above in note 7, see Chris Argyris, Management and Organizational Development (New York: McGraw-Hill, 1971); J.D. Thompson, Organizations in Action (New York: McGraw-Hill, 1967); P. Lawrence and J. Lorsch, Organization and Environment (Homewood, Ill.: Richard D. Irwin, 1969); and Russel Stout, Management or Control? (Bloomington: Indiana University Press, 1980).

17. See for example Larry Kirkhart , "Toward a Theory of Public Administration," in Marini, pp. 127-63; Howard J. Erlich, "Anarchism and Formal Organization," (Baltimore: Vacant Lot Press, n.d.); Theodore H. Thomas and Derick W. Brinkerhoff "Devolutionary Strategies for Development Administration," (American Society for Public Administration, 1978); Steve Andors, "Hobbes and Weber vs. Marx and Mao," Bulletin of Concerned Asian Scholars (September/October 1974), pp. 19-34; Robert T. Golembiewski, "A Third Mode of Coupling Democracy and Administration: Another Way of Making a Crucial Point," International Journal of Public Administration (II, 4, 1981), pp. 423-53; O.P. Dwivedi and J. Nef, "Crises and Continuities in Development Theory and Administration: First and Third World Perspectives," Public Administration and Development (II, 1982), pp. 59-77; and David Korten, "The Management of Social Transformation," Public Administration Review (November/December 1981), pp. 609-18. Two popularized works representative of a larger group which have had some influence are Alan Toffler, Future Shock (New York: Bantam, 1971) and William C. Ouchi, Theory Z (New York: Avon, 1981).

18. See for example George Honadle and Rudi Klaus (eds.), International Development Administration (New York: Praeger, 1979); David Korten and Felipe Alfonso (eds.), Bureaucracy and the Poor: Closing the Gap (Singapore: McGraw-Hill, 1981); Coralie Bryant and Louise White, Managing Development in the Third World (Boulder: Westview, 1982); Louis Goodman and Ralph Ngatata Love (eds.), Management of Development Projects: An International Case Study Approach (New York: Pergamon, 1979); George Honadle and John Hannah, "Management Performance for Rural Development: Local Empowerment, Packaged Training, or Capacity Building?." Public Administration and Development (II, 1982), pp. 295-307; Morris J. Solomon, Fleeming Heegaard, and Kenneth Kornher, "An Action-Training Strategy for Project Management," International Development Review (XX, 1970), pp. 13-20; R. Chambers, Managing Rural Development (New York: Holmes and Meier, 1974); David Korten, "Community Organization and Rural Development: A

Learning Process Approach," Public Administration
Review (September/October 1980), pp. 480-512; D.
Mickelwait, C. Sweet, and E. Morss, New Directions in
Development: A Study of U.S. Aid (Boulder: Westview,
1979).
    19. One of the few exceptions to focus explicitly
on the political dimension is Marc Lindenberg and
Benjamin Crosby, Managing Development: The Political
Dimension (West Hartford, Conn: Kumarian, 1981). For a
discussion of the general neglect of the political dimension in the study of organizations see Samuel B.
Bacharach and Edward S. Lawler, Power and Politics in
Organizations (San Francisco: Jossey-Bass, 1981).
    20. The phenomenon of the expert's role in policy
making has slowly begun to attract attention and has
been approached in a wide variety of ways. As one of
the more explicit approaches, Guy Benveniste's, The
Politics of Expertise (San Francisco: Boyd and Fraser,
1977) is particularly helpful. Other relevant works
include Gary D. Brewer, Politicians, Bureaucrats and
the Consultant (New York: Basic Books, 1973); Arnold
Meltsner, Policy Analysts in the Bureaucracy (Berkeley:
University of Califiornia Press, 1976); Irving Louis
Horowitz, "Social Science Mandarins: Policymaking as a
Political Formula," Policy Sciences (1970), pp. 339-66;
Guy Benveniste and Warren Ilchman, (eds.) Agents of
Change: Professionals in Developing Countries (New
York: Praeger, 1969); E. T. Crawford and A. D. Bider-
man, Social Scientists and International Affairs (New
York: John Wiley, 1969); Jack Hayward and Michael
Watson, Planning Politics and Public Policy: The
British, French and Italian Experience (Cambridge:
Cambridge University Press, 1975); Laurence E. Lynn
(ed.) Knowledge and Policy: The Uncertain Connection
(Washington: National Academy of Sciences, 1978); Jack
Rothman (ed.) Planning and Organizing for Social Change
(New York: Columbia University Press, 1979), and
Frances Pennell Bish, "The Limits of Organizational
Reform," (paper delivered at 1976 Meetings of the
Southern Political Science Association). In the Latin
American context, the most relevant body of work is on
the tecnicos or technocrats and the changing composi-
tion of bureaucratic recruitment. Most of this has
focused on identifying the new groups and their pos-
itions rather than looking at resulting changes in the
policy process. See for example, Grimes and Simmons,
op. cit., and Roderic A. Camp, "The Cabinet and the
Tecnicos in Mexico and the United States," Journal of
Comparative Administration (August 1971), pp. 188-214.
Wynia, op. cit., is one of the few works to focus on
the interaction of the tecnico with other policy
makers.

21. It is clear that there is, within any society, a ranking of expertises with some considered, justifiably or not, more expert than others. What makes an expert an expert, rather than a quack or a dilettante is a complex question, involving general social values and what the expertise is supposed to do, as well as the entire configuration of expertises (i.e., the presence of challengers) and the condition (divisions or unity) of the one in question.

22. Examples include debates between planners over different reform programs, between bureaucratic factions who will lose or gain depending on which program is implemented, and between political leaders supporting different reforms (passage of a stricter merit system of administrative recruitment, for example) whose interests may also be affected in opposite ways. Thus in these situations, alliances could conceivably be formed across the three major groups to compensate for division within each.

23. In discussing the public's role, Benveniste discounts it in the case of economic planning because it ("the beneficiaries") is not directly involved in the policy process. The difference between the situation he describes and that of administrative reform is thus that in the former case the public may be directly and intensely affected but ignored anyway, whereas here, it is ignored, but also not often very strongly affected. (It gets the diffuse benefits). Benveniste, op. cit.

24. Benveniste again notes that the planners tend to ignore the implementers as less important while playing to the rulers. Thus, there already is a tendency for a gap to develop between the two, but in the case of administrative reform it is aggravated by the experts' knowledge that the bureaucratic implementers may be very strongly motivated to intervene. Benveniste, op. cit.

2
Contemporary Reforms: The Latin American Experience

Administrative reform is not a new phenomenon in Latin America.[1] Wherever public bureaucracies exist to implement government programs, it can be expected that minor adjustments will be made continuously, and that there will be less frequent attempts to work more substantial change. In all of the countries examined and in the region as a whole, both types of change are visible from the earliest days of their independent history (and before that, under colonial rule). For example Peruvian administrative historians[2] have suggested that comprehensive reforms have been attempted in that country at thirty year intervals, hypothesizing that this is about the time it takes for new demands and styles of decision making to push existing organizations to their limits.

Still, these earlier reform efforts are different in several respects from the programs begun in the late 1950s. Before that date even the most substantial change efforts tended to be narrowly focused. Although called reforms, they aimed less at a general improvement of administrative performance than at the addition of specific organizations or procedures.[3] They were usually conceived of as of finite duration. While they might introduce new organizations and employ a variety of experts to plot out specific details they did not involve the establishment of reform agencies, i.e., offices staffed with specialists who would plan and oversee the changes.

ORIGINS OF THE MOVEMENT

As contrasted with these earlier examples, the programs developing in the late 1950s represent a distinctive approach to the issue of administrative change. First, they began with a wider notion of the kinds of change needed, and, at the same time, a less specific vision of the solutions to be introduced.

Second, they brought the introduction of specialized organizations with expert staffs to analyze the existing situation, propose changes, and oversee their implementation. Third, although in several cases the earliest proponents apparently envisioned reform as a one-step process with a definite beginning and end, in all cases the programs have lingered on so that administrative reform has become a permanent policy.[4] This permanent status has not meant an equally permanent high commitment of resources. For much of the period covered, these programs have limped along on skeletal staffing and financing. However, the institutionalization of the policy has been important, making it easier to reactivate and also guaranteeing continuities in content and process.

Administrative reform entered this new stage in Latin American politics in the 1950s and early 1960s as the result of two trends. The first was internal and involved the emergence of a general reformist mood in the region's politics and the rise to power of a number of reformist governments. For these governments, and for others seeking a positive image administrative reform came to represent a progressive issue and a symbol of their commitment to breaking with the past. In both senses it was an attractive choice. It promised benefits for all, was less controversial than a number of more substantive and redistributive types of reform, and had a logical connection to the new drive for development in which government was to take a major role.

Administrative reform's availability as an issue and its progressive connotations were conditioned by a second factor. This was an external push, originating in the international development community and a new emphasis in its assistance programs. These programs now defined administrative weaknesses as a primary obstacle to development and promoted reform as a desirable modern goal.[5] The specific types of programs and entities involved in this external push varied considerably, although there was much duplication in personnel, in the recommendations made[6] and in overall effect on the target countries. The immediate result of the program which will be examined more carefully in the next section and in the case studies, can be summarized as a greater awareness of administrative reform as a potential policy among a relatively small group of administrative and political leaders; the creation of still smaller but more actively interested groups of reform specialists; and the establishment at the national level of a more or less permanent program and a reform commission or agency[7] to oversee it. The latter often began life as temporary entities, but later achieved a more permanent status.

The assistance programs themselves began as part of the wider efforts of a number of entities, including the major aid-giving countries (largely the United States, but also several European nations), private foundations[8], and international agencies. They were usually begun as independent undertakings rather than as components of other projects. There is thus a subtle but important difference between admininstrative reform as a contributor to improved performance in all sectors and administrative improvement as an aspect of all sectoral programs. An important early element in all the reforms was the introduction of a corps of foreign advisors to help design and implement them. Although the main thrust of their recommendations and the resulting programs was usually a series of changes in administrative structures and procedures, upgrading personnel was also important. Activities included the creation of training programs and scholarships to improve the technical level of national bureaucracies and to train some individuals specifically in administrative skills. While the assistance was usually well received, occasionally some pressure had to be applied to guarantee its acceptance -- for example the U.S. stipulation that a national planning apparatus be introduced as a precondition for aid under the Alliance for Progress. In other cases, governments were so sold on the idea that they contracted their own administrative advisory team. Whatever their format and whoever their sponsors these early reform programs had several common characteristics: an ambitious set of aims, a bias toward comprehensive change, and enormous optimism as to what was possible.

The common characteristics are not surprising given another common element -- a considerable overlap among their staff. Here the explanation lies partly in self selection and in the specialized set of skills and interests participants were likely to have. It also lies in the reliance on external recruiting. Most of the sponsor organizations did not have a resident staff of expert advisors and so had to contract them, usually from the academic community. Thus they frequently found themselves drawing from the same pool, a likelihood still further increased over time as reputations developed on the basis of past experience. Still more continuity was provided through universities or other professional connections.[9] As donor organizations formed and expanded their own permanent technical staffs there was little break with the earlier tradition as many staff members had either worked with or been trained under the first group.

The participation of many of the same advisors encouraged similarities in outlook both within and between programs established in the various Latin

American nations (and elsewhere as well). Twenty years
after the heyday of the foreign advisory programs, di-
agnoses of national administrative problems and recommended solutions have much in common. Even the occasional disagreements among the foreign experts left a
legacy in terms of the ways issues and alternatives
continued to be structured.

The role of this external push in generating the
region's administrative reform movements and accounting
for many of the similarities in content and evolution
is extremely important. It would nonetheless be a mistake to equate it with a continuing external domination
of the programs. As a result of declining outside interest on the one hand,[10] and an increase in sensitivity to intervention on the other, these programs lost
many of their direct external ties during the late
1960s and acquired a national look. While they continued to receive some external resources (both financial
and technical) and retained an outward focus in their
technology and models, they became sufficiently independent to pick and choose among potential external
influences.

This increasing independence was not limited to
external influences. It also extended to the national
political scene. Once established on the basis of external aid and given organizational form, these programs were able to survive, although often at a minimal
and relatively ineffectual level, without widening
their domestic support and without attempting to tailor
their content to the demands and interests of other
political groups. Their survival is explained by a
combination of the continued availability of external
resources, organizational inertia, and a periodic re-
activation of interest in administrative reform on the
part of the governments involved. It also hinges on
another phenomenon, the emergence of internationally
linked but nationally based groups of experts in administrative reform who have staffed the agencies and
acted as the major pressure group campaigning for this
policy.

EMERGENCE OF THE REFORM SPECIALISTS[11]

In the mid and late 1950s when the first reform
commissions and study groups were established, they
trended to be dominated, intellectually if not numeri-
cally by the foreign advisors attached to them. National participation was of two forms; younger, junior
level members who were to do much of the routine research required while being trained in advanced methods
and approaches, and a few highly regarded individuals
-- either politicians or administrators, one or more of
whom usually headed the commission and so gave it

political weight. The tactic of using these individuals to enhance the programs' prestige was moderately
successful, and often served to protect the groups from
attack. However, having made their names in other
areas, these leaders were usually not overly committed
to administrative reform and tended to see their participation as having a limited duration. Once having
served out their terms they tended to move on to other
areas.

In the three cases examined here, the decisive
changes, and the prelude to the nationalization of the
programs, came with the emergence of a new generation
of specialized reform planners. These individuals were
generally younger than the figurehead group, less distinguished and more inclined to have a personal, professional interest in reform. They came from several
sources, but the majority evolved from the junior staff
of the original projects who had been trained under the
guidance of the foreign advisors. Although most of
this new group already had professional degrees in some
other area -- often law or economics -- they usually
had not practiced that profession and so found this
change of specializations relatively easy. Because
these on-the-job trainees comprised a relatively small
group and one exposed to frequent and intense contact
with distinguished foreigners and nationals, it is not
surprising that the experience made a deep impression
on them. Even those entering unrelated positions at a
later time maintained an interest in administrative
reform and in on-going programs, as well as some strong
convictions about what ought to be done. Still later
some of these former members would become both the
strongest critics and the firmest allies of the official reform movements. They also would be an important source of alternative proposals, not only because
of their interest in the issue but because they "spoke
the language" and had some credibility as experts
themselves.[12]

As the national reform groups began to coalesce
and as the first national leaders emerged, an important
step was taken with the formulation of a reform doctrine or model for each national program.[13] Although
these statements were influenced by foreign input, they
represent a decisive move away from foreign domination
and toward a new independence for the national experts.

In the three case studies the finished products were
an eclectic mixture, borrowing from established national opinion about the administrative problem and its
solution, the more specific suggestions of administrators, organizational and procedural techniques developed elsewhere, and a number of theories and approaches
introduced by the advisory groups or through training
abroad. Where preliminary studies had been done by

30

other organizations in the years past, these were sometimes rediscovered and incorporated as well. The creation or development of some more permanent institutional housing, the emergence of a national expert group,
and finally, this formulation of a reform doctrine were
generally enough to establish each national movement.
An increased national commitment to reform and to the
implementation of the commission's proposals might ac-
company all this or might come years later, but, it was
in some sense the least necessary step of all.

Although these developments and the formulation of
the reform doctrine in particular signaled a breaking
loose from foreign direction, another kind of external
influence was becoming important -- the emergence of a
regional community of reform experts. This community,
composed of leading participants from the individual
countries, and some "nationalized" or "regionalized"
advisors, grew out of and further encouraged contacts
among individual national programs, ranging from the
exchange of documents and members to the establishment
of joint programs. The exchange of information and
ideas further contributed to the cross-national similarities. It also protected the programs from national
and extra-regional pressures. Regionalization of the
reform community provided members with intellectual and
eventually material support. It gave them an audience
and a reference group and so compensated for the relative absence of both on the national level. Regionalization takes its most concrete and institutional form
with the foundation of an United Nations sponsored
Latin American Center for Development Administration
(CLAD).[14] Although the Center's financial resources
were limited, it was able to sponsor exchanges, confer-
ences, research projects and publications, thus providing a forum and outlet for ideas and unfortunately,
further reducing the incentive to seek national support.[15] It was actively involved in efforts to develop
a Latin Amercian reform model as a way of reducing the
reliance on techniques and doctrines originating outside the region.

THE REFORM PROGRAM

One of the most striking aspects of the three
national movements surveyed here is the extent to which
the reform program itself and especially its implementation became secondary undertakings, with the thrust
of the reformers' efforts directed elsewhere. The next
chapters examine the variations in this development as
well as its further consequences, but the general explanation is summarized here. Created with external
support and resources, and directed toward an external
audience even after the more obvious forms of foreign

influence had disappeared, these reform movements and
the reform planners in particular were spared the necessity of negotiating a place for themselves in their
respective national systems. The most obvious way of
accomplishing the latter might have been to gear their
programs to the expectations and demands of other national groups, at the same time calling on their support
at the stage of implementation. However, with the resources they already controlled and in the absence of
any more active national interest in reform (which they
would have had to develop), the planners could continue
to operate, if at a minimal level, without further interaction with other national actors. Because this
minimal level did not include implementation of programs, the diagnosis of existing problems and the formulation of studies and plans became ends in themselves. The presence of the regional community and
organization made these efforts more satisfying through
their function as an audience and reference group.

For all the problems with this minimal strategy,
the periodic efforts at a more activist approach to
reform, one aimed at implementation as well as planning, were not encouraging, even when the reformers
themselves lobbied for the shift. Although not the
only source of renewed interest, the reform planners
have been active as a pressure group, encouraging
political leaders to adopt the issue. Despite this,
the autonomy of the established movements and their
outward focus tended to work against their greater impact. The independence of the existing reform groups
not only discouraged them from looking for greater support; it helped generate opposition by encouraging
their neglect of possible sources of conflict. Two
types of conflict were important here. First, the emphasis on reform as a technical problem caused the
planners to downplay potential opposition from groups
adversely affected by specific proposals. This occasionally produced unanticipated violent protests. It
in turn contributed to the planners' general loss of
credibility in the eyes of the politicians who came to
see them as overly naive and hence dangerous allies.
Second, less violent, but potentially more significant
opposition was created among groups within the bureaucracy who might be receptive to change, but who resen-
ted the lack of attention to their own suggestions and
opinions. Where this occurred, these potential allies
of the reformers, occasionally attempted rival reforms.
At the very least, their reaction was one of alienation
and withheld support.

Thus, ignored, actively protested, or occasionally
challenged by alternative proposals, the ambitious,
highly theoretical, comprehensive reform programs produced by the national movements have enjoyed little

success in terms of implementation.[16] Their failure
hasn't meant the end of the movements. The reform
agencies and their staffs have survived to continue
their studies and in some cases have attempted to adapt
to the less favorable situations with less ambitious
schemes. The details of the programs and their successors are explored in the next chapters.

NINE MISPERCEPTIONS ABOUT THE REFORM PROCESS IN LATIN
AMERICA

As briefly mentioned in the first chapter, the
practical and theoretical reaction against administrative reform has been accompanied by a number of explanations for reform's failure. Some of these were introduced in the literature review; others are derived
from ideas introduced there. Since for the most part
they are inconsistent with the interpretations offered
here and in the case studies, they are briefly summarized as nine propositions on the reform experience.
Unless otherwise noted, they refer specifically to
Latin American administrative reforms, including the
three case studies.

1. These movements have remained dominated by Western
    (read U.S.) beliefs and perspectives and by U.S.
    interests.[17]

Foreign advisors and advisory missions, both public and private, bilateral and multilateral, had a
major role in the initiation of these projects. However, over time the programs have substantially decreased their susceptibility to outside direction. At
present, the tendency is toward an active involvement
in selecting the foreign influences that will be admitted. The unquestioning acceptance of prepackaged
aid programs has been replaced by a situation where
countries request advisors for specific short-term
projects and for the introduction of specific skills
and techniques. Where foreign advisory groups are
involved, there is also a more recent tendency to rely
on international advisors connected with the United
Nations and the OAS and plugged into the doctrines and
perspectives of these two organizations. These movements are still strongly influenced by ideas and perspectives that are hardly reflective of a national
consensus or even of the opinions of the major politicians and administrators; they have been shaped by and
in turn have contributed to an international and regional reform doctrine, on which they now form national
variations.

2. <u>The principal problem with Third World reforms</u>
<u>stems from the limitations of cultural transfer-</u>
<u>rence -- national planners have mistakenly tried to</u>
<u>apply and imitate ideas, techniques, and procedures</u>
<u>which have worked in the more developed nations but</u>
<u>which are not appropriate in a less Westernized</u>
<u>cultural context.</u>[18]

While this explanation may be true in some instances it overlooks the amount of local innovation and
tradition incorporated in these programs. In effect,
the reaction against overt or unintended cultural
imperialism came relatively early on. While acknowledging the lingering influence of some foreign ideas,
the reform planners themselves are a) quick to point
out the shortcomings of across the board imitations b)
equally intent on developing national reforms c) as
influenced by prevailing national beliefs about needed
changes as they are by any foreign assessments. In
some cases, the effort to be unique has led to as many
problems as have the instances of imitation.

3. <u>The reform process itself, that is, the various</u>
<u>steps and procedures involved in a complete reform,</u>
<u>has been patterned after the experience of more</u>
<u>developed countries and is consequently</u>
<u>inappropriate.</u>

If the content of reforms shows a good deal of
local initiative and less imitation than might be im-
agined, this is still more true of the procedures and
strategies involved. For all the early recourse to
imitation Hoover Commissions, the most important models
are based on the experience of other Latin American
nations. This trend continues despite the skepticism
of some participants as to their utility. As in the
case of reform content, there has also been a selective
adoption of techniques and practices developed elsewhere, occasionally leading to severe misapplications.

4. <u>Third World administrative reforms (and perhaps</u>
<u>administrative reforms in general) are insincere</u>
<u>efforts to introduce change -- either aimed at</u>
<u>satisfying the demands of foreign aid donors, or at</u>
<u>impressing local populations with the progressive</u>
<u>nature of the government in power. In both cases,</u>
<u>the emphasis is on doing as little as possible</u>
<u>while appearing to do much more.</u>[19]

This is one of the most serious charges leveled at
these reforms and a common popular assessment. Given

the lack of success it is not an unreasonable conclusion. Certainly, there is an element of symbolic politics in all reforms, and a consequent emphasis on reas-
suring and impressing national and international audi-
ences, but this is not incompatible with more concrete
efforts. Sincerity is difficult to measure, but considering the conflicts they often get themselves into,
most of the reform planners seem to take their jobs
seriously. Insofar as we can trust the planners' perceptions, we can also assume the commitment and sincerity of purpose of at least a part of the political
leaders sponsoring reforms. These leaders have provided the necessary impetus to establish a reform
program or to reactivate interest in it. Their involvement can be traced to a number of factors, but in
many cases, administrative experience has been critical. Where reforms have lost momentum, the decisive
factor has more often been the greater attractiveness
of other issues rather than a loss of interest in
reform.

5. Because administrative organization and procedures
    have political consequences, affecting the allocat-
    ion of values in society, reform is best understood
    as a political act. To understand why one set of
    reform alternatives had been chosen, one must first
    ask who benefits.

    While the assertion that reform is political in
effect (i.e., has an impact on the allocation of values) is unlikely to be challenged, the conclusion that
all reforms are essentially self-serving is an over-
statement and glosses over a number of subtle distinctions. The changes involved in reforms are likely to
affect someone, but it is not obvious that the planners
and decision makers will be directly affected. They
may be completely unaware of the most important dis-
tributive and redistributive effects of their decisions
and so from this standpoint, be neutral. This disinterest may itself be a problem; the case studies include a number of insufficiently political reforms,
planned in isolation from the political system and from
the desires and needs of other actors. Planners, while
aware of the political implications of reform, may attempt to downplay these and create an artificial neutrality. However, arbitrary, disinterested decisions
produce serious conflicts because of their total disregard for the interests affected.

6. Administrative reform is made extraordinarily
    difficult because of the vested interests it
    challenges. These produce the major obstacle and
    opposition to reform.[20]

There is considerable truth in the statement, but
its explanatory powers have been stretched by those who
underestimate how much change is possible. The importance of active opposition has also been magnified
through a tendency to discount lack of support as a
problem in and of itself; where support for a measure
is limited and not very intense, it takes relatively
little opposition to obstruct it.[21] Several considerations further temper the image of vested interests and
opposition. First, because all but the simplest reform
programs involve a variety of very different types of
change, it is likely that opposition will initially be
diffused, directed at specific programs, and of varying
intensity. Second, it follows that the strength of the
opposition and the type of obstacle it poses, depend
both on the resources of the groups involved and the
nature of the political system. For example, because
of their strategic position, where public employees as
a group oppose an issue they present at the very least
a major disruptive threat and thus are likely to win
some compromises. On the other hand, the effectiveness
of bureaucratic alliances with clientele groups to protect interests in individual agencies, seems to be significant only in more pluralistic systems with an
active legislature. In authoritarian systems where
power is concentrated within the executive, such
alliances are much less effective, as evidenced by the
rapid change in tactics after Peru's 1968 coup.

7. The types of changes usually attempted in admini-
    strative reforms are likely to produce so much op-
    position as to be almost impossible to implement.

Once again this statement must be qualified by two
considerations. Administrative reform is generally not
an issue receiving a very detailed scrutiny from the
public at large or even from many of the groups affected. The latter are likely to ignore most proposals
until presented with a more specific idea of the
changes to be made.[22] Thus, there is often a time lag
between the point at which work begins on a project and
the point at which opposition is activated. This delay
is often substantial; adverse reactions may only come
after implementation has begun. It can thus be used to
test out reactions and prepare for opposition. Second,
because programs typically involve many individual
changes, each of which may have its opponents, all do,
in the aggregate, generate a "good deal of opposition,"
but at least initially, each part of that opposition is
more specifically focused. It is a rare administrative
issue on which widespread unified opposition exists
from the start, and even here, with minor changes and
compromises, the intensity and the unity can be

diminished. This suggests that the ways in which
subprograms are presented and timed may be critical:
despite the planners' preference for comprehensive
change, gradualism and the dissociation of issues may
be more practical.

8. <u>One of the major obstacles to effective implementation strategies has been the planners' blindness to
the political implications of their decisions.</u>[23]

The above discussion may suggest agreement with
this point, but there are some important distinctions
to be made. First although administrative experts may
once have ignored the political implications of their
work this hardly seems true today. However, while administrative reform planners (like economic planners)
may be aware of the politics of their task, this may
not be reflected in their planning. In many cases, the
planners' recognition is not shared by politicians and
bureaucrats who prefer to believe in purely technical
solutions (preferably those compatible with their own
interests). This preference strengthens the planners'
control over the planning process, but the insistence
on an image of neutrality and disinterest makes the
delivery of a final product, a plan that can be implemented, much less likely. At other times the planners
may emphasize their own neutrality seeing politics as
an inevitable part of reform, but something which need
enter only at the stage of implementation. They thus
retain a belief in the purely technical nature of their
own decisions, viewing the political part of reform as
best left to the politicians. While this position de-
creases the planners' immediate frustrations, it is not
likely to produce an implementable program.

9. <u>The natural allies of the reform planners are the
progressive change-oriented bureaucrats or technocrats. These groups are more oriented toward performance than toward the rituals and safeguards of
traditional bureaucratic behavior and so will accept change readily.</u>

These more change-oriented groups do exist and in
some sense are the natural allies of the reformers because they are most likely to value change as an end in
itself and least likely to seek security in set patterns and routine. However, these technocratic groups
also compete with the reform planners for control over
change and over the administrative system as a whole.
As practitioners of a related expertise, they are also
likely to challenge that of the reform planners, even
to the extent of presenting alternative reform
proposals.

NOTES

1. Specific studies of Latin American reform programs are relatively scarce. The most comprehensive are those by Roderick Groves on Venezuela and Colombia which are cited in the chapters on those countries and Graham's study of the Brazilian experience. See Lawrence S. Graham, Civil Service Reform in Brazil (Austin: University of Texas Press, 1968). For a discussion of the origins of these and other programs see Ralph Braibanti, "Transnational Inducement of Administrative Reform: A Survey of Scope and Critique of Issues," in John D. Montgomery and William J., Siffin (eds.), Approaches to Development (New York: McGraw Hill, 1966), pp. 133-84, and Organization of American States, Public Administration in Latin America (Washington: August 31, 1955). A series of slightly later studies on selected administrative topics in the region and in a number of individual countries is found in Clarence E. Thurber and Lawrence S. Graham (eds.), Development Administration in Latin America (Durham: Duke University Press, 1973), and in A.F. Leemans (ed.) The Management of Change in Government (The Hague: Martinus Nijhoff, 1976). Reports issued by a number of agencies involved in technical assistance or cooperative programs also provide information on conditions and on reform efforts in individual countries. These agencies include the U.S. Agency for International Development, the United Nations, the Organization of American States, the Center for Latin American Development Administration (CLAD), and the Central American Institute of Public Administration (ICAP).

2. See Peru, Oficina Nacional de la Reforma de la Administracion Publica (ONRAP), Diagnostico preliminar de la administracion publica peruana y propuestas de reforma (Lima: December 1965), p. 1.

3. Typical of these were early reorganizations involving the addition and subdivision of central ministries, or programs in the 1930s to add comptroller generals' offices and other organizations to enhance central coordination and control.

4. In fact, several national programs now speak of the permanent process of reform, although as one long-time participant in Peru noted, he himself was no longer sure what that meant. For a representative regional view on permanent reform see A. Carrillo Castro, "Administrative Reform in Mexico," in Leemans, pp. 185-212.

5. This external push began in the late 1940s as part of a general international interest in development and had taken hold in Latin America by the early 1950s. Several good overviews of the programs and the various

agencies involved are available. The articles by
Braibanti and the Organization of American States are
two examples. For material on the operation of private
foundations and on general assistance strategies, see,
respectively Francis X. Sutton, "American Foundations
and Public Management in Developing Countries," Studies
in Comparative International Development, (XII, 2) and
David S. Brown. "Strategies and Tactics of Public
Administration Technical Assistance: 1945-1963," in
Montgomery and Siffin, pp. 185-223.
     6. These recommendations were based on Western
doctrines of public administration and were in turn
influenced by all the major theoretical approaches --
from Weberian models, Taylorism and scientific management to the human relations school and the various
branches of development administration. Although
American specialists were not the only ones represented
and although other national variations on that doctrine
also had their place much of what was carried abroad
especially in the early years was what Sutton describes
as "the rather peculiar American conceptions of public
administration that had taken shape in the years before
World War II," -- that is, one which took a notably
mechanistic approach to organizational design and managed to maintain a distinction between administration
and politics. For a short discussion of this see
Sutton, pp. 11-12, and Braibanti, passim. For length-
ier and more critical discussions see Alberto Guer-
reiro-Ramos, "The New Ignorance and the Future of Public Administration in Latin America," in Thurber and
Graham, op. cit., pp. 382-422; selected articles in
Dwight Waldo (ed.), "Symposium on Comparative and
Development Administration," Public Administration
Review (November/December 1976).
     7. In many cases these incorporated older, but
less ambitiously focused organizations some of which
had been set up as the earliest public service institutes or civil service organizations. The Brazilian
DASP whose checkered career is described by Graham, op.
cit. is an example of one of these which attained its
first importance much earlier See also Gilbert B.
Siegel, The Vicissitudes of Governmental Reform in
Brazil: A Study of the DASP. (Washington: University
Press of America, 1978).
     8. See Sutton, op cit.
     9. Several American universities have been impor-
tant in this respect, both as sites for the recruitment
of advisors and the training of foreign students. The
Maxwell School of Syracuse University is one well known
example, but there are many others. In terms of other
professional connections, the Comparative Administration Group is particularly important. For a critical
discussion of the latter's impact, see Brian Loveman,

"The Comparative Administration Group, Development
Administration, and Antidevelopment," Public Administration Review (November/December 1976), pp. 616-21.
    10. The declining interest springs in part from a
dissatisfaction with the results of the earlier missions and a loss of faith in the efficacy of generalized administrative reform projects (as opposed to more
specific types of aid in more narrowly defined technical areas). Sutton notes apropos of the Ford program
that this has also been part of the foundation's desire
"to reduce direct technical assistance as more trained
nationals become available." He thus notes a "sharp
decline in the number of project specialists in technical assistance assignments with governments from more
than a hundred at the peak in the late sixties to less
than fifty in 1975." Sutton, pp. 14-15.
    11. This section is based on developments in the
three case studies, but references in the literature to
other reform programs and interviews with a number of
international advisors who have worked elsewhere suggested that they are not unique in the region and that
a similar process of expert creation occurred elsewhere. Graham's work on Brazil, although not focusing
directly on the issue, suggests similar developments
there. See particularly his discussion of the development of Brazilizan theories of administration, Graham,
op. cit. pp. 38-65.
    12. The continuing shortage of people trained in
administrative and managerial skills in these countries
(in part a result of the continued low prestige of the
disciplines) encourages this development. Although
this is not often a highly prestigeous expertise, its
practitioners are scarce.
    13. Although this generalization is once more
drawn from the case studies, interviews with CLAD (see
note 14) leaders (many with experience in other countries) and material published by the organization
stress the formation of a Latin American model of reform suggesting that here too the doctrine is very important. Graham's discussion of the development of
several Brazilian schools of administrative and organizational theory is also relevant as are several publications from the Mexican reform agency. See Graham,
pp. 38-65 and A. Carrillo Castro, op. cit.
    14. Venezuela, Peru and Mexico were the prime
movers in the formation of CLAD in 1972. By 1976 there
were ten national members and eight other nations
participating in programs. CLAD has its counterparts
in Africa, African Centre for Training and Research in
Administration for Development (CAFRAD), and in Asia,
Asian Center for Development Administration (ACDA).
    15. Member nations were required to supply finan-
cial support, but this, given the amounts, represented

far less of a commitment and a very different kind of commitment to administrative reform. The largest contributions up to 1976 had come from the UN ($690,500 over a three year period) and Venezuela where the headquarters are located. CLAD, "The Latin American Center for Development Administration (CLAD) Evolution and Activities" (October 1976).

16. The one partial exception to this is Mexico, where the reformers have been able to get more of their reorganization schemes passed, in part because of a greater interest taken by top leadership. The extent to which the programs have actually affected performance or other administrative characteristics is still another question which can't be answered here, but the case does suggest just how critical support is. See A. Carillo Castro, op. cit.

17. This is the view of the revisionist critics cited in Chapter 1. See for example Norma de Candido, "Further Thoughts on the Failure of Technical Assistance in Public Administration Abroad," Journal of Comparative Administration (February 1971), pp. 379-400; Peter Savage, "Optimism and Pessimism in Comparative Administration," Public Administration Review (July/ August 1976), pp. 415-23; Jose V. Abueva, "Administrative Doctrines Diffused in Emerging States: The Filipino Response" in Ralph Braibanti (ed.), Political and Administrative Development (Durham: Duke University Press, 1969), pp. 536-88; and Loveman, op. cit.

18. See works by Candido, and Abueva. See also Jorge I. Tapia-Videla, "Understanding Organizations and Environments: A Comparative Perspective," Public Administration Review (November/December 1976), pp. 631-36.

19. This represents a piece of popular wisdom as well as the logical extension of the political reorganization literature. While not putting it so blatantly -- and operating in terms of social forces instead of smaller interests -- the numerous historical interpretations of specific reform movements suggest this as well.

20. See Gerald E. Caiden, Administrative Reform (Chicago: Aldine Publishing Co., 1969).

21. This proposition follows from implementation "theory" and its emphasis on the ultimate difficulty of actually implementing even only relatively complex programs, not so much because of overt opposition, but for reasons ranging from inertia to what Bardach calls the essentially "defensive" character of implementation politics. See for example Eugene Bardach, The Implementation Game (Cambridge: The MIT Press, 1977) and

Jeffrey L. Pressman and Aaron B. Wildavsky, Implementation (Berkeley: University of California Press,
1973).

22. This is drawn from observations of programs
in the three case studies. Even where considerable
opposition to a program did arise it often tended to be
slow to do so because the opposed results were not very
obvious.

23. This is a frequent comment of observers who
are quick to suggest that the planners are simply
political babes in the woods -- a not unreasonable
conclusion in view of the political turmoil their
proposals occasionally stir up.

Part II

Case Studies

3
A Comparative Overview

In the next three chapters recent administrative
reform efforts in three Latin America countries --
Peru, Venezuela, and Colombia -- are discussed. These
countries have several nonadministrative characteristics which make them an interesting base for comparison. They also in many senses represent a middle level
of Latin American socioeconomic and political development. Venezuela offers a partial exception to this
statement because of its significantly higher per capita income (the highest in the region), but its wealth
is a relatively recent result of its oil resources and
one with a still limited impact on national development
as a whole. Finally they share many of the problems of
the region and of Third World nations as a group, including imbalances in levels of socioeconomic development, a pronounced, multi-dimensional urban-rural
gap, an agricultural sector with lagging productivity
but still employing a large proportion of the national
work force, high unemployment and underemployment and
dependence on export earnings or straightforward
foreign loans to generate capital for internal
development.

To better establish a comparative framework, the
remainder of this introductory section offers a brief
demographic, political, and administrative sketch of
the three countries.[1] Because the cut-off point for
the case studies is 1979, changes after that period are
discussed in less detail. Some of this material will
be repeated in later chapters as part of a more detailed background on each country. It is presented in
this introductory section to facilitate comparison. In
this form it may be helpful even to those already familiar with the individual countries.

PHYSICAL AND DEMOGRAPHIC CHARACTERISTICS

In terms of territorial size and population, the
three nations occupy the mid ranks of Latin American
countries, falling short of the giants like Brazil and
Mexico, but standing far ahead on both dimensions, of
the smaller Central American republics. This is true
even of Colombia, the most populous of the three and
the fourth most populous country in Latin America.
More important than the sheer territorial or demographic size of the countries, is the distribution of
their populations and resources, which in all three is
very uneven.
Looking first at demographic distribution, all
three have their populations concentrated in only a
portion of the country; roughly one-half of their
territory is virtually unoccupied. In Colombia and
Venezuela the major unoccupied areas are the llanos
(plains) and jungles of the southeast and south, respectively; in Peru it is the eastern jungle. In all
three countries there has been a tradition of denser
settlement in the upland areas although only in Colombia has this remained the most developed and richest
part of the country. In earlier days, Colombia's most
modern areas were located around a number of cities
(Bogota, Medellin, and Cali) in the inland valleys and
upland plains of the Andes. Only more recently have
such coastal cities as Cartagena and Barranquilla
emerged as development centers in their own right.
In Venezuela, and especially in Peru, more rapid
development has occurred, at least in the last century,
on the coast. Although roughly forty percent of Peru's
population still lives in the sierra, they have retained more traditional life styles and economic activities. The effects of modernization have reached them
very slowly. In Venezuela, although the contrasts have
not been as stark (owing in part to the absence of a
large indigenous population like that of Peru) political and economic power and population have shifted
slightly northward in the last decades, away from the
traditional Andean centers like the city of Merida to
the coastal mountain region (Caracas and its environs)
and, secondarily, to the oil-rich Lake Maracaibo area.
In Venezuela, the coastal and northern (Andean) mountain regions, with twelve percent of the national
territory now hold two-thirds of the population.
In all three countries not only population but
also resources are unevenly distributed, both regionally and within regions (including the most modern).
Aside from region, the most important distinctions are
those between urban and rural areas, and between a few
principal cities and the rest of the territory. The
trickle-down effect and government efforts to the

contrary, these kinds of inequities have tended to increase rather than decrease over time. In the simplest terms, this means that a cluster of resources in one region, national capital, or provincial center will tend to attract more resources and thus more growth so that over time the gap widens between it and the rest of the area. This phenomenon takes several forms, all of them posing obstacles to development efforts. It is most noticeable in the presence of a capital city which dwarfs other urban centers and draws population and domestic and foreign resources at a disproportionately high rate. Lima in Peru, ten times the size of the next largest city and with one-quarter of that country's population, is one example, as is Caracas in Venezuela. Even Colombia which has several good sized cities has traditionally suffered from a lesser version of the syndrome. Although a large resource base and higher levels of development characterize more than one urban center, the rest of the country still lags far behind. More disturbingly, there are recent indications that the capital, Bogota, may now be outdistancing the other large urban centers by attracting an ever greater share of new capital and industries.[2] Over the longer run, this may add a second level of maldistribution.

The territorial inequities are simply part of a wider problem of unequal wealth and resource distribution. Thus although per capita income gives some indication of the relative well-being of their populations, it represents an average; these are countries of enormous contrasts in wealth, level of development, standard of living, and lifestyle. These contrasts divide not only regions or rural and urban settings, but also social and cultural groups and economic classes. In its extreme versions, and especially in Colombia and Peru, the resulting situation has been characterized as one of dual societies, cultures and economies or in a more radical interpretation, as "internal colonialism," in which the developed sections of the countries live off the traditional areas.

POLITICS

Politically the three countries offer an interesting comparison. All have suffered in recent times from the instability, violence and other political problems often associated with the region. Venezuela which as recently as 1958 had a military dictator was, by 1978 apparently the most stable of the group -- a result of its oil wealth above all else. Like Colombia, which suffered a brief military dictatorship from 1953 to 1957, it was now ruled through a competitive

party system and had a strong executive with a relatively weaker congress. Still, if Colombia's situation, without the benefits of oil wealth looked less
stable, it was the result of a much longer tradition of
competitive party politics and control by a political
class who had ruled the country since the last century.
In both cases, the ruling elites favored reformist as
opposed to more radical politics, the recognition of
the rights and interests of a large number of organized
groups, and on the whole, an incrementalist approach to
change. The majority of political participants seemed
to share those preferences. More radical ideological
positions were held by minorities on the extreme Right
and Left.

Peru, for much of the period covered here (1960-
1978) constitutes the political exception. In 1968 a
military coup brought it under the control of a "revolutionary" government dedicated to making a number of
radical changes in the socioeconomic as well as political structures of the country. The military government brought a drastic revision of the political power
structure; many former elites were left without much of
a voice and participation, at least in conventional
terms, was significantly reduced. Conditions changed
somewhat after August of 1975 when an internal coup
brought the ouster of the first president, General
Velasco along with some of his more radical colleagues
and the government's shift to a more conservative position. However, the "second phase" military government
(1975-1980) still attempted to limit participation to
those it wished to participate and retained an authoritarian decision-making style in which military and civilian technocratic elites had a major role. One result
of this style and of the exclusion of former elites was
the government's ability to make very rapid and radical
changes in policy, in decided contrast to the more incrementalist approach of the Venezuelan, Colombian, and
pre-1968 Peruvian regimes. In 1980, the Peruvian military turned power back to civilian leaders.

Despite these changes and despite the military
governments' mobilization of formerly nonparticipant
groups (especially peasant farmers), Peru remains the
least politically modernized of the countries. Its
large population of illiterates who have usually been
prevented from voting, and many of whom are Indians
living in rural poverty and often unable to speak Spanish, has kept effective participation in the hands of a
rather small, largely urban-based elite. Political
parties with one exception, the <u>apristas</u>,[3] have come
and gone as fast as their leaders and it has not been
until relatively recently that they have developed much
of a mass base. Finally, like Venezuela, Peru has a

long history of unconstitutional governments, and despite the recent reversion to civilian rule, chances
are that the history is not yet ended.

ADMINISTRATIVE CHARACTERISTICS

Especially in regard to their administrative
structures, all three countries share many similarities, which are also characteristic of the region.
This statement requires some explanation because it
appears to eliminate the need for further investigation
of the origins of the administrative reform movements
or the reasons for the similarities among them. To
dispense with the most obvious qualification first, one
must remember that while the administrative characteristics of the three look similar when compared, say,
with the United States or a Western European nation,
there still are substantial differences among them;
these differences could lead to distinctive definitions
of their problems and to different solutions. Furthermore, even where the "objective" problems are comparable, there is not necessarily one logical solution.
Finally, there is a danger in attempting these charac-
terizations and in identifying "problems" because this
establishes a viewpoint, and a predisposition to reach
certain conclusions and to see certain logical solutions. This obviously poses a threat to an investigation of why and how administrative problems are identified within the countries as well as why one solution
is chosen rather than another. Since there is no way
to avoid this danger and still provide a comparative
description, this explanation is offered in recognition
of the project's contradictory implications.
Turning to the administrative sectors, the first
point to be made is that in all three countries they
are quite large, a function not only of the wider role
government has taken over the past decades, but also of
the public bureaucracy's longstanding status as an employment service for the middle classes The level of
public employment is high and accounts for from one-
eighth to one-fifth of the total work force. The sheer
size of the bureaucracies is also evident in government
budgets as compared to gross national product, but the
importance of the public sector is even greater than
these figures indicate. In all three countries the
impact of government activity is magnified by its direct involvement in strategic sectors of the economy
and by its provision of critical infrastructure needed
to accelerate the rate of development.
As a second point, although one of the three,
Venezuela, is officially a federation, all operate as
unitary systems in which the powers and abilities of
the central government dwarf those of the state or

departmental and local units. The specific form and
powers of the subnational units vary among the three
countries, but they are always limited. Furthermore,
local government tends to be relatively more important
admnistratively (although not necessarily politicially)
than the intermediate level because it provides more
basic services. Both levels are understaffed, underfinanced and regarded as decades behind the national
administrative systems. In Peru there is virtually nothing in the way of a departmental government or administration and even under civilian governments, the one
departmental official, the intendent, was selected by
the national authorities.[4] The Colombian "department"[5]
and the Venezuelan "state" have more complex political
and admnistrative structures although in both the chief
official, the governor, is centrally appointed. Provisions for the selection of municipal authorities vary
by country and by regime; they are currently elected in
all three. In Peru they were appointed by the central
government from 1968 to 1980 and have been for most of
the present century.

The inadequacy of the traditional subnational units in all three countries has led to some discussions
of programs to upgrade the existing units or establish
broadly based regional governments. To date none of
these have gotten off the ground, but they will all be
discussed in the following chapters. It should also be
mentioned that in all three countries the national government determines the powers and structures of local
(and intermediate) governments. Although national legislation may provide for some structural and functional
distinctions among different size local units, there is
still a good measure of de jure if not always de facto
uniformity.

For a number of reasons the national bureaucracies
of these countries tend not to have a uniform structure. The most basic division is between the centralized administration (composed of the national ministries and their immediate dependencies as well as a
growing number of offices attached directly to the
presidency and providing general services) and the decentralized sector which includes a variety of entities
with only loose attachments to the former groups and
performing a number of more specialized functions.
Agencies included here range from nationalized enterprises to scientific research institutes, to agrarian reform institutes. Often the criteria by which
an agency is assigned one status or another are difficult to define; they of course vary from country to
country. Generally speaking the decentralized sector
is a phenomenion of the last four decades. Over time
it has become an important part of the national system,
in some cases now accounting for a larger budget and

more employees than the centralized administration. In
more recent years this has been a cause of concern.
While recognizing the advantages offered by the decentralized status (e.g., greater freedom to operate,
the ability to attract better staff, etc.), critics
feel that it may pose still greater costs in terms of
problems of coordination and control. Each of the
countries has developed its own system for defining,
classifying and supervising the decentralized sector,
but in all concern has been expressed that the supervision is inadequate and that as a result the sector is
not making an optimum contribution to development
efforts.

Heterogenity within the national administration
extends beyond this division. It is also found in both
sectors in the distinction between more traditional and
more modern agencies. The former have less skilled
staff, a less technocratic outlook and often the most
complex structures. However, even the more modern
agencies, although lacking some of these disfunctional
characteristics, face problems of inefficiency, inef-
ficacy and out and out corruption. Generally although
the public sector has been attracting better trained
staff, it is plagued by an inability to hold onto them,
or to compete with the private sector, because of
poorer working conditions, salaries and prestige as
compared to the latter. Although Venezuelan salaries
are relatively higher than those in Peru and Colombia
and although the Venezuelan government has been hiring
bureaucrats from the other two countries,[6] it has
problems retaining its own best qualified employees.
Other common personnel problems, include the influence
of patronage or partisanship in hiring practices, the
ill-defined role of unions, and the simple inability of
the government to keep track of its burgeoning employment rolls.

Another series of common characteristics stems
from the high level of centralization in the bureaucracies, in both a physical and organizational sense.
Government offices have traditionally been located in
urban areas and usually in the capitals, a practice
which was both convenient and logical in the days of a
more limited role for government. However, as governments have taken a more activist position vis-a-vis
national development, and as they have become involved
in providing services for citizens as well as involving
more citizens in their programs, this physical concentration has become less practical. Combined with the
insignificance of intermediate and local government
units it means that many citizens have little or no
contact with government at any level and that what
contact they have is usually not positive (e.g., tax
collection). However, physical decentralization has

been difficult because of costs, the reluctance of
staff to move out of the capital or other urban centers, and the high levels of organizational centralization. Even when field offices exist, central authorities may severely limit their powers. At least two
vicious circles are in operation. In the one, urban
based staff is reluctant to leave the capital for the
less developed provinces; this works against provincial
development which makes the provinces still less attractive. In the other the center refuses to give responsibility to field offices (or to subordinates wherever they are located) because of the lower quality of
the staff; this means that talented people are not attracted to those positions and the staff quality thus
remains low. These are just a few of the many aspects
of the centralization-decentralization theme -- in all
three countries it has been an important political issue and has become even more important as governments
have become directly involved in promoting national
development.

The following tables present these and a number of
other administrative and political characteristics in
summary form. In conclusion, it should be noted that,
on a general level, the common administrative traits of
these countries do suggest that they might develop comparable reform programs. However, we must also consider the different goals of the governments and the
differences in their political styles and resource
bases. Furthermore, although their "problems" have
been presented as comparable they could be diagnosed
differently or a more varied set of alternatives could
be proposed. These and other possibilities will be
examined in the next sections and the three case
studies.

BASIC ADMINISTRATIVE DATA: 1960-1978

Peru: 1978, population 16.8 million; GDP $983.9 pc;
        total government employment 446,200 (245,700
        central administration only); government
        revenues 15.1% and expenditures 19.8% of GDP
        (central administration only).

A. Central Administration
        1966, 12 Ministries:
        Government, Police, Postal Service and
        Telecommunications; External Relations;
        Justice; Labor and Communities (1949); Public
        Education (1935); Finance and Commerce; War
        (Army); Navy (1919); Airforce (1941); Devel-
        opment and Public Works; Health (1935);
        Agriculture (1943).

        1936, 18 Ministries
        Interior; External Relations; Army; Navy;
        Airforce; Economics and Finance; Education;
        Health; Labor; Agriculture; Industry and
        Tourism; Transport and Communications; Energy
        and Mines; Housing and Construction; Fishing
        (1970); Commerce (1973); Food (1974);
        Integration (1976).

        1978, 15 Ministries
        Interior; External Relations; Finance;
        Education; Health; Labor; Agriculture
        (includes Food); Fishing; Industry, Commerce,
        Integration, and Tourism; Transport and
        Communication; Energy and Mines; Housing;
        Army; Navy; Airforce.

B. Decentralized Administration
        1966, called "Independent Public Subsector" SSPI,
        84 in total
        a.   Organs of General Government (65)
        b.   Public enterprise (19)
        1976, number varies by source, from 141 to 171
        a.   Public enterprise
             --Public law
             --Special status
        b.   Nonpublic enterprises
             --State participation 100%
             --State participation 50-100%
Note: the continuity between 1966 and 1976 is even
less than it appears as many of the former SSPI's were
abolished or absorbed into new and quite different
organizations.

Venezuela: 1978, population 13.2 million; GDP $2,399.1
    pc; total government employment 690,000 (280,000
    central administration only); government revenues
    23.5% and expenditures 28.5% of GDP (central
    administration only).

A. Central Administration
    1963, 13 Ministries
        Agriculture; Communications; Defense;
        Development; Education; Finance; Foreign
        Affairs; Health and Social Services; Interior;
        Justice; Labor; Mines and Hydrocarbons; Public
        Works.

    1978, 16 Ministries
        Agriculture; Defense; Development; Education;
        Finance; Foreign Affairs; Health and Social
        Services; Interior; Justice; Labor; Public
        Works; Transportation and Communications;
        Energy and Mines; Environment and Renewable
        Resources; Information and Tourism; Youth.

B. Decentralized Sector
    1959, 38 state enterprises
    1969, 97 state enterprises
    1976, 186 state enterprises
Note: These are divided into three categories
depending on percentage of state participation (from
0.1 to 100%). In 1977, the decentralized sector
accounted for 72% of total government spending and
54.6% of its revenue, not including the 85% of total
government revenues paid by the oil companies. The decentralized sector also includes an additional 88 autonomous institutions and related entities.

Colombia: 1978, population 24.9 million; GDP $747.1
    pc; total government employment 600,000 (110,000
    central government only); government revenues
    9.0% and expenditures 8.4% of GDP (central
    administration only).

A. Central Administration:
    1960-1978, 13 Ministries, 9 Administrative
    Departments
        Government; External Relations; Justice;
        Finance and Public Credit; National Defense;
        Agriculture (1913); Labor and Social Security
        (1931); Health (1938); Economic Development;
        Mines and Energy (1940); Education; Communi-
        cations (1923); Public Works and Transpor-
        tation (1905).

B.   Decentralized Sector:
     1960, 48 entities (39 independent agencies and 9
     enterprises)
     1969, 87 total (72 and 15)
     1978, 121 total (91 public establishments, 13
     state enterprises, and 17 mixed enterprises).
Note: 1978, accounts for 59.5% of government
expenditures.

SOURCES:
     Population, GDP, and government revenue and
        expenditures from Inter-American Development
        Bank, Economic and Social Progress in Latin
        America, Washington: IDB, 1979.

     Decentralized Administration
        Peru
           Centro Latinoamericano de Administracion
           para el Desarrollo (CLAD), Las empresas
           estatales en America Latina. Caracas: c.
           1977.
           ONRAP, Guia del gobierno peruano. Lima:
           ONRAP, 1966.
        Venezuela
           CLAD, op. cit.
           Income and expenditure data from Gene
           Bigler, preliminary draft of unpublished
           doctoral dissertation.
        Colombia
           Jaime Castro, "Las organismos descentral-
           izados," Revista Camara de Comercio de
           Bogota (June 1972), p. 89.
           Colombia, Office of the President, Secre-
           taria de Administracion Publica, Manual de
           organizacion de la rama ejecutiva del poder
           publico, 1978. Bogota: 1978.

     Data on government employment
        Peru
           Actualidad Economico Lima (September 8,
           1978), p. 6.   Figures are for 1977 and
           exclude municipalities (28,000), armed
           forces (80,000), and police (30,000).
        Venezuela
           From Oficina Central de Personal (OCP).
           Figures are for 1978 and exclude municipal
           and state workers (110,000).
        Colombia
           From DASC.   Figures are for 1978 and include
           police, but exclude municipal workers.

NOTES

1. Readers interested in further background on any of the three are referred to the works recommended in the notes accompanying each case.

2. See Alan Gilbert, "Urban and Regional Development Programs in Colombia since 1951" in Wayne Cornelius and Felicity Trueblood (eds.). <u>Latin American Urban Research</u> V (Beverly Hills: Sage, 1975), pp. 241-76.

3. This is the grand old party of Peruvian politics founded in the 1920s by Victor Raul Haya de la Torre, the man who would remain its leader until his death in 1979. Although its platform at its foundation was quite radical, by the 1960s and 1970s it was regarded as moderate to moderate-Right on the ideological spectrum, a function of its own slight movement to the Right and a much larger leap to the Left by public opinion in general.

4. In the last years of the revolutionary government and under the civilian administration to follow there has been some effort to build up departmental governments, but as of mid 1982, it still had brought little change.

5. Some confusion may be caused here by the Colombian usage of the term department (<u>departamento</u>) for both the territorial division ("state") and an organizational unit within the central bureaucracy ("department" or "division").

6. These statements and those made earlier about Venezuela's ample budgetary resources refer to the period prior to the decline in oil prices and the government's subsequent financial difficulties.

4
Peru: Administrative Reform and Political Revolution

"El que quiere darse importancia se crea un sistema"*
--INAP staff member, Lima, 1978

In October of 1968, the Republic of Peru entered a new and controversial era when a military junta headed by General Juan Velasco Alvarado overthrew the civilian president Fernando Belaunde Terry and took power as a self-proclaimed "Revolutionary Government."[1] The new regime justified its action on the basis of a proposed program of massive social, political, and economic change aimed at transforming the national power structure, fomenting economic development, and creating a society whose benefits would be distributed more equitably. Ten years later, if far from achieving these general goals, the government had made varying degrees of progress in the thirty-one specific areas of reform outlined in its "Plan del Gobierno" (Plan of Government).[2] Administrative reform figures in this plan as a separate program area and as a necessary component of other types of change, but over the ten year period the government's achievements here were conspicuously weak, limited to one major reorganization undertaken in 1969, a number of inconclusive experiments in such areas as regional government and the establishment of a series of reform agencies, themselves notorious examples of the inefficiency and immobilism they were created to eliminate. Despite a sudden surge of activity in late 1978 in preparation for the impending transition to civilian rule, it was apparent that the original movement had run it course. What remained had a much less ambitious meaning than ten years before and a much less ambitious set of objectives.

---

*Whoever wants to be important makes himself a system."

ORIGINS OF ADMINISTRATIVE REFORM IN PERU

The concern with the need for administrative
reform predates the 1968 coup although prior to that
time its impact had been minimal. Like many of the
Revolutionary Government's programs, administrative
reform was an inherited issue, with its roots in discussions arising during the first Belaunde administration and earlier. Preceding Peruvian governments had
been exceptionally reluctant to undertake even minimal
reform programs and lagged far behind their neighbors
in introducing any kind of administrative innovation.[3]
The halfhearted adoption of program-budgeting and economic planning in 1963 occurred only after it became
clear that this was a precondition for further U.S.
aid.[4] The unusually strong resistance to change had an
ideological component as demonstrated in the attitudes
of a number of prominent political figures (including
Pedro Beltran, a former Minister of Finance and a presidential candidate in 1962). These individuals favored
a minimal role for the public sector and consequently
opposed any move which might strengthen its influence.
A second aspect of the resistance grew out of the traditional power struggles within the Peruvian politican
system and especially the long-standing rivalry between
the President and the Congress. Given the frequently
delicate balance of power within this system, a proposal to work any major change in bureaucratic organization was bound to be interpreted as a threat to someone's position. The primary beneficiaries of this arrangement were the bureaucrats who were usually the
first to appeal to Congress to prevent any proposed
change, often calling on nongovernmental clientele
groups to support them. Even a reformist president
like Belaunde, who showed some genuine interest in the
reform issue, was reluctant to confront it head on and
limited himself to establishing a study commission
which he subsequently ignored.

ONRAP

Despite a lack of impact during its short life-
time, this commission, the National Office of Rationalization and Training for the Public Administration
(ONRAP) was to have lasting influence. Established in
1964 as a small and poorly financed office, ONRAP inherited the functions of two preexisting and largely
ineffectual bodies, the Peruvian Institute of Public
Administration (a training institute set up in 1958)
and the Office of Administrative Rationalization of the
National Planning Institute. With a budget that barely
covered the costs of renting an office, a solely advisory status, and every indication that Belaunde could

not act on their advice, ONRAP's members might well
have resigned themselves to doing nothing. However,
the lack of support from the domestic political scene
was more than compensated by a strong input of foreign
assistance, most of it provided by the U.S. Agency for
International Development. AID's support of ONRAP
continued through the entire Belaunde administration.
Although AID and its major contractor, the New York
Institute of Public Administration (IPANY), found themselves somewhat at odds with the direction taken by
ONRAP, their participation and material assistance
helped to create a remarkable sense of mission.[5]

ONRAP's internal morale was further bolstered by
the small size of the office (at its peak 30 professionals) and the very fact that over the short run it
was not pressed for results. Thus, despite the likelihood that nothing would come of their work, the ONRAP
staff began an extensive analysis of existing administrative conditions and the elaboration of a comprehensive program of change. The final product was their
Diagnostico de la administracion publica en el Peru
(Diagnosis of Peruvian Public Administration 1965) and
some forty volumes of related and more detailed studies
of various aspects of administrative structures and
procedures.[6] The studies were done rapidly and were
frequently based on only a cursory examination and understanding of existing practices. The specific recommendations for reform sprang from the traditional criticisms of the Peruvian system,[7] some of them (like the
need for greater decentralization) dating back to the
early days of the Republic, and a more formal model
worked out in the Diagnostico and influenced by the
advice of the foreign participants. The result was an
eclectic and inconsistent mixture of imported principles and concessions to national traditions and "national reality." Despite its weaknesses it was unique
in its detailed and comprehensive depiction of a blueprint for reform. With its work largely done, by 1967
ONRAP entered a period of decline and began to lose
many of its most important members, but as they dispersed to other positions they took with them their
conviction on the need for reform and a shared perspective on the directions it should take. Their work with
ONRAP had also established their standing as experts on
administrative problems, and while their reputation was
not widespread, they were the only group who could
claim that title.

ONRAP's Reformers

Because of their impact on subsequent events, it
is worth noting who ONRAP's members were and what interests they represented. The group was a mixed

collection of foreign advisors, professionals in the
administrative sciences, and young technocrats from a
variety of backgrounds. One of the advisors, a Span-
iard, Juan Ignacio Jimenez, is in fact credited with
the development of the ONRAP model. Although the majority were Peruvians, many had received some foreign
training either in public administration or in other
specializations (especially economics). The outlook of
the group thus tended to be international and this was
enhanced by the generally higher status and greater experience of the non-Peruvian members. While some of
the Peruvians had come to ONRAP from other administrative agencies, most had little or no previous administrative experience. Still more significant, was the
absence of politicians and experts in administrative
law, the two groups traditionally most concerned with
administrative reform, although from decidedly different perspectives. The views of these groups would be
influential in shaping the ONRAP doctrine, especially
in its emphasis on tailoring reform to a Peruvian reality (and what observers have criticized as its excessive legalism). Their lack of a more direct participation allowed a departure from their traditional and
often partisan perspectives on reform.

Although the ONRAP group was influenced by a variety of sources, its most impressive characteristic was
its lack of ties with political or bureaucratic factions. Its isolation allowed the emergence of a new,
independent identity. This is illustrated by former
members' references to a strong esprit de corps and to
an initial educational process during which the views
of the group were formed and then passed on to the
younger members. Significantly, while ONRAP's mission
began with a conviction of the need for administrative
reform, the views of individual members on the desirability of wider social and political change were not
incorporated into their collective thinking.[8] Thus,
they represented a distinctive position and interest,
but one without much tradition in Peru -- that of the
public administration generalist and expert in administrative sciences. The particular proposals included
in the ONRAP documents did have a wider appeal in that
many of them had already been voiced by small groups
within the bureaucracy, the legal profession, or the
political parties. However, the appeal was weakened by
ONRAP's political neutrality, its eclecticism, and its
definition of reform as a purely technical problem.
While these constitute ONRAP's unique contribution to
the reform movement, they also were a disadvantage in
attracting allies.

THE REFORM PROGRAM OF THE REVOLUTIONARY
GOVERNMENT: 1968-1972

Had ONRAP never existed, it is likely that the
administrative reform would still have figured in the
military's programs. The Plan del Gobierno (said to
have been drawn up before the coup but not released for
several years) lists thirty-one areas for reform. Most
of these, like administrative reform, were based on
proposals which had been discussed for years. The military's justification for its takeover (which included
mismanagement and corruption on the part of civilian
governments), its decision to expand the state's responsibility for directing socioeconomic change, and
its long-standing interest in clarifying its relationship with the public and private sectors,[9] all can be
seen as encouraging some initial extensive overhauls in
the bureaucracy. However, the new government's proposed reforms were still more detailed and extensive.
Although ONRAP's connection with the Belaunde regime
made it ideologically suspect and led to its immediate
dissolution, the members of the new government were
acquainted with its proposals through individual contacts with its members and through its publications.
Thus, although the source is never credited, the Plan
del Gobierno's discussion of administrative reform
contains many of ONRAP's ideas and recommendations.

The Initial Objectives

The plan's discussion[10] follows its general format
-- an analysis of the existing problems, a brief statement of the general objectives and a list of actions to
be taken. The analysis contains four specific criticisms which are surprising only in their lack of a more
revolutionary perspective. These are the lack of planning, coordination, and control within the administration which is seen as producing excessive centralization and bureaucratization; inefficiency and dishon-
esty; personnel practices dominated by partisan and
group interests; and excessive delay in routine procedures. The stated objective of reform is the creation
of a "dynamic and efficient administrative structure
leading to improved government action and a more effective service to society." Eight specific actions are
to be taken to accomplish this end;

1. The planned and progressive sectoralization of
the actions of the state.

2. The formation of a basic law (<u>ley de bases</u>) for the administrative sector.

3. Regionalization of the public sector.

4. The introduction of more adequate systems of selection, evaluation, classification and training for administrative personnel and of a career civil service.

5. The formulation of improved policies of re- muneration, social security, and welfare for the public servant.

6. Simplification of administrative procedures and the elaboration of the corresponding guides and manuals for the private citizen.

7. Rationalization and modernization of infor- mation and statistical systems.

8. Municipal reform to bring local government into line with other changes introduced by the Peruvian Revolution.

Recommendations elsewhere in the plan include the creation of a number of new ministries and a series of proposals having to do with the management of public funds and specificallly with the reorganization of the Comptroller General's office.

With the dissolution of ONRAP and the announcement that it was "in reorganization" it was unclear what the next step would be, or whether there would in fact be one. Some indication was given on November 4, 1968 when the Minister of Finance, General Angel Valdivia Morriberon gave a televised speech on the general out- lines of the government's administrative reform pro- gram.[11] Stressing the centrality of this program to the government's other objectives, Valdivia noted that efforts in this area would rest on two bases: planning and organization. In regard to the latter he empha- sized the importance of the basic law (<u>ley de bases</u>) which would provide the guiding principles. Although acknowledging the importance of such other programs as training and decentralization, Valdivia stressed that the primary thrust of the reform was the basic restruc- turing and reorganization of the administrative sector, beginning at the ministerial level.

For the would-be reformers and especially those connected with ONRAP, Valdivia appears as a crusading hero of the reform movement, responsible for pushing the government's commitment beyond the merely for- mal.[12] His disappearance from the scene a few months

later (rumored to have been provoked by a personal conflict with Velasco) was an enormous blow, for over the
next few years no major political figure would take
such a personal and public interest in administrative
reform.[13] The government's commitment to other types of
reform made some sort of administrative reorganization
desirable, but it was clearly Valdivia's actions which
provided the impetus for the extensive changes to follow. Within a matter of days a committee was created
to plan a major reorganization and to draw up the ley
de bases to guide it.

The First Reorganization

The reorganization committee had only six members,
but two were former members of ONRAP.[14] It was originally given a deadline of December 31, 1968. Although
this was eventually extended by a few months, time
pressures posed a major constraint on its actions. Despite some opposition within the committee to the use
of ONRAP's schemes, owing to their connection with the
previous government, the time factor defeated all
counter arguments and the committee's final proposals
closely paralleled the ONRAP blueprint. The fact that
the government gave so little direction to the committee, aside from the stipulation that certain key ministries (e.g., Housing and Agriculture) be created,
suggests that it continued to regard administrative
reform as a primarily technical problem and hence one
which the experts could resolve on their own. The committee did attempt to consult with key personnel in the
existing ministries, but the latter, uncertain of their
own positions and deprived of their traditional congressional protectors, came as supplicants and their
influence tended to be minimal. Thus, left largely to
their own devices, the six members presented the plans
they could agree on and when they could not reach an
agreement, often avoided a decision entirely. By
Spring of 1969, their deliberations had produced a general ministerial law specifying the jurisdiction and
responsibilities of each ministry and a series of organic laws describing their internal organization.
Conspicuously absent was the ley de bases which was to
define once and for all the functions and the boundaries of the public sector.

Given the potential consequences, one of the surprising aspects of the committee's decisions was that
they were so often purely arbitrary.[15] The government's much publicized austerity program provoked a
last minute decision to reduce the number of ministries
and so led to the elimination of the old Ministry of
Justice. As the deadline drew near, uncertainties as
to where to put offices that did not clearly belong to

any one ministry were increasingly resolved by giving
them to the Prime Minister. This solution undercut the
central policy making role envisioned for the latter
and converted his office into a catch-all. Although
the military provided definite instructions as to which
ministries were to be created, they gave little guidance on the internal structure. Here the committee
was able to make some important innovations, among them
the creation of the post of superior director, the
chief civilian appointee of each ministry, in charge of
coordinating the latter's activities and responsible
only to the minister, and the up-grading of the role of
the Prime Minister.

As important as this initial reorganization was,
and as much fear as it may have produced among the temporarily powerless bureaucrats, it would be dangerous
to overemphasize its impact. The reorganization essentially consisted of moving existing offices around and
less frequently involved the creation of entirely new
ones. Since many of these offices already functioned
quite independently within their respective ministries,
the consequences were hardly earthshaking.[16] The major
effect was to flatten the administrative structure and
allow more direct attention to problem areas like agriculture that had been promoted to ministerial status.[17]
However, the military's wish that the "sectors" be
neatly separated to eliminate problems of coordination
proved an impossibility and the reorganization plans
already included provisions for intersectoral (interministerial) commissions. Furthermore, the reform
plans had not touched on areas like decentralization
and personnel programs while it remained to be seen
whether the innovations they did include would become
more than paper projects. In the meantime, the first,
and for many, the only stage of the administrative reform was officially concluded as work began on the government's more substantive programs.

The First Eclipse

At this point, the reform movement entered a critical stage in its development. For the reform planners, many of whom had returned to an active involvement in the issue from posts elsewhere in the administration or even outside of the country, the task had
just begun and the most important changes lay ahead.
For the military government, impatient to begin the
real work of changing society, the administrative reform was close to completion. Indicative of the latter
view, the term administrative reform was dropped and
the reorganization of ONRAP concluded with the creation
of three new entities: a Higher School of Public Administration (ESAP); a National Office of Personnel

Administration (ONAP), located in the Prime Minister's
Office and responsible for personnel policies; and an
Office of Administrative Rationalization established
within the National Planning Institute (INP) to formulate the remaining reform (or rationalization) policies. This last move was not welcomed by the administrative reformers It subordinated them to INP's staff
of economic and social planners, a group whose fortunes
were on the rise but which they had never seen as sympathetic to their own cause. The administrative reformers usually explained the difference in terms of the
planners' insufficient understanding of administrative
reform, but it was clearly ideological and political as
well. The INP staff, which had produced many of the
early ideologies of the Revolution and which in its
development of a collective identity much resembled
INAP, was attuned to the issues of redistribution,
participation, and social change, the themes of the
first stage of the Revolution. The administrative
refomers were far more conservative; their main concerns were rationalization and order. They had received their training in the 1950s and 1960s and held
to the view that administrative reform transcended politics, a notion which hardly fit the language of the
new government. Their ties with the Belaunde regime
and with foreign technical missions and their international outlook cast further doubt on their ideological credentials, especially in an era where the emphasis was on peruvianization.

For the next few years very little happened in the
way of further reform. The decision to divide ONRAP's
functions among three separate offices with a consequent doubling or tripling of personnel diluted the
parent organization's sense of mission and weakened the
consensus about the necessary direction of reform.
ONAP and ESAP which inherited few of the original staff
and even less of the old sense of mission, were quickly
caught up in a series of housekeeping activities which
discouraged the elaboration of long-term objectives.
The INP office of rationalization, although it received
a greater portion of the ONRAP personnel, suffered some
of the same problems. Its allocation of personnel and
other resources depended on decisions made by INP which
frequently used the office as a dumping ground. The
presence of a core of ex-ONRAP participants maintained
some internal sense of direction, but there was a continuing tension between the office's commitment to a
specific vision of reform and pressures from its organizational environment which discounted the task's importance and disagreed on the direction it should take.
These pressures, combined with the government's decision that the main burden of reform had been accomplished, once more reduced the office to little more
than a study group.

Reform and Revolutionary Politics

Viewed in the context of the political situation in Peru from 1969 to 1972, the eclipse of the reform movement is more easily understood. The Peruvian military had come to power promising a series of society-wide transformations and had adopted administrative reform as a way of eliminating traces of the previous regime and as a means to these other ends. There was thus a symbolic side to the reform which was satisfied by the initial reorganization, the replacement of top-level personnel and the subsequent exhortations to bureaucrats to be good revolutionaries. Since the more ambitious schemes of the reformers were not widely known and had no direct relationship with other revolutionary symbols, they were superfluous at this level. This line of reasoning suggests that the government's involvement in reform was more than symbolic. In view of the negligible symbolic benefits, their willingness to establish the three new offices and substantially increase their personnel and resources indicates a more concrete interest. The problem is thus one of attention and priorities.

The would-be reformers were not revolutionaries and in many cases were not even good politicians. Their insistence on presenting reform as an apolitical issue, and their failure to tie it to any of the revolutionary themes meant that reform, unlike economic planning, was never seen as a uniquely revolutionary goal. Furthermore, the promises of improvement made by the reformers responded to none of the immediate needs of those in power. These first few years were very optimistic ones; the military as novice administrators seemingly had little idea of the problems they would soon face. In the short run their successes were more obvious than their failures, and they were also able to introduce their own piecemeal reforms by breaking rules that didn't suit their purpose. Many of the highest priority programs (like agrarian reform) were channeled through new and relatively flexible ministries.[18] Even in the older agencies, the uncertainties of the reorganization and new political climate, temporarily reduced some traditional problems. Finally, because the military's shake-up of the existing structure had exacerbated one of the oldest weaknesses, that of control and evaluation, whatever problems developed went unnoticed for some time. As a consequence, administrative reform was temporarily sidelined. For the next three years no one seemed to notice that none of those responsible were doing much of anything about it.

INTO THE SECOND STAGE: 1972-1976

Had the government's programs and the political
climate not taken a turn for the worse, the reform
movement might have remained forgotten for several
years more. However, by 1972, some of the earlier
optimism was dissipating, objectives were clearly not
being met, and after four years in office, the military
may have begun to view its administrative arm in a new
light. In that year, a commission headed by Colonel
Luis Arias was formed to study and evaluate the administrative reform program. Its report was submitted and
forgotten, but one year later, under a new Prime Minister, a second commission was set up to develop the
Arias Commission's proposal for a new reform institute,
the National Institute of Public Administration
(INAP).[19] The six principal members of the commission
included Colonel Jose Guabloche, head of the INP;
Eduardo Urrutia, head of the INP's office of administrative rationalization and a former member of ONRAP;
and Carlos Malpica, director of ESAP and a former educational planner from INP. The commission and its sub-
committees far exceeded their instructions, producing a
sizable body of detailed recommendations for future reforms, but their principal output, and the only part to
bring immediate results, was the brief project of law
which would be used to create INAP in 1974. In accordance with this project, the new office united the
staffs and functions of ONAP, ESAP, and the INP rationalization office. ONAP and the rationalization office
were in effect completely integrated into the new entity although ESAP retained much of its separate identity and mission of training administrators.

INAP and the INAP Model

The creation of INAP marks a change in the objectives as well as the organization of the reform movement. The three years of inactivity had given the
reformers time to rethink their plans and in the INP
office, under the direction of Eduardo Urrutia, the
result was a second administrative model. This model[20]
departed from ONRAP's scheme (or, the "Jimenez Model")
in its tighter, self conscious statement of the principles to govern reform, principles based as much on a
vision of the "New State"[21] as on the old doctrines of
administrative organization. Urrutia's model introduced a new vocabulary of administrative organization,
attempting to distinguish the "normative" from the
"productive" functions of the government apparatus, and

the productive functions that logically belonged to government from those more appropriate to private enterprise. While retaining the term "sector" to describe the different arenas of policy making, it stressed that the sector was more than a ministry and included the private and public activities regulated by a single type of policy. The term "system" was introduced to refer to a series of activities (personnel, planning, budgeting, etc.) common to all the sectors and so organized across them. In the terms of the model, administrative reform thus became a process of reorganizing and restructuring the sectors in accordance with the general principles, and of introducing and strengthening the systems to upgrade performance levels and to establish a second level of control over all administrative activities.

For the reformers this model had the advantage of providing an overall framework to join the policies (personnel reform, decentralization, municipal reform) which were considered aspects of administrative reform. For the government, its appeal was more dubious although in a short pamphlet presenting the model,[22] Urrutia made a number of references to the government's revolutionary goals and the place of administrative reform among them. More ominously, his scheme did not directly address any of the government's immediate problems and in fact implied that many of the decisions made by the military to expand state powers had been in error. Pushed to its logical extreme, it would have required a disbanding of the ministerial empires built up over the past years and the reallocation of a number of other powers (for example that over personnel) that the ministers and other top officials now held.[23] Despite these considerations, the model was not specifically rejected and to some extent was used as a guide in setting up INAP. In light of the military's concern for simply reviving the reform movement, it seems doubtful that they paid it much more attention.

Reformers and Rulers: Two Views on Reform

The government's treatment of the new scheme was symptomatic of the larger misunderstandings surrounding this second stage of reform. Despite the reformers' optimism, it was clear that all was not quite as planned. First, INAP itself only imperfectly reflected the second model; only two of the ten auxiliary "systems," rationalization and personnel, were directly under its control. In principle, INAP was to direct the reorganization of the remaining systems, but its powers here were never specified. Contrary to the expectations of its creators, INAP was not given ministerial status, but remained as an advisory body reporting to the Prime Minister.[24] The organic law founding the institute[25] mentioned none of the specific programs recommended by the commission and simply instructed INAP to "formulate the national policy of administrative reform," "direct the implementation of rationalization and personnel policies" and "coordinate its activities with the entities related to its functions." All of this was, of course, subject to the approval of the government.

While the lack of more specific directions might have appeared ominous, it was welcomed by the reformers who once again had a free hand in planning their programs. This practice of establishing a group of experts to formulate specialized reform programs was not an uncommon one; the government had conducted the educational reform in much the same fashion. There was a difference however in that the educational reform (not an overwhelming success itself) was based in a ministry with its own budget and staff, whereas the administrative reformers depended almost entirely on the cooperation of entities outside their control for the implementation of their programs In principle they were aided by the presence of personnel and rationalization offices (in theory, "little INAP's") within each ministry,[26] but these offices were generally weak and depended on the ministry rather than INAP for their very existence. However, over the short run these problems appeared as minor setbacks before the major accomplishment of reuniting the reform program and removing it from INP's control.

The Reformers Disagree

The most serious problems had still another source, the sheer size of the reform group. During the four preceding years, the growth of the individual reform offices had greatly enlarged the original planning group, and the creation of INAP saw the addition of still more members. These individuals, many of whom had acquired some status in other areas of work, were now reluctant to accept unquestioningly the leadership of the ex-ONRAP group. In particular those who had come to reform planning from INP had a personal and ideological interest in making administrative reform more political and more revolutionary. Thus, as the second phase of the reform efforts began the scene was also set for an increasingly bitter internal struggle.

Two key figures in this battle were Eduardo Urrutia, now the technical director of INAP and second in command after General Guabloche, and Carlos Malpica, the former educational planner from INP and ex-director of ESAP who was now in charge of INAP's Direction of Rationalization.[27] Not an administrative planner by

training and more directly influenced by INP's doctrines of participation, redistribution, and social
change, Malpica was openly critical of the apolitical
technician's approach to reform. Although formally
Urrutia's subordinate, he had sufficient following in
INAP to make his case heard and he was also aided by
General Guabloche's lack of interest in entering internal battles. Unlike Urrutia and Malpica, Guabloche
seemed to view INAP as a temporary post in which he
would be best served by minimizing conflict and preserving the appearance of unity.

Under Urrutia's leadership, further activities
were directed through internal study groups set up to
analyze aspects of the proposed reform.[28] With minimal
direction from the government or Guabloche, the choice
of study areas followed those suggested in the 1973
commission's report and in Urrutia's model, including
decentralization, regionalization, a new ley de bases,
local government reform, and state corporations, as
well as personnel and rationalization. Apart from the
last two, INAP was clearly going beyond its formal mission, but the agency seemed to believe it could define
its own program. This state of affairs was finally in-
terrupted after nine months when the internal divisions
reached an intolerable point. Urrutia proposed to the
government that it either fire Malpica or accept his
own resignation, and when it failed to act, left the
institute, taking with him his most loyal supporters.
Many of the latter went on to jobs in other parts of
the bureaucracy while Urrutia moved to a general advisory position on the Prime Minister's staff.

Unfortunately, Urrutia's departure did not end the
conflict. The INAP staff was no longer polarized, but
those who remained had a variety of views on reform.
Furthermore, now that his antagonist was gone, it became clear that Malpica's position on reform was too
vague to provide much direction to the institute. His
enthusiasm for the revolutionary theme of participation
inspired a series of informal programs to raise bureaucratic moral (including a sportsday titled REDTAP").[29]
Applied within INAP it produced a decision to rotate
staff from one office to another to promote communica-
tion and identification with the institute as a whole
rather than with individual programs. Whether that end
was attained is unclear, but the staff complained that
the rotation delayed further progress. It also meant
that disagreements over objectives and strategies were
never ironed out, but were instead incorporated serial-
ly, producing continual revisions and further delays.

The Second Eclipse

By the end of 1975, work within INAP had effectively come to a halt. The institute had become a
monument to the administrative problems it was created
to resolve. With a staff of around 350 and after almost two years of existence, it was still outlining a
program of action. Various groups within the institute
had progressed to designing substantive programs, but
because the leadership had established no general
guidelines, their plans were contradictory and unmarked
by much concern for the likelihood of their implementation. The ministerial rationalization offices, bereft
of any direction were operating independently amidst
complaints about INAP's incompetence and obstruction-
ism. Even ESAP had ceased its training programs and
entered another period of reorganization.

The two programs on which the government did demand results, a job classification and wage scheme, and
regionalization, were released in record time, but both
encountered problems which held up their implementation. By mid 1976 the personnel scheme was far behind
schedule and because of threatened protests by public
employees over changes in wage scales, had been rede-
fined as a simple job classification. The regionalization plan, presented for public discussion in early
1976, had been shelved indefinitely because of the popular uproar it created. Most criticisms of the latter
plan came from groups in favor of regionalization, but
opposed to INAP's version for reasons ranging from the
purely opportunistic to the ideological. The most important target of complaints was the choice of regional
seats--predictably inhabitants of cities not chosen for
this position protested that the arrangement would work
against them. The INAP staff was still engaged in research on regionalization, but responsibility for the
plan itself had been shifted to the Prime Minister's
advisory group while several offices elsewhere in the
bureaucracy were designing their own competitive
schemes. The one other area in which the government
had shown a specific interest, the simplification of
basic procedures, had seemingly not captured the interest of the INAP staff and was left to the ministerial rationalization offices. The latter saw the
inattention as a further cause for complaints about
INAP's disregard for their needs and interests.

In short, internal morale and the institute's external prestige had sunk to all time lows. While the
office was not widely known, those who were aware of

its existence and purpose acknowledged that it had done
very little and suggested that it even posed an obstacle to further reform efforts. Lower level administrative employees learned of its existence through INAP's
own public relations campaigns, but they seemed uncertain as to its functions. In some cases they came to
see it as an information center on administrative reg-
ulations and a friend in court for individual appeals.
Some observers suggested that this might be INAP's final role. Whatever its future, it was clear that its
decline had now reached the stage of a vicious circle.

REFORM ACCOMPLISHMENTS: 1968-1976

     The reform institutes, INAP and its predecessors,
were in some sense the least successful part of Peru's
administrative reform. While acknowledging their
shortcomings, it is well to keep in mind the accomplishments that were made. These eight years saw less
change than had been anticipated and much which had not
been included in the formal proposals. Still, it would
be a mistake to equate INAP's decline with the total
collapse of the reform effort.
     First, although perhaps least important, were the
changes that the reformers themselves brought about.
The most important of these was the initial reorganization. While its impact may have been overrated, it was
still more than any previous government had achieved.
The 1969 reorganization was followed by a series of
lesser reshufflings of existing and newly created offices, all of which were accomplished rapidly and
fairly smoothly, although the reformers often played
only a minimal role. These changes included the creation of the Ministry of Fisheries, a series of reorganizations in the Ministry of Education, and the
division of the Ministry of Agriculture into two new
ministries in 1974. In terms of its other major programs, personnel reform, regionalization decentralization, and the like, INAP's record was less impressive. With the exception of the personnel programs
none of them got beyond the planning stage where
breakdowns most often occurred because of unresolved
differences of opinion within INAP. That the personnel
program got as far as it did was largely due to its
division into several parts, but after a series of
false starts it remained in the initial phase of job
classification. The wage issue, and the protests it
provoked among public employees who feared any change
would eliminate rather than add benefits, proved the
major obstacle to further progress. Once its resolution was postponed, much of the impetus behind the
classification scheme disappeared as well. Disputes
within INAP over the final objectives of the personnel

programs were also a problem,[30] and probably as critical as the general lack of interest on the part of higher level ministerial staff whose cooperation was essential for implementation.

Still, if INAP made little headway with its programs, its efforts and proposals did encourage a wider interest in and awareness of the need for change. Some of this interest emerged in other administrative offices to produce real changes and a pattern of localized reform efforts. This was especially true of the areas of decentralization, regionalization, and more limited internal reorganizations. Although the government's financial difficulties, which had reached crisis level by mid 1976, proved a severe constraint, by that time most ministries were taking steps to establish or upgrade their own regional offices and some had begun to sponsor experiments in intersectoral regional administration. With the participation and occasionally the leadership of the ministerial rationalization office, discussions of further internal reorganizations continued and some attention was given to the problem of upgrading and modernizing basic procedures to promote greater efficiency. This piecemeal and often short-sighted approach to reform had the potential for creating as many problems as it resolved, but it produced some dramatic changes. One outstanding example is the case of CENCIRA, a highly ideological training institute for campesinos.* CENCIRA's leadership declared a rapid decentralization program, radically reducing their central staff and simply reassigning the surplus to the provinces. Reassigned personnel had only two alternatives--accept the decision or resign.

By 1976 the government had begun to show a renewed interest in accelerating some aspects of administrative change, first pressuring INAP for results and then, confronted with the organization's ineffectualness, taking direct action on its own. By mid 1976, the Council of Ministers had issued two decrees[31] aimed at facilitating and encouraging the delegation and decentralization of ministerial functions, although leaving the details of implementation up to the ministries themselves. The issue of regionalization although temporarily left in the relative limbo of the Prime Minster's office reappeared several months later as part of the government's second five-year plan. Here, and to an even greater extent in the area of personnel reform, the military's interest in change seemed to be accompanied by a major uncertainty as to what ought to

---

*Peasant farmers

be done. INAP's failures contributed to that uncertainty by reducing the government's faith in the experts and by demonstrating that the venture was neither as simple nor as foolproof as it had first appeared. The dispersed sources of potential support for reform within the bureaucracy, demonstrated by the occasional proposals for more limited change, did nothing to resolve the most troubling problem of finding a direction and directors for the reform effort. Until that problem was resolved it seemed unlikely that what remained of the reform movement would regain much momentum.

THIRD STAGE OF REVOLUTIONARY
REFORM: 1977-1978

Despite the scattered signs of government interest, Peru's administrative reform movement appeared to be on its last legs by mid 1976. However, it was not dead yet, and in the next six months it experienced still another revival under a slightly altered set of priorities. The revival is symptomatic of the inherently sporadic nature of wider interest in administrative reform, a function both of the narrow natural constituency (the reform experts) and the difficulty if not impossibility of evaluating reform outcomes and impacts (and so monitoring the experts' performance). More importantly, it is evidence of the trade-off between administrative reform and more substantive types of policy. By 1976, with an increasing number of policy failures behind them, the military government had lost much of its revolutionary zeal and self-confidence. It then turned to administrative reform in the absence of more appealing alternative programs.

New Pressures on the Movement

There were a number of specific reasons for the revival, most of which spring from changes in the political and administrative situation of the country over the intervening eight years. These changes provided pressures and cues from outside the reform group for new priorities and a new short term program. They thus supplied the specific political directives and the unified thrust the reformers had been incapable of generating. Not all of the relevant changes were administrative; those that were, for the most part were not produced by the reformers. Despite the reformers' failures, Peru was undergoing considerable administrative change during this period, much of it the consequence of decisions in more substantive policy areas.

Three major developments are of particular significance for the revival of the movement. The first

and most important was the economic problems experienced by the country in the mid- and late 1970s, cul-
minating in the crisis of 1977-78. The crisis was
characterized by severe inflation, a balance of pay-
ments deficit, and escalating foreign debts requiring a
series of renegotiations with the country's creditors.
Two aspects of the crisis had direct repercussions on
the administrative reform programs. First, although
some of the problems were the result of bad luck, a
good many of them could be blamed on poor policy
choices and plain mismanagement in the public sector.
One conclusion was that the latter was not performing
adequately and that something needed to be done about
it. Second, Peru's creditors and the IMF in particular
entered the renegotiation process insisting that the
country adopt a more conservative economic policy and
suggesting cutbacks in public sector spending in particular. Thus, from these two directions, the economic
crisis pointed to the need for further administrative
change but with very specific objectives.

A second source of pressure for renewed reform efforts originated in the expansion of the public sector
after 1968. This expansion cannot be attributed to the
reform movement itself, although the reformers did benefit from the additional leeway for action it gave
them. The expansion can be measured in several ways
and in all of them it came under the criticism not only
of the IMF and other foreign creditors but also of the
Peruvians themselves. Public sector growth was evident
in the statistics[32] for public employment and spending,
and in the changes in the nature of government activity. During the period from 1960 to 1975 total government employment increased absolutely, from 179,000 to
over 450,000 and as a proportion of the total work
force, from 6 to 11 percent. The government's share of
gross domestic product went from 8 to 22 percent over
the same period (in 1967 it was still only 11 percent).
The revolutionary government's activist stance toward
national development also took it into entirely new
areas of social, economic and political activity, significantly expanded the number of entities, size of employment and budget in the decentralized sector (where
nationalized enterprises and other nontraditional agencies were usually placed), and with the help of the reform movement, increased the number of ministries and
the internal complexity of each. Thus even without the
external economic pressures or the domestic inflation,
the sheer dimensions of the change were enough to provoke demands that it be controlled, redirected, or even
reversed.

There was a final factor contributing to the revival by heightening the sense of urgency. This was

the impending transfer of government to civilian control programmed for 1980[33] and well under way with the
June 1978 election of a constitutional assembly. As
the date for transfer drew near, the military rulers'
tolerance for and interest in experimental projects and
open ended research decreased. At the same time they
were increasingly under pressure to introduce the
changes they did want as rapidly and effectively as
possible. As a result, the government once again presented the reformers with a list of high priority
objectives and projects and once more kicked the reform
movement into action.

Organizational Changes

Characteristically the third stage began with a
personnel change -- the military director of INAP was
replaced with another military leader, General Jorge
Luna Salinas. Surprisingly, the transition did not
involve a change in civilian personnel, and the civilian director, Carlos Malpica remained in his position
as did the other high ranking civilian staff. There
was one important although relatively invisible personnel change, the departure from the country of two
important figures of INAP's early days, the U.N. advisor, Juan Ignacio Jimenez and the ex-head of INAP, Eduardo Urrutia. Although both men had already lost
their formal ties with INAP, loyalty to them and their
ideas remained strong. It took their complete disappearance from the scene to reduce their influence and
the conflicts it provoked. Conflict was further reduced within the institution with the apparent decision
of leaders like Malpica to veer away from the "participatory" theme of the second stage. Thus, with the effective elimination of these two extreme reform positions INAP's staff was able to reunite around a compromise position which, because it was less dogmatic, also
allowed them to work on better terms with the political
leadership and with other administrative bodies.
This last effect of the compromise position is
particularly evident in INAP's new relationship with
other would-be leaders of administrative change. The
era of economic crisis and the demand for reduced costs
was also the era of the rise of the Ministry of Economics and Finance (MEF) to an undisputed central position in the administrative system and the corresponding
decline of the National Planning Instutite (INP). The
latter was in disrepute because of its leftist orientation (unlikely to be popular with the post 1975 governors) and its association with the overly ambitious
policies of the first phase government. All three institutions, INAP, the INP and the MEF, each with its

own institutional expertise, had been rivals for control of the administrative system. The change in relative positions and the changes within INAP, and in the
INP as well, now made it easier for these two to cooperate. In at least one area INAP's "progress" over
these last two years was really the result of its adopting work begun earlier by the INP. Relations with the
Ministry of Finance were not so cordial and led to some
problems for INAP's ongoing programs as well as its
future role.

The first step in the new program was the predictable internal reorganization of INAP, accompanied by
revised statements of the reform doctrines and models.
The principal revisions were really criticisms of the
Jimenez-Urrutia model. An important part of the new
doctrine was thus a formal rejection of elaborate theories.[34] INAP members now complained that the systems
approach was too centralized and too rigid, that it had
been used to equate reform with building systems in the
most concrete sense and that as a result, it only aggravated many of the initial problems of inflexibility.
Future reforms and especially reorganizations would
take into account organizational differences and adapt
to them. Still, the internal reorganization preserved
the basic systems of the old model--personnel (Direccion Nacional de Personal, DNP), rationalization
(Direccion Nacional de Racionalizacion, DNR), and
training (Escuela Superior de Administracion Publica,
ESAP). A new system, supplies (Abastecimiento), as of
the end of 1978 was still contained within the DNR at
the central level although offices were being set up
within the ministries. The reorganization also took
the fundamental "reform function"--presumably basic
research, and the elaboration of plans and models--and
created a new office for it, the Executive Office of
the Administrative Reform Plan (Direccion Ejecutiva del
Plan de Reforma de la Administracion Publica, DEPRAP).
The distinction between the reform function and the
routine work of the other offices was a fine one and
produced some resentment in the latter.[35] Still the
decision encouraged more progress during these two
years by reserving to DEPRAP the more exploratory and
innovative kinds of work. This allowed the other offices and, in the case of personnel and rationalization, their decentralized branches, to devote themselves exclusively to the development and institutionalization of their functions. One longer term result
is that not only the reform program, but INAP itself
received a new lease on life.

Reorganization

Apart from the purely routine work, there were
four main branches of this third stage reform. Three
of them--reorganization, state enterprises, and region-
alization/decentralization--were objects of DEPRAP's
efforts. A fourth area, personnel, remained outside
its province and in some cases, outside the jurisdiction of INAP. The first area in which anything concrete was done was reorganization, a priority of the
government because of its general retrenchment policies
and of its dissatisfaction[36] with the 1969 reorganization and its later modifications. Cutting costs was
a major consideration. This was to be done by down-
grading and eliminating programs and even entire
ministries. Working in conjunction with representatives from the INP and the war college (CAEM), the
DEPRAP team came up with a complex reorganization radically limiting the number of sectors (ministries).[37]
This would be possible through the creation of several
"superministries," within which formerly independent
ministries would now figure as secretariats. The
scheme proved too complex for the junta's needs and
reorganization eventually boiled down to the fusing of
two groups of ministries; Agriculture and Food once
again became merely Agriculture, while Industry, Com-
merce, Tourism and Integration became the ministry of
those areas or MITIC. The confusion resulting from
these initial consolidations--essentially problems of
coordination and redistribution of functions and re-
sources--discouraged the government from adopting the
recommended strategy in other areas. This was hardly
the extent of DEPRAP's intentions in regard to reorganization; it was as much as would be implemented. It
nonetheless continued its basic research in a number of
areas related to the shaping of an entire new legal
structure for the public sector. Its plan of action
for 1977 included almost one hundred major projects
(some to be parcelled out to the other directions)
ranging from studies of forms of rural domination to
restructuring the customs system.[38] Most of this remained untouched, and the likelihood of more progress
being made was further reduced by a number of other
events not foreseeable in 1977 when the plan of action
was set up.

State Enterprises

In the second major area of reform, state enterprises, INAP, ended up doing still less. The problems
here were the size and complexity of the undertaking,
the lack of clear directives from the government, and,

perhaps most importantly, the sheer power of the entities involved. These factors had discouraged work during earlier periods as well, making state enterprises
the area where the reformers would always be working in
the "next stage." INAP did begin studies to diagnose
basic problems and also began establishing contacts
with the "decentralized sector" through the rationalization system.[39] However, the few concrete steps
taken in these years--involving the reprivatization,
scaling down or elimination of enterprises--were done
without INAP's participation, demonstrating the lesser
importance given to the institute as well as the essentially political nature of the decisions. Thus the
initial hopes that INAP might develop a technical
scheme for resolving the problem were not met. INAP's
efforts were also discouraged by the fact that this
whole area, and the larger theme of the extent of
direct government involvement in the economy, were
topics likely to be considered by the constitutional
assembly and the new civilian government.

Regionalization and Decentralization

In the third area, that of regionalization and
decentralization, INAP took more innovative steps
although their combined impact was insufficient either
to turn the tide of overcentralization or establish the
direction of future trends. One problem was that here
even more than in the area of state enterprises a number of political and constitutional issues were involved. It was thus unclear how far the military could
go in making changes and still be fairly certain that
the next government would not immediately invalidate
its work. Still, regionalization and decentralization
became major areas of emphasis for INAP, partly because
of government pressures and partly because of staff
preferences. The resulting efforts can be divided into
three major project areas--decentralization (or deconcentration), local government reform, and regionalization. The fact that these areas overlapped to a considerable degree was itself a major obstacle. Its significance was reduced for the time being by the little
progress made in any one of them.

The first area, decentralization, also overlapped
with reorganization because its major thrust was the
physical (deconcentration) and structural (devolution)
redistribution of functions and resources away from the
existing organizational center. In concrete terms,
this meant establishing field offices to take services
and responsibilities out of Lima and encouraging the
delegation of functions, both in the capital and in the

field. It is in the area of decentralization that reform programs showed the most continuity over the entire ten years, especially in their emphasis on a combination of organizational and territorial decentralization through the creation of regional and zonal offices of central institutions and ministries. The two
decentralization decrees of 1976 and a later one in
1978, offering financial incentives to professionals
relocating outside Lima, suggest a government resolve
to accelerate the process. However, progress over the
entire period was slow, and if anything decelerated
over the last two years as a result of the financial
crisis.

Several factors consistently worked as obstacles
to the program.[40] The first of these was the reluctance of higher level officials to delegate authority
to their subordinates whether in Lima or the field.
While the desire to hold onto as much power as possible
was obviously in effect, the common justification--that
the subordinates lacked the necessary skills and abili-
ties--was not entirely fictitious. This was especially
true of field agency staff who often were of lower
quality, because their jobs were unattractive and gave
them little independent power.

A second factor in the case of territorial decentralization was the difficulty of getting qualified
people to leave Lima for the provinces, or the provincial capitals for more isolated areas. This was partly
a matter of the lack of facilities outside the capital
for the comfort of employees and their families, and as
such was a function of the unequal levels of national
development. It was also a result of a fact of administrative life--officials located outside Lima, even
those in high ranking positions, were not likely to
make the connections necessary to further their
careers.

Finally there was a third problem working against
territorial decentralization and one which became worse
as the decade progressed. This was the shortage of
funds. Thus even if the first two problems were over-
come and officials could be found who would go to the
provinces, there often were simply not enough resources
to set up effective field agencies and to pay the high
quality staff to serve in them.

As a result of all these obstacles, progress in
administrative decentralization was very slow over the
entire period. Although by 1978 all ministries had
established some field offices and made some steps toward moving staff out of Lima, the offices were of
varying quality and generally the most ambitious and
best prepared employees gravitated toward the center.
The ministries with the most decentralized structures
were those, like Education, which had always been more

decentralized. Even here progress toward giving fuller responsibility to the regional and zonal offices and toward upgrading the quality of their staff was pain-fully slow. Unfortunately the "system" tended to work against more rapid progress. As one high ranking mem-ber of an agricultural field agency noted, it was still necessary for anyone with ambitions to make frequent trips to Lima to "sit at his minister's feet."

The second type of decentralizing program, local government reform, did receive a new impetus during the third period, although given its prior neglect, any change would have looked positive. Generally, the mil-itary did not show much interest in strengthening local governments (despite a higher level of interest among some members of INAP) because competing strategies like regionalization were inherently more appealing to them (probably because they looked more "scientific"). Attention was also discouraged by the close association of this topic with the return to civilian rule and the revival of the parties whose leaders were very inter-ested in the issue of municipal elections. However, with the return of the civilians imminent, the govern-ment encouraged INAP to address the problem. DEPRAP's response was a series of studies of current conditions and the development of five alternative models of local government[41]--in essence five model laws setting up different systems. In the end, the decision as to a new law was taken out of INAP's hands and given to a commission of prominent civilians, several of them lawyers and many of them experts on municipal reform. More than anything else, this was a recognition of the traditional parties' stake in municipal reform. In any event, the law itself (D.L. 22250) would not go into effect until the transition was begun. The law selec-ted, as well as most of the INAP alternatives, did re-verse a ten-year trend (and one not channeled through the formal reform movement) of increasing central con-trol over the municipal governments. However the pol-iticians were most interested in this because of its effect on party competition rather than for its admin-istrative implications. It is not clear that their law any more than those of INAP really looked out for ad-ministrative considerations.[42]

The last of the three decentralizing programs and the one which did receive more attention was regionali-zation. Regionalization had been an ongoing concern of the government, but a good deal of it had previously been left to the INP. The rapprochement of the two planning institutes and especially of the INP and the DEPRAP staff allowed a joining of their regionalization efforts as well. Thus part of the apparent progress in these two years was simply a synthesis of the formerly

independent efforts of the two agencies. The most important effect of this synthesis and the one of most
interest to the military because of its likely permanent impact was the shift from a strategy of regionalization through the decentralization of central ministries (with the hope that the next step would be the
emergence of some sort of cooperative endeavor at the
regional level among these field agencies) to an emphasis on first creating regional governments (which the
field agencies could later enter.)

The approach started almost by accident, through
the formation in 1970 of a development corporation to
supervise the post-earthquake reconstruction in the
department of Huaraz. The agency evolved into a relatively independent entity with its own budget and its
own ability to plan and initiate projects. It has gone
through a series of organizational forms and titles
(most recently Ordeza and then Ordecentro), but it has
generally been regarded as a remarkably successful experiment throughout its history. Three years after its
creation, in 1973, a second agency was established in
the eastern jungle department of Loreto (Ordeloreto) to
supervise the latter's development. Then in 1978, the
idea caught on and four new agencies were created;
others were still being proposed both by government
planners and by provincial groups.

By this time INAP, after the failure of its own
regionalization scheme, became interested in the first
two agencies as possible prototypes of a regional government project.[43] It was with this in mind that the
four new organizations were created. Unfortunately, a
shortage of funds, and a number of provincial revolts
organized around these and the related Departmental Development Committees (CDDs), cut the experiment short.
By the end of 1978 INAP planners admitted that the existing six regional development organizations (ODRs)
were likely to be the only ones created for some time.
They were even willing to take a second, if not very
optimistic, look at the twenty-one CDDs already in existence. The latter were unlikely substitutes because
they were little more than coordinating committees with
no power or resources of their own.[44] To date they had
only functioned effectively as centers for organizing
provincial protests.[45] It was clear, however, that
even in the case of the ODRs there were many problems
to be resolved. The most effective example, Ordecentro, owed its success to the large amount of resources
channeled into it and the special circumstances of its
creation. As the reconstruction part of its mission
neared completion it was not at all certain that it
would be able to keep up its past performance.[46]

There was a final setback to the regionalization
projects, the impending transition to civilian government. Because of the potential effect of such regional
organizations on future political contests it seemed
unlikely that the civilian politicians would leave any
scheme introduced by the military without further modifying it to their own needs. Thus although efforts in
regionalization and in the other decentralizing programs had produced some changes and new trends, the
most important determinant of future developments and
of the significance of progress to date was the least
predictable one--the changes that would be made by the
next governments.

Personnel Reform

The final major reform area stressed in this
period was personnel. It was unique among the four
programs in not being dominated by DEPRAP and in some
sense, in not even being channeled through INAP.
INAP's National Personnel Office (DNP) still had as its
first priority for the period, as it had had for its
entire existence, the development of an administrative
career law and the establishment of a uniform civil
service system. The latter was to be introduced first
in the central bureaucracy but was programmed to include the decentralized sector and eventually even the
municipalities. In terms of this civil service system
the major thrust of the DNP's efforts (so far extended
only to the central administration) had involved designing a comprehensive job classification scheme and
uniting it with a uniform pay scale and some system for
fitting in the employees. The DNP's preference in this
last regard had been a rank-in-man system (the career
system). Progress in all these areas had been slow,
first because the DNP was unable to keep up with the
ever-expanding task (and with the constantly expanding
bureaucracy). Other obstacles included the adverse
reactions to its early efforts from civil servants, the
constant ad hoc changes--for example in the addition of
a series of salary supplements[47] which taken together
doubled the official wage--required by the government
for reasons of its own, and the fact that the DNP was
also responsible for interpreting, augmenting, and re-
vising the already enormous body of laws and decrees
governing public employees. For a time during the mid-
1970s it appeared that the office would become little
more than a legal aid service for civil servants. Although it had moved beyond that status by the end of
the decade, its staff still devoted much of their time
to consultations with employees and administrators
about various legal problems.

By early 1979, the DNP was slated to release its administrative career law. Ideally, this would establish the career system and, more importantly, eliminate the need for (and the validity of) much of the previous legislation. The likelihood of this monumental feat of standardization being accomplished with a single piece of legislation seemed minute, but if any government could accomplish it, a military regime was the best bet. Events again conspired against it. Although a project of law was ready for release by the end of 1978, its chances of successful implementation were further reduced by a new personnel policy coming from still another source.

This new policy responded to the IMF pressures and in effect comprised the Ministry of Finance's (MEF) efforts to deal with them by reducing government employment by about 30,000. In August, 1978, the MEF issued two decrees: D.L. 22264 which suggested the ways ministries were to cut back on offices and programs and so on positions, and D.L. 22265 which set up a program of voluntary resignations based on financial incentives. Neither decree pleased the public employees whose immediate reaction was a series of strikes ending in the government's agreement to avoid involuntary dismissals. In the end about 25,000 employees did resign under the provisions of the second decree, but it appeared that those leaving were often the most ambitious and better qualified workers who had other possibilities and could use the financial incentives to realize them.[48] The intended targets of the decree, the superfluous, unproductive employees were the least likely to resign, having nowhere else to go. Voluntary resignations also were more frequent in organizations, like the ministries of Agriculture and Finance, where there had been internal problems. Although the immediate result was decreased conflict, here too it was reported that the better qualified left first. The results were especially disruptive in these cases because entire offices might resign en masse. In one instance, reported in national news magazines, it was rumored that the government had delayed payment of the cash incentives to hold onto professionals from an agricultural field agency who planned to resign together to set up their own company.

Given the size and other problems of the Peruvian bureaucracy, the departure of 25,000 professionals was not a major loss. Replacements could be found, and if those resigning really did represent the most ambitious and best qualified employees, then they might have been still more effective in the less than dynamic private sector. However shortsighted the MEF's strategy, it was less catastrophic than its critics like to believe. It did have more serious repercussions on the future of

the personnel program itself. First, although INAP had
nothing to do with the move, the institute frequently
received the blame and in the minds of many employees
was responsible, boding ill for its future relations
with them. Second, since INAP was one of those agencies beset by internal conflicts, it lost a good number
of its young professionals[49] to D.L. 22265, a fact
which would affect its ability to do innovative work in
the future. Third, and finally, worker dissatisfaction
with the decrees provoked the first effort at a comprehensive organization of civil servants. The resulting
· organization, the Intersectoral Committee of State
Workers (Comite Intersectoral de Trabajadores del Estado, CITE) was a temporary one, but its founders had
set a precedent unlikely to be forgotten. It was also
a precedent with which INAP was unprepared to deal and
alongside which its plans for a career system and a
more humanistic bureaucracy seemed still less
realistic.

Looking back over the two year period and INAP's
revival, it is apparent that in most of the areas of
operation, as in this last example, the institute's
plans and models were relatively out of touch with the
dominant course of events. In many cases the staff,
less committed to a doctrinaire view than it had been
five years before, was well aware of the discrepancies
but was unable to do more, given the institution's limited powers and the instructions they received from the
government. In the end, the specific content of programs devised during these two years seems less important than the act of revival itself or than much of the
routine work (elaboration of manuals, job classification, handling of inquiries about personnel laws) in
which the majority of the staff was involved. In effect these two years may have cemented INAP's future as
a more pedestrian kind of organization, in charge of
the routine housekeeping chores associated with managing a large bureaucracy. While it may keep its involvement in "reform" that reform is more likely than
ever to be a highly legalistic venture. The return to
civilian government can only strengthen that trend and
further reduce the institute's independent role by increasing the bureaucracy's participation in planning
change.

SUMMARY: WHY REFORM FAILED IN PERU

The Peruvian case is a particularly good place to
start a review of reform experiments. Although it was
an extraordinarily ambitious reform, it seemingly
should have gone further than it did. The most per-
plexing aspect of the Peruvian reforms is not that they
failed to produce the promised results; in many cases,

the intended impacts were not clear to begin with.
Where they were, there are many reasons for doubting
that the specific proposals would have produced them.
Failure came long before the impact stage, and for most
of the projects consists of their not being implemented
or even passed into law. Given the size of the reform
program and the proven ability of the military government to implement difficult (if not necessarily well
chosen) programs in other areas,[50] this most basic kind
of failure is particularly puzzling, more so in fact
than a failure of implemented programs to bring about
the desired results. This section examines this first
kind of failure. The second kind, which is related to
the quality of planning and raises fundamental questions about the purpose of administrative reform, will
be examined in the final chapter.

In explaining why the reform movement made so
little progress we can discard two of the most obvious
hypotheses: first, that reform failed because the government never intended that anything be done with the
program, and second, that it failed because of the
overwhelming pressures of opposition to the changes involved. Although one can question the depth of the
government's commitment to administrative reform, especially when it had to choose between reform and other
goals, it is highly unlikely that the program was never
intended as more than a symbolic gesture. It was too
elaborately mounted and endowed with resources on the
one hand, and too severely underpublicized[51] on the
other for it to have been a mere exercise in public
relations. Furthermore, if the lack of commitment was
a response to the programs as they finally emerged from
INAP, as opposed to whatever the government may have
had in mind in the first place, there remains the question of why some more concerted effort was not made to
redirect the institute's activities.

The opposition thesis is also hard to support in
view of actual events. Prior to 1968, the most important source of opposition to administrative change (but
also the most important source of change) had been
groups within the bureaucracy working through the traditional political parties and the Congress to prevent
any challenge to their vested interests. The initial
political changes wrought by the military eliminated
these channels of resistance and at least for the first
few years left most of the bureaucratic factions devoid
of protection. Although a few groups--the economic
planners are one of the best examples--did find military patrons, the type of protective relationship
forged under the civilian regimes was never duplicated.
The bureaucracy's ability to resist reform was at a
uniquely low level.

The opposition thesis also pales when we consider
that with the exception of a few proposals, a substantial amount of opposition was simply never visible.
Even in the exceptional cases-the personnel and regionalization schemes of 1976, for example--it is questionable how important the opposition was in preventing
their implementation. The military's willingness in
such cases to withdraw its proposals, apparently to
avoid further confrontations, constitutes an unusual
sensitivity to popular pressure. When contrasted with
similarly unpopular efforts in other areas, where the
government pressed on despite much greater resistance,
they suggest a lower level of interest, with the out-
bursts compounding the uncertainties and reducing faith
in the reformers' advice. These confrontations in fact
appear less important as displays of opposition than as
blows to INAP's credibility and indirectly, to its political backing. They revealed the agency's naivete in
its failures to predict or prepare for the protests and
gave its bureaucratic rivals another chance to point
out its ineptitude.

Both of these hypotheses could be resurrected by
introducing a more complex explanation based on the
internal politics of the ruling military and their new
found interests once in power. There are some instan-
ces--notably in the creation or elimination of ministries[52]--where such interests did come into play.
However, the notion that significant segments of the
government were either actively or passively opposed to
reform, credits them with giving a good deal more attention to the issue than was really the case. The
reform movement in Peru seems to have languished not so
much from this kind of negative attention as from inattention, but inattention in the form of the absence of
support.

To understand why this was the case, we return to
the initial scheme of reform participants and note that
during these ten years only two of them, the reform experts (with occasional challengers for that position)
and the political leaders were effectively involved.
Only the former had a constant involvement. Because of
their antipolitical perspective and their preference
for technical solutions, the military leaders were willing to accept a highly technical definition of administrative reform and so limit their own involvement to a
bare minimum. However, in surrendering the program to
the experts they also ceded their ability to set its
objectives and guarantee that these would parallel
their own interests. The result was a highly irrelevant reform program, or more accurately, one that was
relevant only to the standards of the reformers themselves. The common characteristic of those programs

that were implemented was their origin in specific directives from the military--often for reasons that had
very little to do with the formal objectves of the
movement. Thus, where the military actively intervened
to make its interests felt, the resulting proposals
were more likely to be carried out. Unfortunately,
left to themselves, the reformers were unlikely to try
to duplicate these conditions.

The isolation and resulting irrelevance of the
expert-dominated reform were structured into the program. The government in creating INAP established an
independent, isolated entity which would operate free
from outside pressure. This was what the reformers
wanted. Their isolation allowed them to focus on reform as a purely technical problem and to develop their
own uncompromised perspective on it. If their independence reduced their immediate need to seek allies in
the bureaucracy, the disincentive was mutual. The reformers' lack of real power discouraged bureaucratic
groups from attempting to work with them. A further
and more disastrous consequence of their isolation,
inasmuch as it affected the thrust of their planning
(accentuating its comprehensive aims), was that it
hindered access to information on administrative conditions, both in terms of a more direct knowledge of
problem areas and as regards the potential difficulties
in implementing their plans. On viewing INAP's efforts, it is hard to avoid the impression that its
members were planning in the dark and that this led
them to underestimate the difficulties as well as overlook the areas where they might have been more
successful.

In the end, the experts' monopoly on the reform
movement was counterproductive. It discouraged support, promoted unrealistic planning, and alienated potential allies in the bureaucracy. Over time, it reduced their sphere of action, further limiting their
initially exclusive control over the planning of administrative change. It did this by encouraging conflict
within the reform group and so decreasing their effectiveness and credibility in the eyes of the government. Although some conflict was probably unavoidable,
INAP's isolation and its members' frustration at their
inability to carry out their programs served to turn it
inward. The result was a high level of visible conflict over issues that had no meaning for anyone outside the institution.

INAP's mode of operation and its members' lack of
political skills also encouraged challenges to its
authority from elsewhere in the administration and from
two key organizations--the INP and the Ministry of Finance and Economics. Conflict among organizations with
a claim to a leadership role in the public sector is

not unusual and is evident to some degree in both of
the other cases. Its usual results, highly visible in
Peru, are the loss of opportunities for cooperation and
the retreat of the losing side into narrowly defined
formalistic versions of their original missions.

One further consideration does emerge from this
case and because of its potential practical applications is worth emphasizing here. This is the importance of the organizational setting to the development
of an effective administrative reform. To blame the
failure of Peru's reform process on the reform agency
alone would be a gross exaggeration, but the organizational factor does deserve more attention because, of
all the variables considered, it is among the most
easily manipulated. There are limits to what can be
done directly about the professional biases of reform
planners, the government's preoccupation with other
issues, the generally low demand for reform, or the
disagreements among potential supporters of reform.
Yet the impact of these variables was visibly accentuated by certain of INAP's characteristics. In terms
of organizational strategies, it appears that the military could hardly have made a worse choice. A less
isolated agency, one with some power to act on its own,
an office with more effective contact with or perhaps
the participation of groups elsewhere in the bureaucracy, or any of a series of other variations might
have proved less vulnerable to the obstacles it faced.
Still, the military's failure to experiment with other
organizational forms is not surprising inasmuch as an
agency like INAP has become the virtually universal
solution to the question of how to set up a reform
program.

NOTES

1. Since the events surrounding and following the
military coup have been described in great detail by
others no more background is given here. Those inter-
ested in further information, or in some of the contro-
versies inspired by the "revolution" are referred to
Abraham Lowenthal, (ed.), The Peruvian Experiment
(Princeton: Princeton University Press, 1975); Alfred
Stepan, The State and Society: Peru in Comparative
Perspective (Princeton: Princeton University Press,
1978); and Stephen H. Gorman (ed.) Post Revolutionary
Peru: The Politics of Transformation (Boulder.
Colorado: Westview, 1982).

2. "Plan del Gobierno Revolucionario de la fuerza
armada," reprinted in Peru, Oficina Central de Informacion, La revolucion nacional peruana (Lima, 1975).

3. Although systematic studies of the Peruvian bureaucracy prior to 1968 (or for that matter, afterward) are scarce this tends to be the judgment of foreign and national observers. The fact that the few Peruvians interested in reform often sought to introduce innovations which they found in practice elsewhere in Latin America supports the idea of a relative lag. For more general discussions of the state of the public administration prior to 1968 see Jack W. Hopkins, The Government Executive of Modern Peru (Gainesville: University of Florida Press, 1967); and Rudolph Gomez, The Peruvian Administrative System (Boulder: University of Colorado Press, 1969). The best overview of Peruvian perspectives is found in ONRAP's documents (See note 6). More specialized works include Dan W. Figgins, Jr., "Program Budgeting in Developing Nations: The Case of Peru" (unpublished dissertation, Syracuse University, 1970); Daniel R. Kilty, Planning for Development in Peru (New York: Praeger, 1967); and Peter S. Cleaves and Martin J. Scurrah, Agricultural Bureaucracy and Military Government in Peru (Berkeley: University of California Press, 1982). Yearly reports (Country Development Strategy Statements and earlier Country Assistance Programs) as well as other material submitted by USAID/Lima provide a wealth of information and a rather rosy picture of prospects for change through most of the 1960s when AID was involved in encouraging administrative reform..

4. It is widely acknowledged that the linking of Alliance for Progress funds to national planning was instrumental in the introduction of the latter throughout Latin America. Interviews with Peruvian participants suggest that the Peruvian Minister of Finance, Pedro Beltran, was extremely hostile to the notion and planned to accept it only at the most symbolic level.

5. The history of ONRAP is taken from interviews with former members and from AID documents. Over the period from 1964 to 1968 the latter show a growing displeasure witn ONRAP's priorities and especially its legalistic approach to reform. They also note interestingly that IPANY staff were too often used as additional researchers rather than as sources of expert advice. See U.S. Agency for International Development, Country Assistance Program, Peru, issued annually, 1962-1968. Earlier and later reports (which have gone under a variety of titles, Country Development Strategy Statement, Country Economic Program) are also relevant

6. The documents are too numerous to list here but all were published under ONRAP's authorship within a period of about five years (1964-68). The key document is the Diagnostic; see Peru, ONRAP, Diagnostico preliminar de la administracion publica peruana y propuestas de reforma (Lima: December 1965).

7. These traditional criticisms came from two basic sources. The first is a series of grand themes like "regionalization" and decentralization which have preoccupied Peruvian political writers and politicians for decades and even centuries. The second includes a series of more specialized, contemporary concerns originating within specific administrative offices and which the ONRAP staff tapped by talking directly to these people (and occasionally because they themselves had experience in those offices). Since in both cases (and especially the latter) criticisms often arose from a knowledge of how things were done outside the country, there is already another level of non-Peruvian influence.

8. As far as can be determined the members' political views ranged from conservative to mildly reformist.

9. This last concern is evident in several of the working papers coming out of CAEM (Center for Higher Military Studies), the much publicized military training institute and "think tank." For a discussion of CAEM's activities see Victor Villanueva, El CAEM y la revolucion de la fuerza armada (Lima: Instituto de Estudios Peruanos, 1972).

10. Plan del Gobierno Revolucionario, Section 27, pp. 110-112. The following discussion of the specific proposals is taken from this section.

11. "Exposicion sobre los lineamientos generales para la reforma de la administracion publica," presented by Gen. Angel Valdivia, Nov. 4, 1968, reprinted in Administracion Publica (Lima: INAP, May-August 1970), pp. 76-68

12. Interviews. Valdivia's interest in reform was not well explained, but he was said to be a friend of a later leader of the reform movment, Eduardo Urrutia. He was also a former head of the INP.

13. It becomes apparent on examining the actions of the military regime, that the interests of individual members were often important in determining the direction of policy, much more so than in an open regime where outside pressures might have outweighed them.

14. Unless otherwise noted, information on the reorganization committee comes from interviews with participants and others in Lima.

15. The examples cited here come from interviews.

16. Interviews in a number of offices in Lima raised this point. Several departments, especially those that were part of the enormous Ministry of Public Works, had been shifted numerous times, but seemed to preserve a good deal of independence through it all. One example is the Direction of Irrigation of the Ministry of Agriculture, some of whose older members

still carried the hope that it could become a separate
ministry.

17. In some cases this did bring a substantial
change, although one apparently unforeseen by the committee, in the character and operation of specific
offices, especially those which the reorganization
allowed to expand significantly. The Ministry of Agriculture is a prime example; once removed from the parent ministry and aided by the government's emphasis on
agrarian reform, it took on a whole new organizational
identity.

18. The nontraditional outlook of these new agencies would eventually create problems but over the
short run it facilitated some major accomplishments--
the massive land redistribution for example. In explaining why so little attention was paid to agricultural production, personnel in the Ministry of Agriculture's field offices explained that despite the formal
job descriptions, land redistribution was all that
counted with the government and was the sole basis for
performance evaluations. This single minded dedication
was unprecedented and in the beginning at least the
costs were not apparent.

19. A summary of the Arias Commission's report
and the final report of the second commission are found
in Peru, Comision para la Evaluacion e Implementacion
de la Reforma de la Administracion Publica, Informe
final (Lima, August 1973).

20. The term model is used here following the
Spanish, but it should be emphasized that this is a
prescriptive model or ideal type. One of the most
concise statements of Urrutia's ideas is found in Peru,
INAP, Estudio de la administracion publica (Lima:
December 1974).

21. This vision was considered more technical
than political and believed to derive logically from
certain universal principles as well as from an ap-
preciation of Peruvian tradition (for example the
insistence that Peru was and would remain a unitary
rather than a federal system). Urrutia's design shows
remarkable compatibility with the corporatist schemes
being developed simultaneously by other groups within
the government (e.g., Sinamos), but there is no indication that either side sought to build on the
similarity.

22. Peru, INAP, op. cit.

23. A particular concern of the reformers, since
the days of ONRAP, had been the expanding number of
state corporations. Although most of their solutions
involved the eventual return of these to the private
sector, they also considered a variety of ways in which
the control and orientation of these entities might be

modified over the short run. The government's reluctance to push reform much harder is sometimes explained
as an effort to protect the vested interests proposals
like these or the regionalization/decentralization
schemes threatened. If this ever was a consideration
it appears to have entered only much later in the game.

24. The lower status of INAP is frequently attributed to the INP's opposition to the former's holding a
position equal to its own. A second, if less widely
held belief, is that to create another ministry (and
thus another minister) at that time would have upset
the balance among the various factions within the
Council of Ministers.

25. Decreto-Ley No. 20316, December 11, 1973.

26. The personal offices were a hold over from
times past, and although nominally connected to the
reform effort, remained for the most part one of the
most unreformed and inefficient sections of the bureaucracy. The rationalization offices (occasionally called offices of organization and methods) were newer ad-
ditions, many of them created with the 1969 reorganization and tended to be much closer to INAP in terms
of orientation and operation, although as often hap-
pens, these similarities provoked some very intense
conflicts between them.

27. The history of the conflict within INAP is
taken from a series of interviews with participants and
observers.

28. A summary of INAP's activities during its
first year is found in Peru, INAP, Memoria anual, 1974.

29. It was Malpica's misfortune that by the time
he became leader of the institute, the first stage of
the revolution (with its emphasis on popular participation) had ended, as had whatever chance he may have had
to implement a "revolutionary" reform.

30. This was made apparent in interviews with
those involved or simply interested in the personnel
reforms, who freely admitted that there were several
schools of thought on the objectives being sought, and
frequently criticized what they perceived as the other
side for not understanding the issues. Considering the
fact that the program was stalemated there was some
fairly ambitious planning being done about worker self-
education and salary equalization.

31. Decreto Ley 21292 (October 21, 1975) and Decreto Ley 21512 (June 8, 1976).

32. The figures cited are from David Scott
Palmer, "Peru: Authoritarianism and Reform," in Howard
J. Wiarda and Harvey F. Kline (eds.), Latin American
Politics and Development (Boston: Houghton Mifflin Co.
1979), p. 208. One indication both of the confusion
caused by the rapid rate of growth and the government's

lack of even the most basic kind of knowledge about its own bureaucracy is the enormous variation in figures given by different government sources. INAP itself did not have direct access to this basic kind of data and generally had to depend on statistics gathered by the Ministry of Finance, the INP or other such better endowed entities.

33. The transfer was made as programmed in July of 1980. The elected president Fernando Belaunde Terry, had been ousted by the military in 1968.

34. Much of this is taken from interviews with high ranking members of INAP and of DEPRAP in particular. Not all of them were in total agreement on the new model. Neither the military nor the civilian director was quite as ready as some of the DEPRAP staff to toss out the systems concept entirely. The path to this restatement was, to judge by the documents left by DEPRAP along the way, long and tortuous, with some of the intermediate versions still more esoteric than the old Jimenez-Urrutia statement. See for example, Peru, INAP, DEPRAP, Definicion y analisis de la problematica de la administracion publica peruana (Lima: December 1977).

35. Some of this displeasure was suggested by an unpublished document elaborated by the DNR staff in which they recommended the elimination of DEPRAP or its subordination to their own office. See Peru, INAP, DNR, "Exposicion a la Jefatura" (Lima: January 1978).

36. One of the particular reasons for this dissatisfaction was the case of the Ministries of Agriculture and of Food which had never sufficiently defined or divided their functions. The Ministry of Fisheries with its enormous budget and staff and its attending rumors of mismanagement and corruption was another cause of displeasure. Generally the initial reorganization had created a number of new entities which had thereafter grown rapidly and without much control or guidance. The results--the misuse of resources, duplication of efforts, conflicts, and poor planning--might have been avoided had the process been slower, so it was not only the reorganization plan that was to blame.

37. See Peru, INAP, DEPRAP, Propuesta de reforma de ministerios (Lima: May 1977).

38. Peru, INAP, DEPRAP, Equipo A, Proyecto del plan general de la administracion publica a mediano plazo (Lima: 1977).

39. For example in November of 1978, the DNR sponsored a three-day seminar for representatives from state enterprises on the development of a system of rationalization for the latter.

40. All of these obstacles were described in interviews with INAP personnel and with representative

administrators both in Lima and in the provinces.
Since no systematic study has been done on any of these
issues either by INAP or by Peruvian or foreign scholars, it is impossible to evaluate the significance of
each supposed obstacle or its real impact. Interview-
ees' assessments of their own situations did indicate
that these factors were at work. For example personnel
in central offices, including those in INAP, frequently
remarked on how difficult it was to delegate functions
to field agencies (or in the case of INAP, to the ministerial offices of rationalization and personnel) because of the lesser abilities of the staff. Similarly,
officials in field agencies often discussed their concern at being passed over for promotions. INAP had
done one partial study of the situation which it published in 1976. Unfortunately, it had to rely on
questionnaires sent to the field offices of central
ministries for the necessary data and the latter as a
result were incomplete. See Peru, INAP, DNR, Problematica de la organizacion y del financiamiento de la
administracion publica en el nivel regional (Lima:
1976).

    41. Peru, INAP, DEPRAP, Modelos alternativos de
gobiernos locales (Lima: c. 1978).

    42. One specific complaint later directed at the
law was that it made all municipal units equal, eliminating much of the tutelary relationship between the
provincial and district councils. Neither the political nor administrative consequences of this provision
are predictable, but they are likely to be unsettling.

    43. See Peru, INAP, DEPRAP, Estudio y propuesta
de decentralizacion administrativa (Lima: December
1978).

    44. A discussion of the CDDs is found in Ibid.,
pp. 55-58. The twenty-one units were created from 1972
to 1977, with about three-quarters of them appearing in
the period 1976-77. A single law regulating their organization and powers was passed in 1978 (DL 22208,
June 1978).

    45. Two famous examples occurred at the end of
1978 in the department of Loreto. The first involved
the city of Pucallpa in the province of Colonel Por-
tillo whose inhabitants demanded the creation of their
own development unit, claiming that Ordeloreto paid
attention only to the area around Iquitos, the capital. The second rebellion took place in Iquitos
itself, whose citizens went on strike demanding the
payment of funds from a 5 percent tax on jungle oil
production. In both cases the complaint was that the
government had defaulted on promises to encourage local
development.

46. One indication of the problems was the fact that in the 1978-80 budget only two of the organizations (Ordecentro and Ordeloreto) had specific funding. The others were to have funds turned over to them by the ministries for projects scheduled for each region, a practice which essentially depended on the generosity of the central government in a period when resources were bound to be tight.

47. These included the remuneracion al cargo (a supplement for the job or position occupied), the remuneracion personal (for each five years of service up to forty percent of the base wage) and a number of supplements figuring as cost of living increases. In total they could double the basic wage and utterly destroy whatever system the DNP had planned to impose.

48. This conclusion is based on impressionistic hearsay--i.e., rumors. However interviews with individuals who had resigned or were planning to do so suggest that they invariably made this move only if they had possibilities elsewhere, an indication that popular opinion was on target. On looking at the laws and the incentives they involved it is in fact hard to imagine how they could have produced other results especially after the government agreed to allow only "voluntary" resignations.

49. By the end of 1978, INAP was down to about 200 employees and had lost a good portion of its professional staff. DEPRAP for example had only a handful of researchers and as a result had to curtail several projects.

50. Several of the government's schemes, especially those having to do with the organization or reorganization of economic and political units (unions, collective farms, worker participation in industries, etc.) had incurred considerably more resistance, but in very few cases did this cause the government to back down as rapidly.

51. Although INAP itself carried on some public relations work, until budget cuts prevented even that, it remained relatively unknown even within the public sector. Outside the bureaucracy few people had heard of it or for that matter of most parts of the reform program.

52. It was commonly suggested by individuals in INAP, elsewhere in the administration and in the public at large that the number of ministries was directly dependent on the number of generals from each branch of the service eligible to head them and on the proportion allotted to each service. Thus, the creation of one new ministry might require two more ministerial level positions to maintain the balance.

5
Venezuela:
The Reformer's Reform

*"Venezuela es el pais que mas estudios y proyectos ha elaborado en materia de reforma administrativa."

--Alfredo Pena.[1]

**... En nuestra encuesta nos hemos percatado de que...existe una disposicion favorable a la ejecucion de la reforma administrativa. Empero no entendemos por que si existe ese llamado 'consenso' aun no se ha iniciado el proceso de reforma.

--Alfredo Pena.[2]

Both comments, taken from a series of newspaper interviews on Venezuelan administrative reform efforts, and the fact, significant in itself, that a paper saw fit to run a series on the topic are suggestive of a number of unusual aspects of the reform process in this country. Taken together, these characteristics comprise what appears to be a favorable setting for reform efforts, especially as compared to the situations in Colombia and Peru. Nonetheless, neither the "so-called

---

*Venezuela is the country which has elaborated most studies and projects on the subject of administrative reform.

**In our survey it struck us that there exists an attitude favorable to the implementation of an administrative reform. However, we don't understand why, if this so-called consensus exists, the reform process hasn't begun.

consensus," the extensive planning efforts, nor Venezuela's most important assets, its great wealth and
relatively less volatile political situation, have
produced much more in the way of realized reforms.[3]
Changes have come about, but as contrasted with the
planning objectives, they are slight. In fact the
trajectory of the Venezuelan movement displays more
similarities with the Colombian and Peruvian experiences than might be expected considering the different
political settings.

The differences that do emerge, most of them attributable to variations in background, leadership or
political style, do not seem to diminish the basic
problems. One of the principal obstacles to the Venezuelan efforts, even more than in Colombia and Peru,
has been the several false starts they have undergone.
The Venezuelan reform movement is really a series of
movements and although these have some continuity, each
stage has also involved the rejection or repetition of
work done earlier. In Venezuela, the multiple starts
and the build-up surrounding each one have increased
popular awareness of the programs, but this does not
seem to have affected rates of implementation in any
positive sense. Of the three countries, this is the
one in which reform has been most widely discussed--not
only by a small group of reformers, but by the political parties, the press, and the public. Interest in
administrative reform has not been high as compared
with other issues, but there is still a greater awareness of its existence, and more public discussion of
the problems it raises.

The opening of the issue to wider discussion has
increased its politicization in the very specific sense
of linking individual proposals to political factions
and tying their acceptance or rejection to the latter's
fortunes in the broader political arena. Politicization has also encouraged conflict between the politicians and the reformers over the question of who will
control the reform movements and what kind of criteria
(political versus technical) will prevail. Unfortunately, because reform has remained of secondary importance for all but the administrative reformers, politicization has not led to higher rates of implementation.
Once the political debates begin, administrative reform
proposals are most likely to be sacrificed in favor of
higher priority issues.

The broadly based conflict is also useful in demonstrating the nature of the differences (type of
stakes and resources) separating the three major groups
of participants (bureaucrats, reformers, and politicians) in the reform process. Although all were active
in the other two countries, the differences among them
were often less clearly visible than the divisions

within each group. In the Venezuelan reforms, both
divisions within and between groups are important, a
situation which increases the desirability of alliance
building between factions of different groups. Although alliance building changes the objectives and
impact of reform, the diversity of resources and interests and the fact that the groups with the most
direct interest in change, the reform experts and the
bureaucrats, have the most limited resources make these
alliances a necessary condition for implementation.
There are a number of factors working against the alliances, most notably the desire of the groups involved
to preserve their independence of action and control
over decisions. However, given the narrow natural constituency behind most reform proposals and the inherent
advantage held by supporters of any status quo, alliance formation becomes a critical strategy for those
proposing change.

HISTORICAL OVERVIEW

The trajectory of the Venezuelan reform movement
from 1958 to 1978 can be divided into at least three
periods, separated by the political events which gave
them their initial impetus. Here, as elsewhere, administrative reform has become a partially symbolic issue,
associated with periods of attempted political change.
Each of the three reform periods accompanies a change
of administration and an effort to define a break with
the past. Unfortunately, once that break is defined
through other developments or simply by the passage of
time, the drive for administrative change loses its
importance. Consequently, the reform process is characterized by a cyclical rise and fall.
The first of these periods, and the one treated
most briefly here since it has been described in other
literature,[4] stretches from 1958 to 1969. It comprises
the period of the first two Accion Democratica ("adeco") governments which followed the ouster of the dictator, Perez Jimenez. Discontent with corruption under
the Perez government, and the desire to establish the
radically different character of the new regime led to
an initial emphasis on administrative reform and to the
establishment of reform entities and programs which set
the pattern for following administrations. This period
has been criticized by later reformers for its lack of
accomplishments and the absence of a coherent reform
program. It was important in establishing administrative reform as a symbol of government's commitment to
change and in turn for setting the general agenda of
issues and introducing the reform mechanisms which
would continue to be influential over the following
years.

As the new government's need to establish a break
with the past diminished, so did their interest in administrative reform. By 1968 the movement had fairly
well wound down. The victory of the opposition party,
COPEI, in the presidential elections of that year once
more raised the need to signal a break with the past
and so brought administrative reform to the fore. In
this second stage, with the formation of a core group
of reform experts (some of whom had been influential in
writing the COPEI platform) and the enlargement of the
reform apparatus, the movement began to take on a life
of its own and the participants to represent a permanent, if not very powerful pressure group within the
government. The persistence of this group and their
ability to retain their influence on policy despite a
low success rate in program implementation were enhanced by their contacts with similar groups in other
countries (notably Peru and Mexico) and their attachment to an international community of reform experts.
Somewhat paradoxically, at the same time that a dis-
tinctively Venezuelan reform doctrine and reform group
began to emerge, both were strengthened by a new set of
international contacts and as a consequence became less
dependent on conditions within the country itself.
    The second stage lasted only through the Caldera
administration (1969-74). Its end was marked by the
change of administration (to another Accion Democratica
regime, under President Carlos Andres Perez), the departure of the leaders of the reform group, and a general cutback both in the reform apparatus and the new
government's commitment to a centralized reform program. Although a core group of reformers remained in
the central office and continued to be influenced by
the second stage doctrine, and although some programs
based on that doctrine were continued, the movement
became more fragmented and the conception of reform
more diffuse, with attention focusing on such concrete
problems as corruption and the performance of state
enterprises.
    During this third period several new tendencies
emerged. First, the formal reform group found much of
its work reduced to a more routine level, particularly
in terms of aiding and advising individual agencies on
their specific organizational problems. While much of
this was done on the basis of the broader reform doctrine elaborated earlier, the immediate objectives were
less ambitious and there was some tendency within the
group to criticize the grandiose efforts of their predecessors. Second there was a tendency for specific
proposals to be promoted or generated by groups outside
the formal reform circles, in part motivated by special
interests. The incidence of this opportunistic reform
was not high but it offered an important precedent in

challenging the reformers' monopoly on planning. Finally, the discussion of reform came to be merged with and in some cases eclipsed by a broader debate over the role of the state, shifting the focus from an effort to improve and expand existing organizations to an attempt to define what it was those organizations should be doing. This shift also threatened the reformers' control of planning since it entered an area they had never defined within their jurisdiction.

All of these periods and the specific proposals to which they gave rise are discussed in greater detail below. One preliminary generalization can be made about an obstacle common to all periods--the lack of wider specific support for administrative reform. Despite the more open discussion of reform, at least as contrasted with Peru and Colombia, the reform planners remained the only group for which it constituted a high priority. Because no one was likely to oppose reform publicly the movement once begun was never eliminated. Still support has rarely progressed beyond the diffuse level and then only on a limited number of issues. The lack of support is not surprising as the changes involved were not perceived as having a direct benefit for a wider audience. Yet despite their discussion of the need for participatory reform (referring to the need to seek the aid and cooperation of bureaucrats in particular), the reformers made little effort to surmount this problem and at times prejudiced their case through direct confrontations with political and administrative groups.

STAGE ONE: LAYING FOUNDATIONS, 1958-1968

As this period is described in a number of other studies, it is only briefly summarized here. Generally, Venezuela's contemporary administrative reform movement is considered to have its real beginning in 1958, during the provisional government headed by Vice-Admiral Wolfgang Larrazabal which replaced the Perez Jimenez dictatorship (1948-58). There had been some preliminary signs of interest even prior to 1958. During the reformist civilian government in power from 1945 to 1948, a Commission for Financial and Administrative Studies (CEFA) was set up in the Ministry of Finance. CEFA's activities were limited and were focused almost exclusively on the financial part of its mandate, but it presence did indicate a general interest in administrative reform within the Accion Democratica leadership. Although it considerably reduced CEFA's powers and resources, the Perez Jimenez government moved in another direction by financing a number of independent studies at the ministerial level most of which were done by foreign consulting firms. For the

most part these narrowly based studies produced no further action; Groves[5] attributes them to a desire to improve the regime's image more than to any real interest
in reform.

In the generally reformist atmosphere following
Perez Jimenez's removal the next step was taken when
the provisional government invited a United Nations
Technical Assistance Mission, headed by Herbert Emmerich, to do an analysis of the country's administrative
needs. Emmerich's report[6] which called for broad reforms in just about every area, included a recommend-
ation for the establishment of a "Hoover Commission" to
do a more extensive study and reform plan. As a direct
result, the Public Administration Commission (CAP, Com-
mision de Administracion Publica) was set up in the
months preceding the presidential elections. Its introduction preceded by several months that of the Central Office of Coordination and Planning or Planning
Ministry (CORDIPLAN); as in Peru, these two agencies
enjoyed a rocky relationship. CAP's eight members were
distinguished representatives of all the major political forces--the parties, business, and the military.
Its first director, Dr. Carlos Lander Marquez, a business leader, had pushed for the reform program and was
also close to the Junta president, Larrazabal. Despite
the auspicious send-off, there were problems from the
start. As one observer notes[7] the Commission's status
was unclear in two regards: its relationship to the
Ministry of Finance under whose jurisdiction it was
placed, and its connection to CEFA which remained in
existence but was never mentioned in the legislation
establishing CAP. Another problem emerged with the
transition to the first elected government, the Accion
Democratica administration of Romulo Betancourt. Betancourt was visibly less committed to administrative
reform than his military predecessor, a result of personal preference and of the politically difficult times
his government faced.

The lack of support from Betancourt and the new
administration's out and out rejection of the Commission's proposals for a reform of the presidential office brought Lander's resignation. In his few months in
office he had set a major precedent for the Commission
by contracting with three U.S. consulting firms to do
studies in the basic reform areas (two areas, organization and methods, and personnel were taken from Emmerich's report and a third, procedures, was added by
Lander). The Emmerich report had suggested such an
action, but on a much smaller scale. Emmerich apparently believed that the Venezuelan staff was capable of
doing the essential research and that consultants
should be called in only on very technical matters.
The initially more important position given the foreign

consultants by Lander and his own declining interest in
the project meant that the Commission's work came
increasingly to be directed by outsiders, and specifically by a series of technical advisors on loan from
the United Nations.[8] These advisors were particularly
instrumental in building up a fourth area of commission
work, training. The arrival of a U.N. expert in this
area led to the creation of a comprehensive program
aimed at the Venezuelan analysts.

Under the Betancourt government, Lander was followed by two other directors, Benito Raul Losada (1959-
1960) and Alberto Lopez Gallegos. The latter, a lawyer,
had a personal interest in administrative reform, having served as both a governor and municipal president,
as well as being an ex-director of the Advanced School
of Public Administration of Central America. He was
also one of the original eight members of the commission until his resignation following a disagreement
with Lander.[9] Given this background, Lopez's efforts
at imposing his own perspectives on the Commission came
as no surprise. Lopez's major change was to shift from
an emphasis on comprehensive reform to a focus on a
limited number of areas and agencies. The personnel
program received a major push under this strategy especially in such steps as the formation of ministerial
and agency personnel offices and the completion of a
job classification scheme. A civil service law, designed by one of the consultant teams, was never passed
because of congressional opposition. However, considerable progress was made possible by means of an executive degree issued at the end of the period. Lopez
also cut back the number of foreign advisors, apparently as much from personal conviction as for the
official reasons of economy. Finally, he lobbied successfully for the formation of an Institute of Public
Administration. Although the institute remained understaffed and underfinanced for several years, it set a
base for future action.

From the end of the Betancourt period, when Lopez
resigned his position on the grounds of poor health, to
the end of the Leoni government (1963-68) no other major steps were taken. The work begun by Lopez in implementing the civil service decree was continued, most
of it involving such routine measures as the elaboration of manuals and control procedures, the establishment of more ministerial and agency personnel offices,
and the creation of training programs for their staff.
Two major accomplishments were the completion of an
initial job classification scheme and the first salary
schedule.[10] There was also a continuing effort to
centralize the entire system through CAP's personnel
division and the presidency in turn. To the extent
that both offices now received notification of a large

portion of major personnel actions taken within the
central bureaucracy, the program was generally considered to have been successful. It was not clear,
however, that this had any greater impact on personnel
policy except for eliminating some potential for gross
mismanagement.

The routine nature of the personnel work and the
limited impact account for CAP's ability to work unop-
posed. In addition, although government support for
administrative reform as a whole had languished, that
for the personnel program remained high.[11] Efforts
were further aided by support or at least lack of opposition from the public employees who, after some initial protests, came to see the possible advantages of
the new system in terms of job security and related
benefits. By the end of the Leoni administration much
of the preparatory work toward the enactment of a career system had been completed. However as the out-
going president showed signs of a considerably lessened
interest, the Commission members saw themselves with
little future and a mass exodus of professional staff
occurred.

SECOND STAGE: REFORM UNDER THE CALDERA GOVERNMENT,
1969-1974[12]

The reform program seemed to have reached a dead
end at the close of the Leoni administration. It got a
second chance with the 1968 presidential elections and
COPEI'S decision to include administrative reform in
its platform. This decision was in part the result of
such chance factors as the COPEI candidate's acquaint-
ance with one of the chief proponents of reform and the
man who would be picked to head CAP, Allan Brewer-
Carias. Judging by the willingness of the other parties to adopt the issue, it also appears to have had
some appeal for the political leadership, a probable
legacy of the earlier program. The renewed interest in
reform was also a product of the changing political
situation. As the country moved into a more stable
era, and after the implementation of the first round of
social and economic reforms, new issues were needed.
It was now possible to turn to a variety of less urgent
projects, including administrative reform.

The issue's reemergence cannot be traced to wider
public demand. As before, it originated in pressure
from within the political leadership and from the
would-be reformers themselves. Particularly important
were a number of COPEI policy makers[13] with an interest
in what they termed "organization for development" and
a new group of administrative experts linked to COPEI
who were already forming contacts with reform groups
elsewhere in Latin America (and notably in Peru and

Central America). Thus, with the COPEI leadership's
interest in establishing new policy directions as a
facilitating condition, the experts were on their own
to design a new program.

The New Leadership and Its Program

As the presidential campaign got under way, the
reform program was developed by a small group led by
the man who would dominate it for the next years, Allan
Brewer-Carias. Brewer was a young lawyer and professor
of administrative law, who had studied in Paris. He
was already making a name for himself as an outspoken
critic of the existing administrative situation and
gained still more attention with a widely publicized
speech he gave in May of 1968[14] which became the basis
for COPEI's platform on reform. In the speech and in
the platform, the emphasis was on the state's responsibility for national development and the inadequacy of
the existing administrative structure to fill that
role:

> *Se resume en una sola frase: ella no responde ni
> desde el punto de vista estructural ni desde el
> punto de vista funcional a las exigencias del
> desarrollo nacional[15]

Elaborating on points raised by Brewer in his
speech, the government program further commented that
the existing structure was the product of an "alluvio-
nal and irrational growth and proliferation"[16] of both
central ministries and state enterprises and was characterized at the central, state and municipal levels by
duplication of function, inadequate resources, and
overcentralization. In terms of other specific problems, criticisms were directed at the absence of legal
norms, the lack of definite objectives and adequate
control and coordination, and the inattention to prin-
cipals of scientific organization. The program stressed the inadequacies of the personnel system, citing
the prevailing popular opinion that "the personnel at
the service of the state were numerous and inefficient"[17] and attributing this situation to insecure
tenure, the lack of a career system, the prevalence of
patronage in hiring, and the absence of any kind of
personnel planning. The proposals for reform[18] covered

---

*It can be summarized in one sentence: it [the struc-
ture] does not respond either from the structural point
of view or from the functional to the requirements of
national development.

all these areas and began with the reorganization of
the entire system, to be directed through a number of
offices attached directly to the presidency (a Secretary of Planning, of Popular Promotion, of Administrative Reform, etc.). Regional and municipal reform was
also stressed as was the introduction of an updated
personnel system which would encourage "honesty and
efficiency."

This first cut at a reform plan was relatively
vague, largely juridicial in focus, and distinguished
from its predecessors most notably in its extremely
broad scope. It was, as its chief creator later characterized it, "an invention."[19] It had little in the
way of an empirical base, as is suggested by a reliance
on mechanisms like the interministerial committee, a
device which despite its logical appeal has rarely
worked well in practice. There were a few new elements
which were either the product of past experience with
reform or responses to the contemporary political climate—for example, an emphasis on popular participation
in decision making (which was never defined much further than that) and the reassurance in the section on
personnel reform that its objective was not a cutback
in employment. On the whole, the proposals were so
general that, like the overridng goal of national development they were almost undebatable.

Organizational Changes

With the victory of the COPEI presidential candidate, Rafael Caldera, the next step was his invitation
to Brewer to head the old reform agency. Given his
participation in writing the COPEI program, Brewer was
a natural choice, but the move had further implications. Although higher ranking copeyanos had shown
some interest in the program, it apparently was not
enticing enough to do more than attract their support
and they offered Brewer no competition. Brewer's selection also suggests several things about the way the
program was viewed. Since he was chosen for his technical expertise rather than a political background, it
is apparent that the program was defined as a technical
one. The fact that he was put in charge rather than
serving as assistant to a political director reinforces
this point and also suggests the politicians' reluctance to enter the area. Whether this was because
reform was viewed as politically less interesting and
promising or as too sensitive to warrant the risk is
not clear, but the absence of a political volunteer for
the position is significant.

Prior to taking over the new position, Brewer
began to make contacts with reform groups outside the
country, building up the international connections that

would be influential in shaping the Venezuelan program.
A trip to Mexico on another project provided contacts
with the Mexican reform commission. A subsequent trip
to Peru as legal assessor for the Andean group also
allowed meetings with the Peruvian commission and its
president, Eduardo Urrutia. (The U.N. advisor, Juan
Jimenez who had been influential in Peru later visited
the Venezuelan CAP). Contacts with both these groups
were maintained even after Brewer's departure from the
Commission, and the reciprocal influence is evident in
the schemes developed in all three countries.[20] Thus
although under Brewer the use of technical aid missions
from international organizations and the United States
declined, and the Commission exercised more discretion
in selecting its foreign advisors, this new type of
foreign influence came to be more important.

With the entrance of the Caldera government,
Brewer was apparently feeling secure enough to set further conditions on his acceptance of the CAP director-
ship. The first of these he termed "absolute liberty
to invent" (libertad absoluta para inventar)[21] meaning
that the shape of the reform would be left to the Commission rather than being dictated by the government.
The latter could veto any proposals but only after the
Commission had first presented them. The second condition which was met only in part was the Commission's
direct attachment to the office of the president. Here
the more powerful Minister of Planning, Luis Enrique
Oberto, intervened with the result that CAP was attached to the planning office, CORDIPLAN. CORDIPLAN
did not have veto power over CAP's proposals, but the
reformers saw this as a subordinate position, although
one with temporary advantages owing to CAP's low prestige. A final condition was that CAP's decreto de
reglamento[22] (a decree law finalizing its form and
functions) be approved immediately; this was done in
July of 1969.

These conditions were interpreted as victories by
the CAP members and they did facilitate their activities over the short run. It is also clear that they
were easily met because of the low level of interest in
the program and the tendency to view it as a purely
technical matter. Brewer's "freedom of invention" was
no problem in a situation where no one else had other
suggestions; for similar reasons, the decreto de
reglamento, written by the Commission, was accepted
without modification. None of this involved the approval of anyone but Caldera and his closest advisors
and they had more pressing concerns. Later this lack
of direction and autonomy of action would be a problem,
especially for proposals requiring wider support for
their implementation.

In writing the reglamento, Brewer and his collaborators tried to strengthen their position by introducing an executive committee chaired by the Commission's
director and including the viceministers of CORDIPLAN
and Finance. They planned to involve representatives
of the most important ministries and so enhance the
Commission's status.[23] Furthermore, the reglamento
specified that any proposals having to do with administrative reform had to go through the Commission before
they could go into effect. Although CAP had no veto
power and was limited to offering its opinion, this
would, if respected, give it further leverage.

First Steps and First Conflicts[24]

It was this section of the reglamento which produced the Commission's first conflict with the government. Shortly after Brewer took office he received a
copy of a projected resolution from the office of the
Minister of Finance. It proposed a reorganization of
the Ministry in accord with the general reform program
and the creation of a ministerial reform office to direct it. This followed an earlier proposal from Finance
suggesting a general plan for creating similar offices
in all ministries. Interpreting these projects as a
move by the Minister of Finance, Pedro Tinoco, to undercut the Commission's power, Brewer went to the head
of CORDIPLAN with the complaint that Tinoco's proposal
could not be considered by the Council of Ministers
without CAP's prior opinion. Then, he and the Commission struck back with a counter proposal establishing
ministerial administrative reform councils or ORCAs
which would be directly linked to CAP. This move not
only provided the Commission's first victory against
efforts to ignore it into ineffectiveness, but it accelerated the first stages of the reform program, forcing the reformers to take steps they might have delayed for months or years. The creation of the ORCAS
was one example--while CAP might have eventually promoted some such organization, its preliminary plans had
not envisioned anything of the sort.
The inauguration of the ORCAs also provided an
opportunity for further publicizing the reform within
the bureaucracy with a series of speeches given as each
council was installed over the next two and a half
months. In these speeches the reformers began to elaborate the details of their own program and to devise a
model of the reform. It was here that the three fundamental divisions of macro-, micro- and functional reform emerged as well as the guidelines for the ministerial councils (which were responsible for the micro-
or internal reforms).[25] Brewer kept a tight watch over
all of this, writing many of the documents himself,

which in the long run would lead to criticisms of over-
personalization of the reform. Still, the speed with
which the Commission set up its initial program was
widely noticed and helped to dissipate some of the
reputation for inactivity it had earned in the preceding years.

Personnel Reform

In these preliminary efforts, the Commission had
been working on its own initiative with virtually no
direction from the presidential office. This was an
initial advantage because it allowed the reformers to
take potential opponents by surprise. In 1970, CAP was
thrown back into the wider political arena as the opposition (Accion Democratica) controlled Congress[26]
moved to review the long pending administrative career
law with an eye toward finally passing it. The motive
here was highly political--the law which had been opposed for so long because of its potential effect on
the political control of appointments now was viewed by
the adeco Congress as a way of preventing the copeyano
government from stacking the bureaucracy with its own
followers.[27] Meanwhile, neither CAP nor the Caldera
administration, the latter having promised a civil service reform, was adverse to taking advantage of the
sudden turn of events.

The Commission did object to the version under
consideration, which it viewed as entirely out of
date. At Congress's invitation it produced a new
reform which was accepted with only minor changes.[28]
Among the changes imposed by Congress was the removal
of the central personal office from the Commission's
control. Brewer and his group raised no objections,
realizing this would give them more time for other
aspects of the reform and free them from the wealth of
details the personnel program would now entail. Their
reaction suggests a lesser commitment to the supervi-
sory and implementation aspects of reform as well as a
disregard for power politics. It also clearly limited
their self-defined role to drawing up the optimal reform scheme; in this vision their responsibility ended
once that scheme had been passed on to the President
and Congress.

The New Reform Doctrine

With the Commission's part in the personnel reform
completed, its members could turn their attention to
the wider task of reorganizing the entire bureaucracy.
Here again outside events intruded to accelerate their
pace of work, this time in the form of a proposal for
creating a ministry of housing.[29] The Commission and

Brewer in particular interpreted this proposal, originating in the executive office, as another infringement
of their jurisdiction. In January 1970, they thus presented a protest to the head of CORDIPLAN, stating that
no ministry could be created until the criteria for
ministerial reform had been defined. The protest
would, over the next year, produce a series of confrontations with a number of ministers, including those of
Public Works and Finance (Tinoco). In a meeting of the
Council of Ministers attended by Brewer, it was finally
suggested that instead of isolated reforms, CAP would
have to produce an alternative in the form of a comprehensive plan.

The Commission members spent the second half of
1970 on this project. They worked in relative secrecy
fearing opposition from interested groups within the
bureaucracy and government. In January 1971, the final, six-volume report was submitted to the Council of
Ministers where its size and detail effectively stilled
opposition. This document eventually became the 1,000-
page Informe, ("Report") outlining the proposed reform
of the entire public sector. By the time this final
work was presented the Commission had lost any hope of
implementing its scheme. It was then mid 1971, the
middle of the government's term and it was clear that
partisan based congressional opposition would prevent
any further progress. Even the so-called microreforms,
internal reorganizations of individual ministries which
were to be enacted through the budget law were blocked.
The only successful ministerial reform was that of Finance, accomplished because of Minister Tinoco's influence with Congress. The finished report was also Brewer's parting statement. Following its submission in
June of 1971, he resigned his position and left the
country for two years to study and do research abroad.

Up to Brewer's departure, and despite the political opposition, CAP had worked with the strongest sense
of internal mission it had ever had. The speed at
which it worked and the size of the project kept internal disputes to a minimum. Alhough the Commission's
reports complain about limited staffing and budgets, it
had grown from earlier days to a maximum of 125 employees and seven million bolivares in annual budget. The
Commission also made use of the ministerial councils
(ORCAS) especially in working out its diagnosis of
existing conditions and in planning the microreforms.
The ORCAS were the intended vehicles of "participatory
reform".

   * La idea por tanto es que la responsabilidad
      de la reforma debe ser compartida por la
      Comision de Administracion Publica con todos
      los organismos administrativos, y esta es

> precisamente la orientacion, tanto del
> Decreto No. 103 de 23 de julio de 1969 como
> del Decreto No. 141 de 17 de septiembre de
> ese mismo ano, que institucionalizan todos
> los Consejos de Reforma Administrativa. En
> esta forma la Comision de Administracion
> Publica, de organo que pretendia imponer una
> reforma desde afuera, ha pasado a ser un
> organismo normativo, orientador, coordinador
> y evaluador de las reformas que los Consejos
> de Reforma Administrativa haran e inciaran en
> todos los Ministerios e Institutos
> Autonomos.[30]

Despite these provisions, the Commission clearly reserved the dominant role for itself. This was possible not because of its "normative and evaluating" status, but rather because of the inexperience of the ministerial councils, their lack of power and prestige within their ministries, and especially in the early years, their dependence on CAP for guidance. Where, as in the case of the Ministry of Finance under Tinoco, or Public Works under Curiel, a minister himself took an active interest in reform and reorganization, this dependence on the Commission was decreased or even eliminated. However, so long as reform remained of limited interest to higher level administrators, the ORCAs languished unattended and developed little on their own.

CAP's Decline

The central role played by the Commission and its early victories in confrontations with Congress and the Council of Ministers in the end cost it dearly. Even before the end of Caldera's term the reform movement was again in decline; there were many who welcomed this development. In the beginning, opposition to the Commission was of two forms, based on vested interests and

---

*The idea is thus that the responsibility for reform should be divided by the Administrative Reform Commission with all administrative entities and this is precisely the orientation, in Decree 103 of July 23, 1969 and in Decree 141 of September 17, that the Councils of Administrative Reform institutionalize. In this form CAP, from an entity attempting to impose reform, has become a normative, directing, coordinating, and evaluating entity in relation to the reforms that the Councils of Aministrative Reform will make and initiate in the Ministries and autonomous institutions.

on a fear of what CAP might do. Individual administrators like the Minister of Finance, Tinoco, whose position gave them a bureaucracy-wide power, saw CAP as a
rival and opposed it on that grounds. Congress's opposition although stemming largely from partisan hostility, was also based on a fear that the proposed
changes figured as a political power play that would
benefit COPEI. As of 1974, CAP had not only managed to
keep those fears alive, but had also created a series
of new enemies both in Congress and in its own government. Brewer's leadership was responsible for a good
part of this; although his outspokenness and willingness to discuss issues with the press heightened attention to the Commission, it antagonized the targets
of his criticisms. The confrontations with the government in general and with individual ministers lost the
Commission the backing of potential supporters who felt
the director had overstepped his role.

     With Brewer's departure the Commission's prospects
did not improve. Under the new director, Manuel Rachadell, a protege of Brewer's and himself a lawyer, CAP
moved into a number of other reform areas touched upon
in the Informe but with less attention than the basic
reorganization. These areas included regionalization,[31] public information, a study for a proposed
reform of the state enterprises, and sectoral studies,
the latter resulting in some twenty unpublished reports
on the situations in the various sectors (Ministries).
In all of this, the Commission was aided by a special
U.N. advisory project.[32] From 1972 to 1977, the project brought some fifty experts to the country on long
and short term programs to advise on specific aspects
of administrative reform. Although some progress was
made in all areas, the work of the Commission from 1972
to the end of Caldera's term in 1974 produced far more
studies and reports than it did programs. This had its
inevitable effect on morale and the CAP staff began to
leave for other posts. Those who remained were well
aware of the limited prospects for their program and
for themselves. Their resulting cynicism earned them
the title of the "iconoclasts of CORDIPLAN."

THIRD STAGE: RETRENCHMENT AND AN UNCERTAIN FUTURE

     With the third stage we move from a period of rel-
ative concentration of the reform in the Commission,
and after 1970, the Central Personnel Office, to one of
much greater dispersion. The two offices remained in
operation, although CAP's structure was modified and
its powers diminished. In addition, new groups and
organizations began to enter the picture with a consequent widening of discussion and a further fragmentation of the program. This was partly the result of the

politicization of some issues, a process begun with
CAP's confrontations. This more threatening side of
CAP's activities, combined with its own failures apparently suggested to many political leaders that administrative reform might be too important to be left
to the experts, and especially experts with different
political sympathies. It was also the result of the
departure of a number of the CAP leaders from that organization and their continuing involvement in reform
from other positions either in the private or public
sector. Thus, although the resulting conflict was
minor compared to that generated by other issues, it
became clear that there was no longer one acknowledged
group of reform experts sharing a unified position.
The reformers had become divided among themselves while
a number of outsiders began to challenge their position
charging that the experts' perspective was too narrow.

The Perez Government and Reform Policy

By 1974, with the advent of the Democratic Action
president, Carlos Andres Perez, it was apparent that
the Commission could accomplish little more. It seemed
that it might simply disappear over the next years.
CAP's association with the Caldera government and COPEI
made it highly unlikely that the adecos, who now controlled both the executive and the legislature, would
attempt to revive it or to follow through on any of its
plans. Despite new leadership in the Commission, this
partisan hostility was compounded by CAP's general un-
popularity with those it had fought. Finally, CAP's
presumably temporary status provided the Perez government with a convenient rationale for ignoring it.
Within its own plans CAP had figured as the predecessor
of a more generously endowed executive agency which
would supervise implementation of its reforms. While
there was no indication that the new government intended to create this entity, it clearly was time for some
sort of transition during which CAP could be still further neglected.
Two steps followed, stemming from the desire to do
something with the Commission and from pressures within
the government related to certain aspects of the reform. First, in response to these pressures, the government set up a second reform commission, the Commission for the Integral Reform of the Public Administration (CRIAP) or Tinoco Commission, after its leader.
CRIAP's status relative to CAP was unclear. It was
evident that despite the comprehensive title, its members' interests were much narrower, focusing on the
situation of the state enterprises. Claiming that the
inefficient public bureaucracy would damage the performance of these entities, Tinoco and his collaborators

presented a plan[33] to establish a separate system of
state enterprises. These would be coordinated through
a series of large holding companies all run by a Minister of State for State Enterprises. Tinoco's plan
immediately aroused charges that it was a plot by private business to gain control of state holdings. It
was strongly opposed within the Council of Ministers
for this reason and, probably more importantly, because
it threatened to undercut the ministries' own power.
The status of the state enterprises would remain a major issue over the next years, although it had been
barely touched upon in CAP's report. The Tinoco plan
made any immediate solution unlikely. It stirred up so
much controversy that the Congress avoided future proposals for fear of what might lie behind them.[34]
     The Tinoco Commission remained in existence and in
uncertain relationship to CAP until 1977. In the meantime, CAP was being transformed by a second set of government policies. In the beginning the Perez administration apparently had little idea of what it would do
with CAP and so settled for simply replacing its director with a political appointee, Enrique Azpurua Ayala,
a former copeyano deputy who had supported AD in the
1973 elections and received the position as a reward.
Azpurua, with no particular background in the area,
offered little in the way of leadership. He uninten-
tionally contributed to CAP's declining prestige within
CORDIPLAN by siding with the reformers' criticisms of
the Tinoco plan. Thus once Azpurua left the director-
ship, the Minister of Planning, Gomercindo Rodriguez,
initiated steps to liquidate the Commission and turn it
into an office of administrative planning within
CORDIPLAN.

Relocating the Reform: DPA

     The liquidation process took two years and in-
volved two new directors both of whom submitted reports
and recommendations on the agency's future. The first
of these directors came out of CORDIPLAN and was less
than sympathetic to CAP although he at least recommended it remain as a CORDIPLAN bureau ("direccion").
The second, Alfonso Salazar, took over in 1976 and
served until CAP was abolished in 1977. Salazar was a
lawyer with a background in administration and was more
enthusiastic about the prospects of a continuing reform. He thus concentrated on holding what remained of
CAP together while the new office was being set up. As
a consequence the remaining members of CAP stayed on to
supply some continuity in perspective as well as in the
concrete projects. Salazar's second contribution was
his insistence that practicality was important over the
short run and that the Direccion should attempt to

prove its usefulness. This advice was acceptable to
the remaining reformers who were not the superstars of
CAP's heyday and so were willing to concentrate on
smaller aspects of the large problem.

With the 1977 budget, CAP's transfer to CORDIPLAN
was completed. The new office was much reduced in size
(approximately twenty-five people) and less visible.
(It had also lost its connection with the National
School of Public Administration, ENAP, which was transferred to the Ministry of Finance becoming the National
School of Public Administration and Finance). Despite
its tighter attachment to CORDIPLAN, the new Direccion
of Administrative Planning (DPA) benefitted from that
institution's lesser interest in reform; except for the
restrictions imposed by its limited resources, it was
able to direct its own program with relatively little
interference. Under Nelly Antonorsi, director from
1977 to 1979, and one of the ten remaining members of
the old CAP, the office thus concentrated on what they
termed "focal" reform--that is concentration on a few
problem areas rather than on a global plan in the style
of CAP. The CAP report was kept as a guide and model
in the belief that while reform could not be implemented globally, it required global targets in order to
be effective. Because the reorganization came in the
middle of a presidential term, and moreover during one
that was not entirely friendly to the reformers, the
latter were once again caught with insufficient time
and resources to implement more ambitious programs.
Thus with an eye to the future, they worked on building
alternative strategies for the next administration,
hoping that they would thus be able to go to the new
president, whoever he was, with a program ready for
implementation.

Redefining the Reform Task[35]

The on-going work of DPA was divided into two main
areas. On the one hand, was what the members regarded
as the routine aspect, that of overseeing reorganization attempts throughout the administration. The office was aided here by its good relations with the personnel and budget offices, both of which enhanced its
power by refusing to pass changes which had not been
approved by the Direccion. This routine work was not
the first choice of the reformers, who set a much
higher value on their research into a number of more
broadly based administrative problems. This research
included the development of a model of a planning system, a study of the decentralized enterprises, a number
of regionalization projects, and a pilot project on
ministerial reorganization (to comply with the Law for
the Centralized Administration, based on the old CAP

project and passed in 1976 but still unimplemented for the most part two years later). Most of these projects were really a combination of planning and applied research. For example, in the work on regionalization, some effort had gone into creating two regional planning bodies and training personnel for them, as well as advising the ministries on their own regionalization plans.

This work required more participatory reform than had been attempted by CAP, for the practical reason that the new office was limited by its size. There was a problem, however, in attracting the attention of people of a sufficiently high level to have some impact. While it had been logical to work through the "offices of systems and organization" (the old ORCAs) these had remained relatively underdeveloped and as a consequence, not very important. Thus, the amount of assistance they could provide was often limited and they usually lacked political leverage within their own ministries. This put DPA in a position of constantly having to seek entry to the system, finding someone who was interested or could be made interested in a specific plan. Support from the executive was sufficiently low so that even the existence of a law or decree calling for a change did not give the office much more advantage in getting it implemented. This has been true of such major legislative steps as the Law for the Centralized Administration (reorganizing the ministries along the lines of CAP's plan) and the Law of Regionalization (both that passed under Caldera and the modified version issued by the Perez administration). Consequently even in advising entities on adapting to these laws, the Direccion had to go begging, making appeals and trying to convince administrators of the desirability and necessity of compliance. In this, DPA acted with little support from CORDIPLAN or the executive. It was further hampered by an increasing lack of credibility, based on what appeared to be the impermanence of reform decisions. The two regionalization laws struck a major blow here; while some ministries did attempt to comply with the first, the announcement of a second law changing the number of regions and making a few other seemingly arbitrary modifications considerably reduced the incentives to comply.[36]

The Central Office of Personnel[37]

The other formal reform institution operating during this period, the Central Office of Personnel (OCP), also faced problems of limited resources, staff (150 professional and administrative employees), and leverage, as well as the uncertain fate of its own programs under the next government. Its progress was somewhat surer, both because it had not suffered the substantial reverses experienced by CAP/DPA and because its main work was the implementation of an existing law for which much of the infrastructure was already in place, and for which there was wider support within the government and among the bureaucrats. Although like DPA, OCP needed the cooperation of other entities, that cooperation was easier to get. It required less extensive changes of behavior on the part of the bureaucracy as a whole and focused most directly on a group whose power would be enhanced by many of the changes, the ministerial personnel offices.

In effect, the greatest obstacles to OCP's progress in building a unified and uniform personnel system were not direct opposition, of which there was little, but rather the size of the task, the scarcity of trained staff (especially at the ministerial level), and the likelihood that the civil service legislation even though revised in 1970 was still outdated in many aspects and was becoming increasingly so at an accelerated rate with the rapid expansion of the public sector.[38] Given the propensity of each new administration to overhaul programs completely, there was also some question about the eventual fate of any effort to update the system. However, the greatest problem was simply the size of the task and the number of employees to be covered. With some 280,000 actually covered by the Administrative Career Law, another 300,000 on collective contracts, 110,000 in municipal and state government and another 110,000 working as teachers, the personnel system had a potential coverage of roughly twenty percent of the national labor force.[39] OCP had temporarily limited most of its programs to employees in the central administration but even here they lagged far behind in completing the most basic tasks. As of mid 1978, eight years after the law's passage, less than 10,000 of those eligible had been formally incorporated into the career service, a step which at that point required only the issuing of a certificate after ten years of service or after a six-month probationary period following entrance by an approved examination.[40]

Meanwhile, despite the problems with organizing the system as established in 1970, OCP was busy planning a radically new version. Like the Peruvians with whom they had been exchanging information, the Venezuelans' goal was to modernize the system to bring it more into line with perceived present and future demands, moving it further away from a strictly Weberian model.[41] Two aspects were emphasized--first the development of some sort of human resource planning (which would be largely the responsibility of CORDIPLAN) and second, a change to a system of rank-in-man rather than in job (the present system) which was seen as allowing

more possibility for human development within the
bureaucracy. Although the future of this scheme was
unclear, a good deal of effort had gone into it as it
was of more interest to the personnel planners than the
routine work of implementing the existing law. It was
also indicative of the relative lack of external pressure on OCP and its lack of externally defined goals, a
situation which allowed the office to spend more time
on this internally derived project. It would be fair
to say that while a small, but influential segment of
Venezuelan political and administrative figures were
aware of and concerned with a number of specific personnel problems--notably those involved in attracting
and holding high quality personnel[42]--a widespread
interest in a comprehensive new program and particularly one aiming at a human development potential, was not
present.

One additional point should be made about the personnel program, although its importance only becomes
truly visible in comparison with the situations in Peru
and Colombia. The Venezuelan Administrative Career Law
does allow civil servants to unionize and there is a
national federation of "white collar" (empleados)
workers.[43] This organization, FEDE-UNEP (Unitary
Nacional Federation of Public Employees) is affiliated
with the Accion Democratica dominated Confederation of
Venezuelan Workers (CTV), the most important national
labor confederation. The relationship of FEDE-UNEP
with the OCP was surprisingly friendly. The personnel
office held special programs for individual syndicates
and for the federation, while the latter featured
articles in its official magazine on OCP's efforts.
The anniversary issue (celebrating twenty years of
union activity) contained an article in which the
director of OCP explained the proposed humanistic
career scheme.[44]

FEDE-UNEP's position on the Administrative Career
Law was extremely positive, largely because it saw the
law as guaranteeing job security. Individual unions
had offered some initial resistance, including a strike
threat by workers affiliated with the CTV, in the mid
1960s when CAP began a job classification program in
three ministries. However, the national confederation
decided against the strike for strategic reasons and
since that time, organized opposition to this or any
other part of the program was virtually nonexistent.
Just what FEDE-UNEP's reaction would be to the changes
now proposed was unclear, but at least for the time the
employees' unions did not, as they did in the other two
countries, pose a major additional problem for the personnel planners. For the most part their members
seemed satisfied with the status quo, but observers

also suggested that their complacency had its roots in government and party control and manipulation.

Redefining Responsibilities

After 1974, although OCP and DPA remained as the offices officially responsible for planning and to varying degrees, implementing administrative reform, much of the discussion and decisions having to do with the broadest kinds of change took place elsewhere in government, and to a lesser degree, among private pressure groups. In some cases, as in the passage of the Law for the Centralized Administration, (December 22, 1976), and the second Regionalization Law (Decree 1331) this had less to do with the issues being seen as too important or too political than with the government's style of decision making. Not incidentally, a reluctance to work too closely with the COPEI influenced organization may have come into play. Thus, in the case of these two laws, although the models posed by the old CAP were clearly influential and while former CAP members were consulted informally,[45] the decisions were made within the executive office by a small group of advisors and associates of the president. They were passed onto DPA only afterwards for minor revisions and later, for help with implementation.

In other cases, as with the still pending Law for the Decentralized Administration[46] the issues first raised by the reformers had captured the attention of other groups and become the subject of wider political debate. This meant that they were no longer regarded as purely technical matters and thus the province of the administrative planners. While the latter were still exploring these topics, they remained peripheral to the real centers of decision--first within the Tinoco Commission and then when its report was discredited, at other levels within the government and outside. By the time of the 1978 presidential elections there were three issues related to administrative reform which had become part of popular discussion and figured in the campaigns: corruption, the quality of public services, and the role of the state in the economy.[47] Of these three, the Commission had worked directly only on the last as the state enterprise issue. This not coincidentally was the most technically defined question and the one which seemed to capture the attention of the most specialized outside groups as well. The other two issues, corruption and public services, had drawn more widely based attention. However neither was a theme treated directly by the reformers who tended to see them as too popularized and as peripheral to their real mission.

AIMS AND ACCOMPLISHMENTS OF THE VENEZUELAN REFORM
MOVEMENT: 1958-1978

If there is a single generalization to be made
about the twenty year period, it is that the aims of
the reform were not only more ambitious, they were also
more varied and more numerous than the accomplishments.
This stands to reason in that, given the constraints
posed by the political and administrative systems, certain kinds of changes will be easier to make time after
time--which explains why reorganizations are more frequently carried out than decentralizations. Still, at
a more abstract level, the reformers' objectives also
showed a good deal of continuity. Although changing
leadership accounts for variations in the emphasis of
each period, when left to their own devices and not too
vigorously reminded of the potential obstacles, the
reformers advocated a comprehensive reshaping of the
administrative system, imposed from the top down (despite the participatory theme), and based on universally
applicable deductive models. These models, with their
emphasis on functional specialization and clear chains
of command, obviously owed a good deal to the principles of scientific management and a whole related tradition of administrative science. In addition, in
their vocabulary of macro-, micro-, and functional reforms, their emphasis on cross-cutting administrative
"systems," and their discussion of a humanistic bureaucracy, the influence of the Peruvian and Mexican movements[48] (and their versions of several newer trends in
management theory) was evident. Although the reformers
were not adverse to empirical research and to the incorporation of more problem-specific solutions, they
for the most part preferred to begin wih a grand model
to guide change. Even where they did pilot projects,
the emphasis was usually on the educational or demon-
stration value of the effort (for convincing others of
its worth) rather than its utility as a means of tes-
ting a plan.[49]

This obsession with a model, with logically as
opposed to empirically derived remedies, and with order
and symmetry as the keys to efficiency was not without
problems. In many cases, it was not apparent why the
recommended change should work any better than the situation it replaced. In some cases, it did not work as
well. For example, the head of one ministerial personnel office noted that he had to revise the basic decentralization scheme which duplicated, at the regional
and subregional levels, the offices in operation in the
national ministry. Although the arrangement had a logical appeal, in practice it was unduly complicated and
stretched scarce human and material resources beyond
the limit. This example also suggests something about

the values maximized in the reformers' models. One observer has characterized these as efficiency as opposed to efficacy.[50] However, if this was efficiency, it was an efficiency that was not measured in time or resources saved, but simply in the guarantee that tasks would be done in a set predictable fashion on command.[51] If the only alternative was the kind of random malfeasance or simple ineptitude still plaguing the worst corners of the Venezuelan administration (and most other administrations as well), then this constituted an increase in both efficiency and efficacy. However, the emphasis on routine and predictability was also likely to compound a number of other problems--slowness, red tape, nonresponsiveness--suggesting that even if implemented, many of these programs were at best partial solutions.

In practice, much of the system never got this far; whatever ones evaluation of the reformers' programs, their most immediate failing was nonimplementation. Despite Brewer-Carias's pessimistic departure from the Commission in 1972, the reformers' programs produced four major pieces of legislation; however the subsequent history of each was difficult. The Law for the Centralized Administration, passed by the Perez government in 1976, was a long way from implementation two years later. Its two major effects to that date were the creation of several new ministries[52] with an accompanying redivision of responsibilities (macro-reform) and the provision for a number of changes in the internal organization of all ministries (the micro-reform). This "micro-reform," which was left to the individual ministries, had only been skeletally implemented by the end of Perez's term. While some changes, like the larger role for a number of systemic offices (personnel, budget, etc.) had begun, much of the rest of the proposed standardization of form and function semed likely to be achieved only nominally if at all. Once again, the underlying notion that this standardization would bring increases in efficiency, efficacy or any other desired characteristic seemed questionable. More recently, the Commission had to back off on the standardization for practical reasons, instead tailoring its reorganization plans to the needs and desires of individual agencies.

In the case of the regionalization scheme (which produced two laws, proving that more is not necessarily better when it comes to encouraging compliance) and the proposals for state enterprises (represented by the long debated Law for the Decentralized Administration) the situation was more complicated, owing to the higher level of controversy surrounding both issues. Unlike reorganization these were not unquestionably administrative issues, and perhaps in response to this, the reformers were willing to go beyond their intuitive

sense of what seemed correct to base their recommendations on real systems in operation elsewhere. However, the search for empirical models was hardly exhaustive and the choice among those sampled, in the
last resort, seemed arbitrary. In both areas, there
was the further unresolved question of how the reformers' expertise should interact with that of other
groups (economic planners, or politicians for example).
As the reformers themselves noted in the case of the
regionalization schemes, there were many criteria that
can be used to define regions--geographic, economic,
cultural, administrative, political and so on. Their
suggestion that administrative criteria be considered
was thus valuable, but hardly the last word on the
subject.[53]

The shortcomings of the reformers' unique contributions to the regionalization issue suggest some other
problems with their approach. Their recommendations on
the internal organization and operation of the new regional units were among the least inspired of their
proposals, as they themselves admitted. Despite the
focus of popular discussion (and opposition) on regional boundaries (i.e., which states are included, or whether existing subnational units should be considered at
all) it is the regional governments and their interaction with the national administrative system which have
proved the major stumbling blocks to most regionalization schemes. The problem is a complex one. First,
regionalization proposals, as a type of decentralization, face a universal reluctance on the part of more
centralized organizations to surrender power. They
also face a number of practical problems involving the
reallocation of resources and personnel.[54] Second,
even where a measure of decentralization has already
been achieved by elements of the national administrative system and other entities (labor unions, for example) it is unlikely that it will match the territorial patterns of a single regionalization scheme and so
may be difficult to transfer to the new system. Third,
even in the absence of these two types of resistance
from above, there is still the problem of creating some
kind of subnational governmental unit with sufficient
resources, independence and purpose, to exist on its
own. The reformers' proposals did not come to grips
with this particular problem as their lifeless models
of regional government demonstrated.[55] Despite the
optimistic hope (first harbored by CORDIPLAN's economic
planners who developed it) that the Guyana Development
Corporation (CVG) might serve as a more dynamic example
in another vein, followup projects in other regions
have been less successful. Both the economic and administrative planners admit that the CVG's unique status may have been the major factor behind its success.[56]

Finally, the reformers' major innovation, their
decision to reduce intraregional conflicts by establishing multiple regional centers (instead of the
single regional capital favored by the Peruvians) further complicated the basic task of creating a viable
governing and decision making unit. In short, although
the immediate obstacle to the regionalization schemes
has been the disincentive posed by the second law, both
proposals shared serious shortcomings, which argued
against their longer term success. Here as in the case
of the "decentralized administration" (state enterprises) the blame cannot be placed entirely on the administrative reformers who share responsibility with competing planners from other backgrounds.

In terms of actual implementation, the personnel
program came furthest. This is hardly surprising given
its much earlier legislative base in the Administrative
Career Law of 1970 and the still earlier enabling decrees. It was also indicative of the advantages of the
program's more restricted focus and the OCP's greater
control over implementation. The program was not without problems, which ranged from the low rate of accomplishment relative to its own objectives to the much
larger question of its real impact on the administrative system. Despite the progress made, by late 1978,
the program was still behind schedule in even the most
basic areas. It was hampered by personnel shortages
and its inability to keep up with the rapidly changing
administrative system. This was true of such fundamental and routine tasks as job classification, the
elaboration of uniform pay scales, and the introduction
of examinations and other standardized procedures for
recruitment and promotion. Although the OCP's efforts
were for the most part limited to career employees
(about one-fourth of total public employment) even here
the system was not complete and several aspects (job
classifications, pay scales, lists of qualifications)
were out of date and scheduled for revision.[57] Inadequate resources account for part of the delay, but it
also stemmed from OCP's apparent desire to oversee directly as much of the implementation and routine actions
as possible. This reflected the office's distrust of
the skill level in the ministries, but its overall
effect was to dilute the program's potential impact.

The problem areas uncovered as the personnel program developed indicated the reality of OCP's worst
fears as a justification for continued central supervision. The question remained as to whether outrageous
cases of misconduct like the lists of "phantom" (nonexistent, but salary collecting) employees discovered
in at least one ministry or the less scandalous but
more frequent instances of nonmerit appointments, in-
equitable salaries and irregular promotions might be

better prevented by the narrowly based but highly sup-
ervised procedures already in use or whether a loosely
directed program with a broader focus might not only be
more rapidly implemented but might also be just as effective in this regard. There were also indications
that OCP was neglecting or even aggravating a number of
critical problems, like that of attracting and holding
highly skilled personnel who may be frustrated by a
system better at preventing arbitrary dismissals than
at rewarding merit.[58] The office's experiments with
innovative schemes and its model of a humanistic bureaucracy were aimed at this kind of problem, but their
future was uncertain given the radical departure they
represented. At the least their adoption would mean
still another comprehensive revision of the entire
personnel system and the negation of most of the
achievements to date.

To discuss accomplishments only in terms of the
implementation of major pieces of legislation is, however, to omit a good deal. The reform movement has
done much beyond these major programs and it is in fact
in these other areas that its most significant achievements may lie. First, it encouraged a wider awareness
of and interest in administrative problems; the effect
of this change in attitude clearly extended far beyond
its own ability to provide solutions. It generated a
large amount of information about the state of the administrative system as well as demonstrating where the
remaining gaps in that information lay. It was also
important in collecting and centralizing the information that did exist but was not easily accessible.
Thus, although the reformers themselves downgraded this
function, much of the basic data central authorities
have today on the size of government, the number and
identity of employees, the shape and size of the decentralized sector, and the relationships and inter-
actions of the various parts of the system are available through the efforts of the reform agencies.

Beyond this, the reform agencies were directly and
indirectly responsible for a number of smaller and more
isolated changes. They inspired the independent efforts of other offices which either accepted the notion
of reform or were so threatened by it that they tried
to anticipate likely changes and make them first. After 1972 CAP/DPA was increasingly willing to adopt an
advisory role vis-a-vis individual agencies and to help
directly with isolated reforms on request. It is un-
fortunate that it came to this role so late and after
having stirred up so much hostility. Despite the negative image it had to live down, its limited resource
base, and its own reluctance to see this as its major
function, the agency was slowly developing in this direction. It remained to be seen whether its position

was sufficiently stabilized to allow it to continue or
whether the next administration would further contract
or expand its responsibilities. OCP was less willing
to take a back seat in the reform process, a bias which
might not serve it well in the long run. However, for
the short term it was helped by its greater ability to
enforce its own programs.

This review of the reformers' accomplishments
raises one more point; if these accomplishments are not
measured against conventional standards (and especially
the goals set by the reformers themselves as well as
the expectations they provided for the public) they
need not be as minor as they first seem. Furthermore,
given the questions that can be raised about some of
the movement's more ambitious goals, their most important, and least debatable achievements may be in these
less spectacular areas--the provision of information
about the state of the system as opposed to its comprehensive reshaping; the discussion of the problems posed
by the high level of centralization, as opposed to a
comprehensive and not very well planned regionalization
scheme. In this light the Venezuelan venture raises
several further questions about reform. There is the
question of how much a central agency can do and what
kinds of improvements it can really effect with its
universal, comprehensive, generalized reforms. There
is also the possibility that it may be its own worst
enemy in creating the expectation of this kind of
change, which is both hard to produce and plan, and
also difficult to relate to the interests of other
political actors. Finally, there is the question of
what kind of improvement is really included in the
notion of reform. As one long-time participant suggested, and as is indicated in the new attention to
public services, for the majority of the population,
reform is only likely to be felt when it affects efficiency and efficacy at the point of contact with the
bureaucracy--that is in the delivery of services. This
type of reform may eventually follow from improvements
in control, planning, and coordination. However, its
distance from those targets suggests a need for more
direct attention to the public's view of the problem,
or at least to a view that treats programs as well as
abstract administrative variables. It is clear nonetheless that if this perspective is to be tried, it
will involve changes in the orientations of the reformers themselves. With their background and professional biases it is unlikely that they will spontaneously
redefine the basic problem in these terms.

NOTES

1. Alfredo Pena, Democracia y reforma del estado (Caracas: El Nacional, 1978), p.292.
2. Ibid, p. 253
3. For further information on this period in Venezuelan politics, see articles in John D. Martz and David J. Myers (eds.), Venezuela: The Democratic Experience (New York: Praeger, 1977).
4. See for example, Roderick T. Groves, "The Venezuelan Administrative Reform Movement, 1958-1963," in Clarence E. Thurber and Lawrence Graham (eds.), Development Administration in Latin America (Durham: Duke University Press, 1973), pp. 47-80.
5. Ibid., p. 49.
6. United Nations, Department of Economic and Social Affairs, Public Administration in Venezuela (New York: United Nations, 1961).
7. Groves, pp. 51-2.
8. Ibid., p. 60. In my own interviews, informants supported this view, suggesting, as one stated, that the Venezuelans were "secondary."
9. Ibid., p. 63.
10. A discussion of these projects is found in Venezuela, Comision de Administracion Publica, "El factor humano en la administracion publica; caso de Venezuela." (Caracas, 1973).
11. This was stressed repeatedly by informants who participated in the program in the 1960s or in later periods.
12. Much of the information in this section was supplied by participants in the program, some of whom have written their own accounts. See for example Allan R. Brewer-Carias, "Administrative Reform Experience in Venezuela 1969-1975," in A. F. Leemans (ed.), The Management of Change in Government (The Hague: Martinus Nijhoff, 1976), pp. 213-37; Manuel Rachadell, "La reforma de la organizacion y el regimen del factor humano en la administracion publica venezolana," (Caracas: n.d.); and Venezuela, Comision de Administracion Publica, La reforma administrativa en Venezuela, 1969-1971, (Caracas: 1971).
13. For a discussion of changes in COPEI leadership during this period see John D. Martz, "The Party System: Toward Institutionalization," in Martz and Myers, pp. 93-112.
14. Brewer attracted still more attention through an interview and one-page article published in El Nacional a few months later (August 26, 1968, p. C-1). Through his public statements and articles he is single-handedly responsible for creating a wider public awareness of the reform issue although his efforts have

clearly not always been appreciated by others involved
with the policy.

15. Programa de Gobierno de Rafael Caldera, Presidente de Venezuela, 1969-1974, (Caracas, 1971), p. 68.

16. Ibid. p. 68.

17. Ibid. p. 70

18. Ibid. p. 247-62.

19. Interview, Caracas, 1978.

29. These contacts were stressed by a number of
informants, one of whom received a package of documents
from the Mexican program during the interview. The introduction to the famous Informe also contains references to Brewer's initial contacts and to those made
and maintained later. Venezuela, Comision de Administracion Publica, Informe sobre la reforma de la
administracion publica nacional, Vol. I (Caracas:
1972) pp. xxxiii-xxxix.

21. Interview, Caracas, 1978.

22. Informe, I, pp. 109-13.

23. Interviews, Caracas, 1978.

24. This section is based almost entirely on
interviews with participants, although relevant documents can be found in both volumes of the Informe and
in the other CAP publications listed in it.

25. These divisions are outlined and explained in
the Informe, but they basically refer to reorganizations of the entire scheme of ministries and other
public entities (macro-reform); internal reorganizations of individual ministries (micro-reform); and the
establishment of what the Peruvians termed "systems",
the crosscutting functional programs common to all
entities (e.g., planning, budgeting, etc.). A very
concise summary of the entire scheme is given in Allan
Brewer-Carias, "Reform Proposals for the Venezuelan
Public Administration (1972)," Journal of Administration Overseas, (October 1974), pp. 524-35.

26. Caldera had won the presidential elections
with only twenty-seven percent of the total vote because of a division within Accion Democratica. The
latter party, however, maintained its congressional
majority.

27. There is no indication that the copeyanos had
serious plans to this effect or more to the point, to
fire adeco supporters. However patronage appointments
had tended to be the rule (much more so in fact than
dismissals) and it is widely agreed that well founded
or not, the adeco fear was the major factor behind the
law's passage.

28. Ley de Carrera Administrativa (August 25,
1970).

29. This account is based on interviews, but the
official correspondence and documents relating to it
are included in the Informe, I, especially pp. 579-83.

128

30. *Informe*, I, p. 19.

31. A first regionalization law was passed in 1969, under the Caldera government. It was the product of the work of both economic and administrative planners within CORDIPLAN although most of the credit can be given to the former. The *Informe* itself gives less attention to regionalization; the eighty-page section on regional reform is largely an explanation of the first law. See *Informe*, I, pp. 386-461. Brewer himself later published a more extensive work on regionalization, Allan Brewer-Carias and Norma Izquierdo Corser, (eds.) *Estudios sobre la regionalizacion en Venezuela* (Caracas: Universidad Central de Venezuela, 1977). A short summary of the progress to 1974 is found in Gene E. Bigler, "Regionalization of the Public Administration in Venezuela" (Paper prepared for 1975 Meetings of the American Political Science Association). A discussion of the experience of one ministry in its efforts to comply with the first law is found in Mark Hanson, "Decentralization and Regionalization in the Ministry of Education," *International Review of Education* (1976), pp. 155-76.

32. The total budget of this project was roughly one and a half million dollars, one-third of which was contributed by the Venezuelan government. Its numerous reports have been published by the U.N. The project summary also contains a list of the other published proposals and reports. See United Nations, Project VEN 44, "Reforma administrativa en Venezuela: Informe final de proyecto," Appendix V, Vol. I (VEN/71/534/01/01, Caracas: 1977).

33. A discussion of the Tinoco Plan and interviews with participants in the Commission as well as with its critics is found in Alfredo Pena, *Democracia y reforma del estado* Tinoco himself also wrote a book expressing his views. Pedro Tinoco, hijo, *El estado eficaz* (Caracas: Italgrafico, 1972).

34. This was at least the suggestion of former CAP members who had watched the Congress's discussion of a Law for the Decentralized Administration in 1977 and who attributed its lack of success to the Congress's fear of the Tinoco plan. Interviews, Caracas, 1978.

35. The discussions in this section are taken from the most part from interviews with DPA staff. Relevant material is also found in Venezuela, CORDIPLAN, *Plan de accion de la reforma administrativa 1976-1980* (Caracas, 1977).

36. In mid 1978, a year and a half after the issuing of a presidential instruction giving the ministries six months to establish their regionalization

plans in accordance with the Perez law, only one ministry and two state enterprises had done so. DPA officials could offer no explanation for the second law and regarded it as inferior to the first in some respects. One of them summed it up as "change for the sake of change." Interviews Caracas, 1978.

37. Discussions in this section are based on interviews with members of the OCP.

38. Neither the job classification scheme nor the salary schedules had been comprehensively revised (as opposed to "patched up") since 1970 and the versions adopted then were in large part based on still earlier studies, some of which dated as far back as the original 1960 reports. Interviews Caracas, 1978. See also CAP, "El factor humano...."

39. These figures were made available by OCP staff members.

40. In general the entrance requirements as applied by the ministerial offices were not strictly according to the legal provisions, but the OCP was once again far behind in devising and checking examinations. It had still not supplied all those with ten years or more of service with certificates, but followed a practice of issuing certificates whenever one of these employees was brought to their attention for another matter. This in effect meant that if their status was questioned they were more likely than not to be officially enrolled. Interviews, OCP, Caracas, 1978.

41. Interviews, OCP, Caracas, 1978.

42. See the interviews in Pena for a discussion of the views of political and administrative leaders on this matter.

43. The blue-collar workers or obreros are organized separately. They were first legally able to unionize in 1965. As of 1973, there were 150,000 in FENODE, the National Federation of State Workers, all of whose working conditions were regulated by collective contracts. CAP, "El factor humano...," p. 8.

44. Revista UNEP, 1978, pp. 12-3.

45. It is reported that Brewer-Carias and other high ranking former CAP members were brought in by the President and the Presidential Secretary to work on these laws (and on the Law for the Decentralized Administration) although credit has never been openly given to them and the amount of influence they actually had varies according to who is telling the story.

46. Bigler notes that as of 1978, there was a new de facto policy for decentralized structures in operation and based on the Law for the Centralized Administration. It included the use of coordinating councils, and according to Bigler the end result was a tighter connection to the central administration. See Gene Bigler, "Characteristics and Significance of the

Decentralized Public Administration" (draft of chapter
for dissertation).

47. It is worth noting that only the issue of
corruption became a popular campaign theme with all
other parties charging the adecos with misuse of
funds. The other two themes were more of interest to a
narrower group of political leaders and other elites
many of whose views are cited in Pena. Midway through
1978, Brewer publicly, entered the scene again and in
the process tried to stir up interest in these two
themes. The format was an article in a popular news
magazine. See Allan Brewer-Carias, "El estado venezo-
lano carece de contemporaneidad," Resumen (July 16,
1978), pp. 18-34.

48. Although the Peruvian movement was more
visibly influential because of the exchanges of personnel, the Mexican group also left its mark. For a
comprehensive summary of the Mexican reform and reform
model, see A. Carrillo Castro, "Administrative Reform
in Mexico," in Leemans, pp. 185-212.

49. More recently, the DPA group may have soft-
ened on this position. In 1978 in regard to their
pilot project of ministerial reform, they referred to
this as a kind of test which might be extended to the
other ministries if it worked.

50. William S. Stewart, "Public Administration"
in Martz and Myers, p. 228. See also Stewart, Change
and Bureaucracies (Chapel Hill: University of North
Carolina, 1978).

51. It is highly unlikely that the CAP reformers
would accept this characterization of their efforts,
but in examining the Informe model with its emphasis on
order, symmetry, and set lines of coordination and com-
munication, it is hard to avoid this conclusion.

52. Two of the most controversial of these are
the Ministry of Youth (Juventud) and the Ministry of
Information and Tourism.

53. Regionalization was in fact first reserved
for the economic planners who drew up the first regionalization law. The law was passed onto CAP for
modifications and since that time the administrative
reformers have kept an interest in the subject, although attempting to work with the CORDIPLAN group.

54. This problem may have reached its peak in the
Venezuelan case and now be on the decline. DPA members
reported that owing to the urban congestion in Caracas,
people who formerly would never have considered a job
outside the capital were anxious to move. It is unclear, however, just how significant a group this
really is. Interviews, DPA, Caracas, 1978.

55. The two models of regional government devised
for the two laws, COREGOs (Regional Committees of

Government) and COREDIs (Regional Committees of Development) respectively, were never satisfactory even to their creators. One immediate problem was the question of who would preside over them--the decision to rotate the position among the relevant state governors was a coompromise that no one ever expected to work. A discussion of the two regionalization laws (Decree 72 and 929 of 1969, and Decree 1331 of 1975), is found in Norma Izquierdo Corser, "Comentario critico a los decretos de regionalizacion..." in Allan Brewer-Carias and Norma Izquierdo Corser, op. cit. pp. 163-91.

56. This unique status refers not only to the fact of its being first but also to such characteristics as the region's vast resources and relative under population. The director of the CVG wielded so much power that he was referred to as the "Viceroy." Although there has been some pressure from other areas wanting to be incorporated into regions, it was recognized by the planners, as one of them put it, that "in the end what the regions wanted was money." (En el fondo las regiones lo que querian era el dinero.")

57. For example, as the OCP staff noted, although they had examinations for 160 of the most basic positions by mid 1978, most of these were already out of date because the students were better educated and would naturally do extremely well. Furthermore a spot survey of the ministries' recruitment procedures had determined that less than half were complying with the requirement for use of a list of eligibles (that is a list derived from those who had passed a general examination and from among whom positions would be filled as they open up). Interviews, OCP, Caracas, 1978.

58. A survey done by the National School of Public Administration (ENAP) in 1973 for example established that public employees generally perceived the system as one ruled by patronage and pull and that they saw any effort on their part to further their professional development as going unrewarded. See, CAP, "El factor humano....," Anexo V, pp. 6-7.

6
Colombia:
Institutionalized Reform

*"Dos leyes de sociologia politica colombiana.... todo
gobierno busca reorganizer la administracion segun sus
propios criterios; dichas reorganizaciones no las lleva
a cabo el Congreso a traves de la ley sino el gobierno
mediante facultades extraordinarias que recibe de
aquel."

      --Jaime Vidal Perdomo[1]

    Despite the differences in their political set-
tings, the Peruvian and Venezuelan reforms demonstrated
surprising similarities in content and development. By
contrast, the Colombian case, which at first glance
politically most resembles Venezuela (competitive party
system; pluralist, nonideological decision making,
etc.), is quite different from the two on both dimensions. A part of this difference and especially that
in content can be traced to a distinctive initial pattern of outside influences and to Colombia's continuing
lesser involvement in a regional reform movement. A
number of political factors also come into play in the
development of Colombia's program. However, these are
not the most superficially obvious ones. Instead, the
most important political variables are those which
directly affect the experts' role in the process and
thus the question of who controls reform.

---

*Two laws of Colombian political sociology... all
governments try to reorganize the administration
according to their own criteria; these reorganizations
are not carried out by the Congress through normal
legislation but by the government through the extraordinary powers it receives from the latter.

133

Colombia's experience is distinctive in several
respects. Unlike the situation in the other two countries the Colombian reforms have not been dominated by
a group of specialists. While such a group has existed, it never had the monopoly over reform enjoyed by
its Venezuelan and Peruvian counterparts, and it has
not produced a systematic reform doctrine to guide its
programs. For these reasons, reformers in the other
two countries see the Colombian movement as less successful, although it has also been argued[2] that the
Colombians have implemented more reform proposals. As
in Peru and Venezuela, reform efforts in Colombia have
been sporadic and closely tied to changes of administration. Observers note that every incoming administration finds it necessary to announce an administrative reform program to indicate its determination to
improve on its predecessors' performance. There is a
major difference in the procedures introduced for
implementing the Colombian reforms--the extraordinary
powers granted to an incoming president to enact certain specified administrative changes.

Two further characteristics differentiate the Colombian reforms from the other cases. First, they have
generally been less ambitious than those proposed in
Venezuela and Peru, limited to what the Venezuelans
termed "micro-reform"--that is, the reorganization of
individual entities rather than of the bureaucracy as a
whole. Second, they have usually been drawn up by committees of bureaucrats and politicians. The official
reform agencies have taken a lesser role which, over
time, has been limited to the simple revision of proposals originating elsewhere. Personnel reforms constitute a partial exception as they have been done on a
wider scale and have usually been drawn up by the professional staff of the Administrative Department of the
Civil Service (DASC). Even here, most changes have
been incremental and have been realized through the
device of exceptional presidential powers.

POLITICAL BACKGROUND[3]

A few facts about Colombian political history are
essential to understanding the reform movement. Colombia is unusual among Latin American nations for the
relative persistence and stability of its party system
and for having had only one period of military dictatorship (1953-57) since the early twentieth century.
Colombia has a two party system, in itself a rarity;
still more unusual is the fact that the same two
parties, the Liberals and the Conservatives have dominated its politics since the mid-nineteenth century,
in large part through their success in developing a
mass base. Popular identification with the parties is

remarkably high for the region and is often strongest
among groups like the rural poor who have benefitted
least from the system.

The Colombian phenomenon is not a classic two
party system[4] and its longevity hinges on a number of
idiosyncracies. First, strictly two-party open competition has not usually been the rule; the traditional
system has been "characterized by the hegemony of one
of the parties"[5] although often with some minority rep-
resentation. A party not in control of the executive
and the Congress would often refuse to participate in
the next elections claiming that fraud would prevent it
from winning anyway. Periodically, the level of conflict between the parties would escalate and combine
with other tensions to produce nationwide outbreaks of
violence like those in the 1920s and more recently in
the late 1940s and 1950s. This last disturbance which
began in 1948 and was known as la Violencia (the violence) approached the proportions of a civil war with
over 100,000 casualties. Although it started as an urban phenomenon, its spread to rural areas quickly put
it beyond the control of national leaders. In response
to this situation and to the military dictatorship os-
tensibly begun to put an end to it, the leaders of the
two parties reached an agreement to create a national
front and to share government office for twelve (later
sixteen) years. According to this agreement[6] the
parties were to alternate control of the presidency and
to divide equally all other elective and appointive offices, except for those which were part of the politically neutral civil service. This arrangement was
seen as a way to curtail a major incentive for the
partisan hostilities, the scramble for government jobs.

To the extent that it may have prevented another
outbreak of violence the Front, which ended in 1974,
can be considered a success. It can also be considered
successful in respect to another less publicized objective, that of maintaining the two parties' joint control over government. That control was most seriously
threatened in the 1970 elections when ANAPO, a party
formed by the former dictator, Rojas Pinilla, ran its
leader for president and almost won. ANAPO did pick up
some seats in Congress, creating further problems for
the elected, Conservative, president, Misael Pastrana,
under whose party label the anapistas most frequently
ran. It also damaged Pastrana's position because of
the lingering suspicion that his victory had been en-
gineered and that Rojas had actually polled the most
votes. Despite these setbacks, the Front was clearly
in the interests of the traditional parties, and their
leadership, a traditional political class with a decidedly upper class outlook. This political elite is
another anomaly in a region where politics has more

frequently been taken over by the middle class. It is
not so obvious that the Front or the continued domin-
ance of the two parties has been to Colombia's best
interests.[7] Critics charge that the parties although
electorally successful are too traditional and elitist
in their outlooks and do not respond to the interests
of new classes and groups. They have also charged that
the pluralist, incrementalist, nonideological policy
making style is best suited to perpetuating a nonegal-
itarian status quo. These questions go far beyond the
scope of the present study, but some of the same conditions, including the high level of institutionalization and the diffusion of power within the traditional
political system, are of interest because of their
direct effect on the administrative reform process.

COLOMBIAN REFORM EFFORTS: THE FIRST STAGE, 1958-1962[8]

The idiosyncracies of the Colombian reforms have
not prevented their sharing one major trait with the
other two cases--a close association with changes of
administration. The limited role played by reform
specialists has accentuated this trend so that the
stages and changes in the direction of reform efforts
neatly correspond to the five presidential terms covered in this period. Each stage is marked by an enabling law, giving the president extraordinary powers to
effect administrative change by executive decree; Law
19 of 1958 (Alberto Lleras Camargo); Law 21 of 1963
(Guillermo Leon Valencia); Law 65 of 1967 (Carlos
Lleras Restrepo); Law 2 of 1973 (Misael Pastrana
Borrero); Law 28 of 1974 (Alfonso Lopez Michelsen).
These laws find their origin in the limited powers of
the executive to make changes in the central bureaucracy under normal conditions and in the Congress's
lesser interest in the details of administrative reform. Congress has maintained some control over the
process by requiring that the enabling legislation
stipulate fairly specifically the nature of the changes
to be made and by the further requirement that the decrees enacting them be issued within a set period of
time (ranging from two months to two years). While
these stipulations were meant to put limits on the
executive's powers they have had a more important effect in curbing the role of the reform specialists.
The requirement that the executive issue a specific
statement of the details and direction of reform has
given political leaders a dominant role in the process
as compared to Peru or Venezuela while limiting the
specialists' room for independent action. The arrangement has also generated some criticisms because of the
inconsistencies it may encourage. As one observer has
remarked,

*... Algunas veces las reorganizaciones se
hacen solamente al gusto de funcionario de
turno...[9]

The five major stages of the reform movement have
thus been shaped by the desires of individual administrative and political leaders. They have also been
shaped by changes in the political climate, so that new
political themes are constantly reflected in the changing objectives and emphasis of the reform movement.
Finally the institutionalization of the reform process
and of the extraordinary powers mechanism has had its
own impact. Not surprisingly the first reforms were
more ambitious than later efforts. Law 19 of 1958 was
broader and less specific in the powers it gave to the
president than were the other enabling laws. It set
forth the goals of reform and established the institutions through which reform was to be conducted.
Although subsequent legislation and informal adjustments would substantially modify the role of these institutions, the movement as begun in 1958 bore strong
similarities to the Venezuelan and Peruvian efforts.
These similarities are particularly evident in the comprehensive nature of the reforms envisioned, in the
areas stressed (reorganization, extensive personnel
reforms and the introduction of a merit based civil
service system, training, etc.) and in the use of
centralized institutions.
      Many of the similarities spring from the early
influence of foreign advisors who, as in the other two
countries, were heavily relied on in the early years.
During the 1950s Colombia was visited by four major
foreign missions all focused on areas related to administrative reform.[10] One important difference accounting for some variations in detail was the greater
influence of French as opposed to American advisors.
The French impact was particularly strong on the early
civil service legislation and has been blamed for many
of the latter's failures.[11] A still more important
factor demonstrating similarities with the Venezuelan
situation in 1958 and the Peruvian one in 1968 was the
political context in which the reform began. In 1958
Colombia was emerging from a decade of civil strife and
violence which had begun and been sustained by the outbreak of uncontrollable hostility between members of
the two traditional parties. Thus, as in the other two
countries, administrative reform first represented part

---

*Sometimes the reorganizations are simply done
according to the whims of the incumbent official.

of a widely defined new start. In the Colombian case,
the National Front also had a more specific goal, that
of eliminating the conditions which had encouraged
partisan conflict. Political control of and conflict
over bureaucratic employment was seen as a major contributing factor. Thus a major goal of the reform
movement was to depoliticize the public service as much
as possible through the introduction of a merit civil
service system.[12]

Early Objectives

Although the elimination of the spoils system was
the primary objective of this first stage of reform it
was not the only one. Alberto Lleras, the first president under the National Front, had a more personal interest in the wider issues of administrative reform,
inspired by the increasing disorganization of the public sector during the years of civil strife and civilian and military dictatorship. The specific recommendations of the four foreign advisory missions were influential here. The first enabling law (Law 19 of
1958) was relatively broad in its scope, stating in its
first article that the reorganization of the public
sector had as its objective:

> *...asegurar mejor la coordinacion y la
> continuidad de la accion official conforme a
> planes de desarrollo progresivo establecidos o
> que se establezcan por la ley, la estabilidad
> y preparacion tecnica de los funcionarios y
> empleados; el ordenamiento racional de los
> servicios publicos y la descentralizacion de
> aquellos que puedan funcionar eficazmente bajo
> la direccion de las autoridades locales; la
> simplificacion y economia en los tramites y
> procedimientos; evitar la duplicidad de labors
> o funciones paralelas; y propiciar el ejecu-
> tivo de un adecuado control administrativo.[13]

---

*... to better guarantee the coordination and
continuity of official action in accord with the
development plans established or to be established by
law; stability and technical preparation of the public
employees; the rational ordering of public services and
the decentralization of those which can function
efficiently under local control; simplification of
basic procedures; elimination of duplication of
functions; and the provision of the executive with
adequate administrative control.

The law which was passed on November 25, 1958 gave the executive until July 20th of 1960 to issue a series of decrees which would, among other ends:[14]

1. Create a National Council of Economic Policy and Planning

2. Create an Administrative Department of Planning

3. Create ministerial planning offices

4. Organize the civil service and administrative career systems with the aid of an Administrative Department of the Civil Service and a Commission on Recruitment, Promotion and Discipline

5. Create a Chamber within the Council of State for the Civil Service

6. Create an Office of Organization and Methods

7. Develop university level public administration courses

8. Decentralize some services to the provincial and local level

9. Encourage community action

10. Give technical assistance to public entities and local governments

While many of these goals were not met or were realized only at the most basic level, the immediate results of the first effort included 153 executive decrees and a number of new entities which would be responsible for carrying out the initial reform and for continuing after the July twentieth deadline ran out.

Organizational Beginnings

One of the most important characteristics of this first period and one which would have still more impact later was the division of the reform program into three distinct and largely independent agencies: the Administrative Department of the Civil Service (Departamento Administrativo del Servicio Civil, DASC), the Higher School of Public Administration (Escuela Superior de Administracion Publica, ESAP) and the Administrative

Reform Commission (<u>Comision de la Reforma Administra-
tiva</u>) with its Office of Organization and Methods
(<u>Oficina de Organizacion y Metodos</u>), later to become
the Secretariat of Administrative Organization and
Inspection (<u>Secretaria de Organizacion e Inspeccion de
la Administracion Publica</u>, SOIAP) in the Office of the
President. Since their creation these entities have
maintained relatively cordial relations and in some
instances have managed substantial cooperation. Still,
their independent status and occasionally overlapping
functions have also produced conflicts and decreased
the power of the reformers as a group. In recognition
of the actual and potential conflicts a coordinating
committee (<u>Comite de Coordinacion de la Administracion
Publica</u>)[15] with a representative from each institution
was created in 1961. However, problems have continued
to be resolved on an <u>ad hoc</u> basis through informal
agreements among the institutions involved.

In the early years and especially through 1960 the
most important reform work fell to the Administrative
Reform Commission and its successor the <u>Secretaria</u>
(SOIAP). Prior to the latter's formation in March of
1960, the Commission had a simple if broad mandate to
formulate recommendations on the general outlines of
reform. The three commissioners (one from the United
Nations and two distinguished Colombians, one from each
party) were aided by a staff of nine U.N. advisors and
by the Office of Organization and Methods with its
eighteen Colombian members.[16] Most of the latter were
young economists or lawyers who would receive more
specific training on the job.

After the creation of the <u>Secretaria</u>, with the
broadening of its functions through Decree 1709 of
1960, and the enlargement of its staff to forty-eight,
work centered on the task of reorganizing the executive
branch. Decree 0550 of 1960 (drawn up by the Commission and modeled on a pilot study of the Ministry of
Health) set the basic criteria for this reorganization,
outlining the respective functions of ministries, territorial departments and local and municipal authorities. In April of 1960 a further step was taken with
the submission of the "Report on the Reorganization of
the Executive Branch of the Government" (<u>Informe sobre
la reorganizacion de la rama ejecutiva del poder pub-
lico</u>). Background material used in the report included
a series of interviews with high level personnel and
specific documentation (collected and analyzed by the
technical staff) on the legal bases, organization, resources, and internal operations of all major public
entities.[17] Although the recommendations of the report
were never collectively legislated into effect, as had
apparently been the intent of the Commission,[18] they

served as the basis for many of the changes subsequently effected by decree under Law 19.

These products of the Commission's early days
represent the closest this body or its successor would
come to a reform model or doctrine. The major thrust
in each was the standardization of organizational forms
within the various ministries (at least to the extent
of the adoption of a uniform nomenclature), an appropriate level of delegation and decentralization of functions, and the addition of a number of advisory and
coordinating entities like the ministerial offices of
planning and of organization and methods. However, the
Colombians were realists in applying these norms. From
the start they accepted that any general standards
would have to be adjusted to the characteristics of
each agency and to the biases of the officials in
charge. The latter in particular required long periods
of consultation so that:

> *...En muchas oportunidades el intercambio de
> ideas fue un proceso bastante prolongado hasta
> lograr que por ejemplo un Ministro aceptara el
> cambio de estructura de su Ministerio.[19]

Because of the strict time limits under which it
worked, the Commission devoted most of its efforts to
reorganizing the central bureaucracy. This was seen as
the prior step to any other reform. In other areas included in Law 19--for example public enterprises, systems and procedures, local government, etc.--its actions were limited to preliminary studies with recommendations for future action. In the case of departmental reform and the delegation of powers to departmental governments, pilot studies were done in three
departments ranging from the most to the least developed.[20] These pinpointed the major obstacle to
improved performance as limited finances and the solution as improved systems of taxation and tax collection. A second problem was identified as the lack of a
departmental civil service and the consequent absence
of professional staff. As a result of these studies,
one of the departments used, Boyaca, became the first
to introduce a civil service and career system. Real
progress there and in the other departments has continued to be slight owing to the persistence of the
financial and political obstacles to change.

---

*Many times the exchange of ideas was a fairly drawn
out process so that, for example, a Minister would
accept a structural change within his ministry.

Law 19 had provided for the establishment of a series of entities to oversee the civil service system: the Administrative Department of the Civil Service (DASC), the National Civil Service Commission (or Commission on Selection, Promotions and Discipline), and the Civil Service Chamber in the Council of State. Once established these institutions operated independently of the other administrative reform bodies, proceeding on the basis of the powers and responsibilities given them in Law 19, in the legislation accompanying their actual creation, and in the Civil Service and Administrative Career Law (Decree 1732 of July 18, 1960). These powers and responsibilities were also the source of many of the subsequent problems of these agencies which soon found themselves overextended. For example, the original notion that the proposed civil service system would include not only national employees but those at the municipal and departmental level as well, and the central role of DASC, which among its other tasks was to serve as the immediate channel for all entrants to the national career service, proved counterproductive in their application. By February of 1962, it became necessary to make provisional authorizations for the appointment of 5,212 new employees[21] through the direct actions of the ministries and agencies involved because DASC was simply incapable of keeping up with government demand. It was estimated at that time that just to keep up with the yearly turnover and new positions at the central level, the department would have to provide 12,000 candidates.[22] Fortunately, no effort was ever made on the local systems except for an occasional study at the request of individual departments.

A further problem was posed by political pressures. Although public opinion had originally favored the career service concept, the concrete proposals were met with opposition. Politicians saw them as a way of circumventing the parity concept introduced by the National Front; public employees interpreted them as a threat to their jobs.[23] Thus, during this early period progress toward the implantation of a national career service was made very slowly and many of the original provisions (like the early civil service law) were later revised on the theory that their initial complexity hampered their effectiveness.

THE INSTITUTIONALIZATION OF THE COLOMBIAN REFORM: A SUMMARY OF POST-1962 TRENDS

In the following sections some of the highlights of the subsequent years are discussed. Because many of the details of the years up to 1973 have been reported elsewhere, the major trends from the next four periods

are outlined first. Each of these periods corresponds
to a presidential term; thus the objectives of the reform movement and the importance assigned to it were
dependent on the changing political climate and the
preferences of the individual leaders. Despite the
resulting fluctuations, some very strong patterns
emerged over the period as a whole, as the policy area
itself became more institutionalized.

The first of these patterns or trends is the emergence of extraordinary executive powers as the chief
mechanism of reform. Except in the case of Pastrana,
who faced problems with Congress, presidents requested
these powers early in their terms to allow enough time
to make the required changes. Because Congress continued to require that the intended reforms be specified
in the enabling legislation, much of the general work
had to be done still earlier, sometimes before the president took office. This in turn meant that much of the
initial work was done by political leaders (perhaps as
part of the party platform) and that the reform offices
would only be called in at a later stage, further reducing their role.

A related trend involves the emergence of administrative reform as a program expected of each president, in part because of its symbolic value, in part
because of pressures from special interest groups within the bureaucracy and the political system as a whole
(see third point below). Furthermore, as reform itself
became a tradition there was a tendency to incorporate
other political themes within the reform program. This
made reform more current and probably increased the
chances for political support and interest throughout
each term, but it also decreased continuity over the
long run. As an example President Valencia, whose government faced a financial crisis, stressed reform as an
economy measure and emphasized its utility in eliminating duplication and waste. Valencia went so far as
to set up an additional (temporary) reform body, the
Committee on the Reduction of Public Spending (Comite
de Reduccion de Gastos Publicos) to work with the
SOIAP. Meanwhile, Lleras Restrepo who had an interest
in economic planning as a result of decades of experience with the public sector, stressed this theme in his
reform. This attachment of the reform to the executive
made the likelihood of implementation dependent on his
political strength and skills. Pastrana, who aside
from his problems with Congress, was simply not a
strong executive, had one of the least extensive reforms, while Lleras, an unusually strong figure, was
able to do much more.

Finally, there is a closely related third trend.
As bureaucrats and others came to realize that each
administration would enact some kind of administrative

reform and do it through the device of extraordinary
powers, they began to anticipate this event and prepare
for it.[24] Given the obstacles to introducing changes
under normal conditions (that is with the direct supervision of Congress), administrators wishing to make
modifications in their organizations found it more
convenient to save their proposals for the next request
for extraordinary powers. Thus there emerges a pattern
of a period of considerable administrative readjustment
once every four years alternating with longer periods
when things remain more stable. This also meant that
reforms became more disjointed, tending towards col-
lections of mini-adjustments in which the voice of the
reform experts was further weakened.[25] In a similar
fashion the effect of the presidential theme was reduced; whether it was economy, planning or decentralization that was officially stressed, most of the individual changes were of the same sort as always.

Aside from these three trends, a number of other
developments are also apparent. For example, as time
went by, the rather ambitious scope of the first reform
(drawn from Law 19) was reduced when it became obvious
that many of the early goals would not be reached in
the foreseeable future. The clearest example is found
in the personnel reforms and the decision in 1968 to
remove many of the centralized powers of DASC, giving
them instead to the ministerial personnel offices. At
the same time, many of the impediments to enrollment in
the career service were removed (Decree 3079 of 1968)
making it easier for those already holding public employment to join automatically and so further reducing
the work load on the personnel offices. The work load
was also reduced with the earlier de facto decision to
make the departmental and municipal civil service systems optional and separate. As a result few local units ever attempted much in the way of a formal system.

Another more complex development involved the
shifting powers of the three main reform agencies and
in particular the Secretaria's loss of functions to
ESAP. This process moved ahead rapidly in 1973, as a
result of resistance by administrative agencies to the
Secretaria's reform plan, drawn up without their participation and thus bringing charges of "imposed reform."[26] In the plan that was finally accepted in that
year and in the 1976 reforms, the Secretaria took a
less dominant role, limiting itself to reviewing agency
proposals. Although in theory, the Secretaria could
still delay specific reforms by withholding approval,
it voluntarily limited its criticisms to instances of
noncompliance with legal norms or with the formal mission of an agency. It did not again attempt to impose
a single model on the agencies' proposals or otherwise
shape them to its own preferences. As we will see, the

Secretaria's actions were so restricted that the office, even after substantial cutbacks in personnel was able to adopt another function, that of investigating complaints of administrative malfeasance and inefficiency.

The Secretaria's decline coincided with ESAP's assumption of a more active and varied role in the reform process, a role which not only included activities once performed by the Secretaria but also some shared with DASC. ESAP's increased activity was not the result of conscious government policy or a direct consequence of SOIAP's fall from grace. It was the product of greater funding and more external aid which simply gave the school more freedom of action. With its greater financial and human resources, the latter in the form of staff, advisors, and students, ESAP undertook a number of projects that might more logically have fallen to the Secretaria or DASC.[27] Many of these were studies of the administrative and personnel needs of organizations at all levels of government. As time went on and ESAP's reputation spread, an increasing number were done at the request of individual entities which actively sought out ESAP for this purpose.

The reallocation of functions was not limited to these three agencies alone. After 1968 when Lleras Restrepo upgraded the national planning apparatus, the Department of Planning (DNP) began to enter some areas of administrative reform, notably that of regionalization. Law 19 had stated the desirability of decentralization of the central bureaucracy and the transfer of powers to reorganized and reformed departmental and municipal governments. All three reform agencies had done studies relating to these themes, but little more had been accomplished. DASC and more recently ESAP had provided aid to a number of departmental governments desiring to upgrade their bureaucracies, but limited financial and human resources, and political obstacles, had prevented the latter's following through on the recommendations.

Since the efforts of the three reform agencies were turned toward strengthening existing subnational governments it remained for the planning office to first raise the issue of creating new units, the larger nontraditional regions. The economic planners' interest in regionalization was not surprising given the importance of that concept in their discipline.[28] The fact that it remained to them to introduce and develop it does suggest once again the more limited role taken by the administrative reformers. It also demonstrates their lack of involvement in the kinds of innovations promoted by their Venezuelan and Peruvian counterparts.

The reformers' continued noninvolvement meant that regionalization remained the province of the economic
planners. Both official regionalization schemes (1970
and 1979) and most pilot projects and studies were directed by the Department of Planning without any effort
to coordinate them with the strictly administrative
reform plans.[29]

There is a final pattern in the later reforms
which offers an interesting contrast with the Venezuelan and Peruvian experiences. This is the continuing absence of any core group of reform specialists
directing and dominating the movement. There were no
Colombian reform superstars; the individuals mentioned
as prominent leaders of the movement were usually politicians, and had generally earned their fame in areas
other than reform. One reason for the experts' lesser
role was undoubtedly the continuing division of the
movement, not only into the personnel and administrative divisions, but into a third branch, ESAP, as
well. Other reasons include the constant involvement
of political leaders and their participation in setting
the goals for each new reform period.

The absence of expert leaders did not prevent the
creation of a staff of professionals within each of the
agencies. This was particularly true of DASC whose
director during the Lopez administration had come up
through the ranks of the organization, as had many of
the other top personnel. The more erratic growth of
ESAP and the Secretaria made this kind of background
less common, but it did not preclude a professional
outlook in their younger and generally less experienced
staffs. The difference in all three cases, as contrasted with the Venezuelan and Peruvian examples, was that
the Colombians' professionalism focused on a narrower
conception of the job and one which featured enforcing
policy decisions rather than determining them. A primary factor accounting for this difference was the Colombians' greater sensitivity to political constraints.
Reformers in all three countries talked about political
obstacles, but only the Colombians seemed to see them
as an inevitable, necessary, and natural part of the
job.

REFORM IN THE 1970S

The last big push for reform came in 1968 under
the Lleras Restrepo government and utilized the extraordinary powers granted with Law 65 of 1967. This reform is generally regarded as less far reaching in its
impact than the changes made under the earlier Lleras
Camargo government (1958 to 1962). It was important
both for the new steps it took, especially in the area

of national and sectoral planning, and for the read-
justments it made in the earlier reforms, and especially in the civil service system.[30] As a result, the
economic planning office (<u>Departamento Nacional de
Planeacion</u>, DNP) reached the height of its power in the
period from 1966 to 1970. For a time it also looked as
though the bottlenecks in the civil service system
might be eliminated. Subsequent events proved that any
optimism about either development had been exaggerated,
but new trends had nonetheless been established.

During the two following administrations (Pastrana, 1970 to 1974 and Lopez, 1974 to 1978), political
problems and the end of the National Front (with Lopez
as the "bridge" or first non-Front government) obstruc-
ted reform efforts and diverted attention from them.
Pastrana's weakness as a president and his conflicts
with Congress delayed the granting of extraordinary
powers until near the end of his term (1973). Despite
a more auspicious beginning, Lopez became embroiled in
conflicts over his conduct in office and such controversial proposals as the calling of a constitutional
assembly.[31] More important than the lack of presidential leadership was the absence of strong leaders within the reform group itself. Those figures involved
earlier, for example under Lleras Restrepo, had either
retired from the scene or gone on to other issues. For
the political leaders who had actively backed reform in
the earlier years the chief concern was now that of
managing their own careers with the end of the National
Front.

With the loss of its political leadership, the
Colombian movement's initial advantage of not having a
dominant core group of specialists began to work
against it. By the mid and late 1970s reform planning
continued on several fronts, but the wider sense of
purpose and its concrete objectives had disappeared.
The absence of external and internal leadership and the
uncertain future had their impact on the work of the
reform agencies, many of which were engaged in projects
which might never have a chance of implementation. In
response to this situation, the reformers began to emphasize smaller scale programs with the idea of making
themselves useful and so guaranteeing their future
existence.

By the late 1970s with the addition of the national planning office (DNP), administrative reform
efforts were being conducted through four largely
independent bodies which, although they maintained
contact with each other, carried out their functions
separately. The <u>Secretaria</u> had by this time decreased
its staff to an all time low of thirteen, only half of
whom were actively involved in its original reform

mission. Meanwhile, both ESAP and those offices of the
DNP engaged in relevant work had grown in size and
taken on a number of functions which might more logically have fallen to the Secretaria. DASC, despite the
elimination of a number of its powers in 1968, had expanded and after further setbacks in the career system
had still managed to increase its work load by developing a number of peripheral functions.

The organization suffering the greatest decline
and with the least apparent prospects for future growth
was the Secretaria (SOIAP), the core of the original
reform movement. Its decline occurred in stages and
was attributable in part to such factors as a decreasing wider interest in administrative reform, and the
growth and expanding role of such entities as DNP and
ESAP. The Secretaria also hastened its own decline
with its efforts, in 1973, to introduce a more theoretical reform into the normal reorganization process. Until that year, the normal procedure had been
for specific proposals to be drawn up by a committee
composed of members of the agency under reorganization
and the Secretaria. This method was too slow for the
short period allowed in 1973 and in the end, the Secretaria's members wrote up the reorganization plans on
their own, taking the opportunity to introduce a more
uniform and systematic format. The agencies involved
protested the move, calling it an imposed reform. As a
result, the basic procedure was changed so that in
1976, the agencies were first allowed to submit their
own proposals which the Secretaria then reviewed. After the failure of the "theoretical" reform, that review was based largely on legal criteria with the
Secretaria making no effort to give some more uniform
direction to the changes.

Given the periodic nature of the reform efforts,
even were the Secretaria to take a more active role,
its staff would be unoccupied much of the time. Thus
over the years the office assumed a number of additional functions all related to its original role.[32] For
example, one of its principal tasks became that of reviewing contracts made by central agencies with private
firms. This arose out of the Secretaria's old role of
approving contacts with private companies for reform
related studies and was reinforced by Decree 1050 of
1976 which made those public officials signing contracts responsible for them. Other new functions included the review of modifications of statutes for
decentralized entities and studies on the administrative implications of projects of law put forth by various offices. In all of these instances, the opinion
of the Secretaria was not binding and might not even be
required. It was usually requested as a precaution, to

guard against a proposed change being held up by unforeseen legal and administrative details. In the case
of proposed structural changes within the central bureaucracy, the Secretaria's role was strengthened
through an informal agreement with DASC whereby the
latter would not approve changes in staffing without
the Secretaria's prior consent. As of late 1978 the
impact of that arrangement was weakened by the Ministry
of Finance's failure to cooperate.

Beginning under the Pastrana government, the Secretaria's other major activity, involving almost half
of its staff, was the review of the performance of individual administrative entities. Here the Secretaria
functioned as a cross between an ombudsman and an efficiency expert.[33] Although in the course of its inves-
tigations, it might uncover instances of individual
malfeasance, the emphasis was on improving performance
through changes in structure and operating procedures.
With its small staff the Secretaria's potential impact
was limited, but its first major project was an ambitious one—an investigation of the Social Security Fund
(Caja de Seguridad Social), undertaken in response to
the large number of complaints it had received against
this entity. The Secretaria's findings in an investigation of this sort were not binding. In order to have
an effect it had to work closely with the targeted entity's staff and directors. In theory, this type of
investigation could be done through the decentralized
offices of organization and methods which had gradually
been set up throughout the centralized administration
following the first reform period. However, in 1968
these offices were transferred to the ministerial
(economic) planning sections and as a result have remained understaffed and less effective than they might
have been working on their own.

In a final area in which it was first intended to
operate, departmental and municipal reform, the Secretaria's lack of staff and the availability of another
agency, ESAP, curtailed its activities. The office
still maintained some interest in this area and in 1978
began a survey of the administrative structures of the
departments and municipios with the idea that this
might be used as a basis for evaluation and later reform. However, its small staff and the fact that few
people were even aware of the Secretaria's existence
prevented a more active role. In terms of actual aid
to municipalities and departments, ESAP took over where
the Secretaria retreated, working from the advantage of
a larger staff and a body of students it could utilize
as researchers, as well as its greater funding and
visibility. Toward the end of the decade, ESAP had
completed or had in progress a number of departmental

advisory projects begun at the request of the departments involved and for which it charged only its
costs.[34] In 1978, the Congress contracted it to undertake a study of its own administative services, a
highly visible project and one likely to bring ESAP
still more business. Interviews with ESAP staff on the
departmental studies in particular revealed that they
were not too optimistic about the changes that would
result. However, they also suggested that given the
backwardness of the departmental bureaucracies, even
minor, rudimentary reforms could have substantial pay-
offs. The limited resources of the departments and the
political pressures supporting the status quo made it
unwise to expect more. As one staff member noted,
there were simply too many benefits in the existing
local systems for those involved, to make many changes
possible. Despite these qualifications, and despite
ESAP's continued involvement in training programs for
prospective or actual public employees, these studies
remain its most significant contribution to reform to
date and the one with the most potential for development. Although ESAP's creators, working under French
influence, had envisioned its role as more like that of
the French National School of Administration (ENA),
with the end of producing a select corps of top level
career administrators, this never materialized. The
products of its courses were a mixed lot, still too few
in number and too widely dispersed to have a measurable
impact. Like other such schools in the region, ESAP
faced a prejudice and an ignorance about its mission
which made it difficult to attract top candidates.

AREAS OF REFORM: PERSONNEL ADMINISTRATION

    Because it was the key issue of the early reform
movement, the fate of Colombia's civil service reform
is a particularly significant indicator of the problems
of administrative reform in that country. Administrative reform first emerged as a means to resolve Colombia's political problems--by removing the patronage
element from civil service employment and creating an
administrative career class. Although neither goal was
reached, the institutions created for these purposes
remained and grew. Over time their functions were modified and their objectives became less clearcut. While
it would be politically risky to suggest the elimination of either the original goals or the institutions
involved, the changing political system has made the
former less urgent. This raises the questions, still
not addressed, of what the ends the institutions and
the civil service system as a whole should serve and of
whether those ends in the 1980s bear any relation to
what they appeared to be twenty-five years earlier.

Early Problems and Revisions

The shortcomings of the civil service system as created in the period from 1958 to 1960 emerged gradually so that several partial solutions could be attempted along the way. The first problem was that the original legislation (Decree 1732 of 1960) was nearly impossible to implement. In the initial version, all but the most routine personnel functions were centralized in DASC which was to administer tests, select candidates and send them to the ministries. The process was so complex that only about one percent of the employees was actually selected this way;[35] as a result only a small portion of the public servants entered the career system. DASC was so incapable of meeting the actual demand that in 1962 legislation was passed allowing agencies to take on new staff without going through the formal procedures. By 1968 it had become apparent that even these stopgap measures were inadequate. In that year, DASC's position was transformed to an almost entirely advisory one and the ministerial personnel offices were allowed to assume many of its functions. Under the revised system for entrance into the public service and the career system, the ministries were to select their own candidates and establish their own lists of eligibles subject to general standards set by DASC. In practice this system could be circumvented in a number of ways, but even this was unnecessary. The new process did not become compulsory until 1973, pending the passage of a reglamento (decree 2400) which was delayed by a lengthy political battle. For the five intervening years, the ministries operated pretty much on their own, filling their staffing requirements as they chose.[36]

In the meantime, one of the most critical problems behind the drive for a career system--that of unstable employment--had failed to materialize. In the absence of a uniform system and with the ministries able to hire staff virtually at will, patronage had not been eliminated, but it was now visible in hiring rather than firing. Although massive dismissals of employees with each change of administration had not been unknown before, they were now seen as impolitic and were replaced by the practice of creating more jobs for political followers. This produced a new problem--an unprecedentedly rapid growth of public employment, but it was one political leaders were reluctant to tackle head on. The change eliminated much of the interest in reform among the politicians and bureaucrats and created a further disincentive for the latter to seek

entry into the career system. Even when further
changes were made to allow existing employees to initiate their own entrance into the career service, few
took advantage of this. By the late 1970s only about
ten percent (11,000) of the 110,000 employees eligible
were classified as career service members.[37]

Changes made in 1968 and after reduced the ambitious scope of the career service, excluding not only
the departmental and municipal employees, but also
those in the decentralized enterprises. There were
also a number of separate career systems in operation
(teaching, diplomatic, judicial and military) which
further reduced the number of potential members out of
the total 600,000 paid by the central government. Further reductions seemed likely as a number of public
entities (for example the Ministry of Finance) had
proposed the creation of their own independent career
systems.[38] Trends like these arose in the uneven
development of the public service as a whole, the
different levels of patronage or merit appointment
operative in different agencies, and the possible
advantages separate systems might offer in terms of
attracting and retaining qualified personnel. Since
DASC still maintained its ability to set salary levels
and regulate the creation of new positions, this last
factor was particularly critical.

Further Setbacks: Lopez's State of Siege and the 1978 Strike

We can only guess at the changes which might have
resulted from the 1973 law because the situation was
further complicated soon after its passage. In 1975, a
teachers' strike provoked President Lopez to declare a
national state of siege which, among its other provisions, froze entry to the career service for its duration. The striking teachers had been the target of
this move aimed at eliminating their job security, but
Lopez found it more prudent to extend its coverage to
all public employees.[39] The immediate results were as
follows: the ministries could go back to hiring new
employees as they wanted; all new entrants and those in
office but not covered by the career service, lost job
security and could be fired from one day to the next.
The ten percent of all employees officially enrolled in
the career system retained their job security but were
threatened with six to twelve months suspension if they
went on strike. The first state of emergency was lif-
ted after a few months but was almost immediately re-
instated so that for virtually all of Lopez's presidency the growth of the career system remained at a
standstill.[40]

The past experience with the career system meant
that the situation was not much lamented by the employees, political leaders, or members of DASC. The
latter had expressed a good deal of skepticism about
the revised legislation and early in 1978 requested
faculties to begin working on still another revision
which they believed more likely to be implemented.[41]
Although the faculties were granted, the revision never
got under way--owing to the political backlash provoked
by their preliminary work on salary scales and job levels. It appears that DASC's main interest was in simplifying the system still further to make it more man-
ageable and less subject to abuse. Interviews with
DASC members indicate that they still accepted the idea
of a career service but saw little hope for the existing system even as revised in 1968.

In the meantime, DASC continued to expand its
activities despite the suspension of its original central function. During the Lopez administration, the
emphasis was increasingly on the general management of
the personnel system through training, social welfare,
legal advice and the control of the creation of new
posts.[42] As a consequence DASC expanded its organization, creating a division of human development (responsible for in-service training) and a division of systems, one of whose major projects was the creation of
an up-to-date computerized registry of all public employees. In most of these efforts, the office was hindered by its largely advisory role. While it could
establish new programs and supply information and advice to offices throughout the executive branch, it
could only in limited instances require that those
offices adopt or implement programs.

DASC's effectiveness in developing the personnel
system was also hindered by the nature of its relationship with the decentralized personnel offices throughout the bureaucracy. Although it had been instrumental
in the creation of these offices, after 1968 the latter
were formally able to operate in relative independence.
Their subsequent development and activities hinged more
on ministerial policies than on the central system, as
indicated by the enormous variation in their size,
structure and activities. In the larger ministries
(e.g., Public Works and Finance) they tended to be
quite big (up to 250 members) while in the smaller
ministries (e.g., Mines) they might be staffed with
only a few people and capable of carrying out only the
most routine work.[43] At both extremes the offices were
unlikely to be responsive to DASC, in the one case because of their limited abilities and in the other because of their own complexity and importance. DASC
contact with the ministerial and agency personnel

offices tended to be limited as well, sometimes restricted only to official communications, like the
transmission of norms, the monthly reports on personnel
movements or occasional orientation programs. Thus the
offices maintained considerable independence as witnessed by their lack of uniform procedures for the most
routine activities.

DASC's major remaining point of control was the
area of salaries and position classification. Here the
office not only established norms; it also set the legal levels for all of the centralized sector potentially within the career system. More recently there had
been a movement in the office toward the standardization and simplification of these levels as a preliminary step in the introduction of a more functional
career system.[44] Although this move worked against the
ministries' tendency to introduce complex wage scales
and positions (as a means of attracting and holding
employees) it was opposed most fervently not by them
but by the civil servants themselves, creating the
first major political battle directly engaging DASC.

The conflict occurred in the spring of 1978 and
produced a civil service strike capped by the hanging
in effigy of DASC's directors. It centered around four
attempted reforms, each of them aimed at simplifying
and upgrading the existing system. (This would affect
all 110,000 employees eligible for, and not only those
officially enrolled in, the career system). The proposal included:

> 1) a salary reform (as part of a general
> increase, but objected to because it gave
> minimal increases to the higher levels and
> collapsed the existing system into a smaller
> number of salary levels)[45]
>
> 2) a provision stipulating that any increase
> in the number of positions in a specific min-
> istry would have to be linked to programs (so
> that as programs were eliminated, positions
> would disappear as well)
>
> 3) the introduction of minimal educational re-
> quirements (as opposed to experience alone)
> for professional positions (feared by those
> who had entered without meeting those require-
> ments)
>
> 4) a change in the number of basic categories
> of positions from four to seven, which also
> established a separate wage scale for each
> (eliminating the necessity of moving from one
> category to another if salaries were to be

increased, but also bringing the complaint
that this was an elitist solution).

In the end, after the uproar died down these reforms
were passed in only slightly modified form.

DASC's Outlook

The confrontation is most interesting not for
these results, but for what it illustrates about DASC's
position. Unlike the Venezuelan and Peruvian civil
service reformers, the Colombians were not attempting a
particularly theoretical reform nor were they attempting to change the main thrust of the system as set up
in 1968. Instead frustrated by their own inability to
act and by the misuse of the present system, they had
set about to simplify it and so reduce its susceptibility to manipulation. Here they used their one means of
leverage, their control over salary and classification
scales. They saw themselves as pitted against the ministries with their tendency to increase positions, job
categories and salaries whenever possible as part of
their own drive for expansion and as a way of respond-
ing to pressures from employees. The intent was thus
not to change the basic thrust of the existing system
but to reinforce it. In introducing these changes, the
DASC had taken care to consult with representatives of
the ministries and of the civil service unions, but the
latter in particular had not foreseen the implications
of the changes. Thus it was only five days after the
passage of the new decrees that the conflict broke out.
Significantly, DASC had not consulted with members of
either the Secretaria or of ESAP, neither of which became involved in any part of the debate.

In order to make peace with the civil service
unions, a series of further meetings was held resulting
in some modifications of the original reforms. The
salary issue was resolved by establishing a sixteen
percent minimum raise for all personnel, the provision
that further employment would be linked to programs was
dropped, and the original provision allowing experience
to substitute for formal education was retained both
for new and old employees. The change to a system of
seven basic career lines was retained as were the
changes in salary scales both of which allowed a considerable simplification of the basic scheme. This,
the DASC hoped, would facilitate future management of
the system and cut down on the potential for its manipulation. In the end, however, the career system remained untouched and any hopes of rewriting the basic
legislation were indefinitely postponed.

Civil Service Unions[46]

These events had two further results with uncertain long term implications. First, they had prompted the first nationwide strike of civil servants and encouraged the emergence of a much greater union strength. Colombian civil service unions have been organized and continue to be organized through the ministries with two national federations weakly affiliating them. Thus, the success of the combined efforts of the unions in forcing modification of the reforms seemed to have given a push to the unionization effort and to the possible strengthening of broader groupings. Second, the experience set a precedent for collective agreements with civil servants as opposed to the previous system where new conditions were simply fixed by law. Both effects demonstrate as in our other cases that one result of attempts to strengthen the civil service system is, for good or for bad, the strengthening of civil service unions as well.

It is evident however, that DASC's early dealings with the unions and the 1978 reforms in particular did not set a good precedent for further efforts to introduce change. DASC's self-image as a kind of policeman of the civil service system, pitting it against the manipulative ministries and employees did not help much in this regard. While its vision of the existing system and of the pressures encouraging the manipulations was a realistic one (and much more so than the idealized visions pursued by the Peruvian and Venezuelan offices), it also defined the situation as one of conflicting interests from the start. The conflict was further complicated by its three cornered nature--pitting DASC, the ministries and the unions against each other--and by the varying strengths of the unions and of the personnel offices with which they dealt directly. This also meant that there might be more room for agreement among the parties than DASC was willing to believe. Thus, for example, although members of DASC's directorate suggested in interviews that the unions were opposed to a further extension of the career system because it would weaken their own power, the union of DASC employees claimed to support the system and to be in favor of fuller coverage. Union members indicated that their objections to the existing system were similar to those the DASC staff had cited-- specifically the continuing role of patronage and the various means by which provisions for merit appointment could be circumvented.

The status of the civil service unions themselves was another issue which DASC had so far not attempted to touch. As in the other countries this was viewed as a legal and political matter and thus not one over

which the civil service office should have any monopoly
of jurisdiction. Although the office consulted with
the unions on some matters and otherwise took them into
account in making policy, it had not developed any
special programs for dealing with them nor made any
effort to consider their impact in any of its studies.
The unions correctly perceived the issue as one of concern to the wider government and made their most general complaint about the government's de facto policy
of trying to keep them divided. The most important division was that between the trabajadores (blue collar)
and empleados (white collar). The former's status and
privileges (including the right to strike) were similar
to those of private workers; the latter were more
strictly constrained by existing legislation. One of
the major goals of the civil service unions was the
elimination of this distinction.[47]
     The second major type of division was more a
function of the historical development of the unions
than of any conscious government policy. This was the
orgnization of the unions on a ministerial or agency
basis. Although national federations existed their
coordinating abilities were weak, and they could not
meddle in the internal affairs of individual unions.
The latter also made their own decisions about such
collective actions as national strikes. One of the
major factors preserving union autonomy was the enormous variation in the power and effectiveness of individual unions. Each of these generally dealt directly
with the entity to which it was attached and through it
with the government. Union power was thus a function
of the level of organization and the critical nature of
the work performed. Some of the stronger unions were
those in key ministries--Public Works or Finance.
There were also a number of agencies which still lacked
unions, largely because of a reluctance on the part of
employees to form them. As is generally the case
throughout Latin America, upper level workers tended
not to be members and those agencies--like the Contra-
loria--with a more professionalized staff were slow to
form unions.
     To summarize the status of personnel reform in
Colombia the following generalizations can be made.
The movement got under way and the first legislation
was passed because of the agreement among the politicians and the bureaucrats on the need for the elimination of political patronage particularly as it affected the job security of employees. The urgency of this
early goal was eliminated over the first years as it
became apparent that the massive firings envisioned by
the old system's critics were not taking place and that
public employees had a relatively high degree of security. This development, combined with the unworkability

of the first career system and the shortcomings of the
revised system introduced in 1968 produced a crisis of
objectives in the reform movement. By the 1970s it was
no longer clear what goals it should be realizing.
While there was general agreement on the desirability
of a merit based career system which would attract and
retain higher quality employees, the conflict of aims
among the various parties involved--notably the political parties, the bureaucrats, the ministries, DASC,
and the civil service unions--produced a ten-year
stalemate. The problem was complicated by the fragmentation of power within the system, a characteristic
of the administrative reform movement as a whole.
Where power is so dispersed, but where every major
group is still able to operate within its own sphere,
the chances for change are much less than in a situation where one or more groups are prevented from acting. So long as this balance of power remained and
there was no out and out crisis, it was unlikely that
the existing complaints--for example the proliferation
of government jobs, or the low salary levels of higher
level employees-would provoke more decisive change.

The status quo was also supported by the practical, untheoretical outlook of DASC, the core institution, whose members saw themselves more as enforcers of
the existing system than as having a mandate to change
it to something substantially different. While their
suggested reforms provoked conflicts with the unions
and produced one massive general strike, they still
restrained themselves to tinkering with the existing
system rather than introducing more radical change.

AREAS OF REFORM: DECENTRALIZATION AND REGIONALIZATION

Although decentralization and regionalization
remained important themes in Colombian politics, these
two topics (and related issues like departmental and
municipal reform or even the status of decentralized
institutes) were the orphans of the administrative reform movement. The reasons for this were both political and organizational. Politically, the relatively
greater fragmentation of power in the Colombian system
and the fact that the changes entailed in regionalization and departmental and municipal reforms could significantly affect the electoral base of the national
parties made these issues more sensitive and kept political leaders involved in their discussion. Although
these areas have been claimed by the administrative
experts in Venezuela and Peru, they were not viewed
this narrowly in Colombia. What one economic planner
said of the regionalization issue--that it was an area
where everyone felt entitled to an opinion--was true of
all the decentralization themes.

Organizationally, it was the very fragmentation of
the reform movement that has worked against a more concentrated attention to these issues. In the division
of functions among ESAP, the Secretaria, the DASC, and
later the DNP, jurisdiction over these issues was never
settled. As a result everyone has done a little to
produce a number of partial and not strictly compatible
schemes. Of the four offices, only planning had a
clear and independent jurisdiction over the regionalization issue. Even here, the Lopez administration's
proposals for a limited constitutional assembly to discuss, among other issues, regional reforms, sidestepped
the DNP's Office of Regional and Urban Development
(Unidad de Desarrollo Regional y Urbano, UDRU) which
thus declined to take a major role in the
discussions.[48]

In all of these areas, the major problems were the
lack of leadership, both political and administrative,
and the rather vague mandate provided by even the early
discussions of decentralizing reforms. Although everyone was in agreement that the Colombian administrative
and political systems were too centralized, this was
the reform area in which the problems and objectives
were least clearly defined and the methods to be used
most uncertain. Changes in emphasis brought by different adminstrations (for example the Pastrana administration's focus on urban areas as opposed to Lopez's
stress on rural improvements) and the distinctive focus
of each agency working on related projects further complicated the situation. By the end of the Lopez administration in mid 1978, although small steps had been
taken in several directions, the future thrust of the
regionalization and decentralizing reforms was still
unclear. It was also evident that several of the projects were working at cross purposes. Still, the progress in any direction had been too slight to create
much waste. In some sense the various projects figured
as experiments among which a future administration
might choose.

Municipal and Departmental Reform

The choice facing any such future administration
is a big one, involving the specification of both objectives and strategies. It will have to decide whether decentralization will involve the strengthening of
existing institutions (departmental and municipal government) individually or in some collective form, or
whether the move will be toward a new form of organization perhaps involving the introduction of regional
governments. The 1958 legislation stressed the former
strategy under the heading of municipal and departmental reform. For a number of reasons, including the

higher priority of other reform measures, little progress was made here. Other factors working against
reform in this area were the enormity of the task,
especially at the municipal level, which meant that
even at the height of its powers the Secretaria lacked
the staff and other resources to undertake it; the limited resources of both departments and municipalities
which limited the kind of change they could realistically undertake; the power of locally based vested interests; and the difficulties of meddling in a system
which was tied to the power of national parties and
politicians.[49] All of this discouraged the introduction of comprehensive reforms at either the departmental or municipal level. It did not prevent a series of
more limited efforts many of which utilized the voluntary participation of local entities. The simplest of
these efforts involved the use of advisory missions to
individual departments or cities to conduct studies of
existing conditions and help in directing reforms. All
three of the original reform agencies--ESAP, the Secretaria, and DASC--conducted such missions, although in
more recent years, the Secretaria ended its participation because of inadequate staffing. As a result,
ESAP's involvement increased although even with its
ability to utilize students as well as staff, it managed to conduct only a handful of such missions. Lacking a formal program, DASC had still been available to
departments and municipalities requesting aid in setting up civil service systems or otherwise reforming
their personnel systems. Over the two decades it co-
operated in this regard with a small number of local
units.

Generally participants from all three entities had
similar impressions of their experience.[50] They stressed that the changes that could be made were not great,
given the resource constraints and other obstacles. As
one ESAP staff member noted, even where reforms were
implemented, they were likely to be reversed in time as
local officials succumbed to the pressures which gave
rise to the problems in the first place. On the positive side, all felt that even small changes were worth-
while and that this was one area where their experience
and knowledge could provide a real help. As one member
of DASC suggested, whatever problems the office faced
at the national level, it was still twenty years ahead
of the departments and municipalities in personnel
techniques and could provide assistance in some very
basic areas. Given that these efforts were the primary
responsibilities of none of the agencies, the fundamental obstacle was the size of the task compared to the
time they could devote to it. That problem was unlikely to be resolved until and unless a still more

fundamental decision was made on an overall decentralization strategy and the place of these programs within
it.

Municipal and Departmental Associations[51]

A second type of reform and one that attempted to
deal with the problem of limited central and local resources included a number of attempts to encourage municipal and departmental associations. Both of these
were channeled through the DNP's regional development
office although neither was systematically coordinated
with simultaneous efforts in regionalization. Although
begun in 1975, the municipal associations had come to
naught by 1978. Of the four in existence by the latter
year, only one was judged to be working well. The DNP
blamed internal conflicts for the poor results, but the
planners' lack of interest in the scheme was probably a
factor as well.

The departmental association project began in 1974
through a contract with the Organization of American
States to cooperate in setting up a pilot project in
the underdeveloped Atlantic coast departments. The
resulting association, ADCA, and its regional planning
office SIPUR, were later termed a disaster by the DNP,
principally because of conflicts that broke out between
the national and regional planning bodies. From the
central office's point of view, the source of these
problems lay in the political appointment of many of
the local staff members who had little training in
planning. Complicating and contributing to this
conflict was the reluctance of the various central
ministries to offer cooperation.

Despite these inauspicious beginnings, the formation of departmental associations continued so that
by 1978, twenty-two of the twenty-three departments belonged to one. Much of the impetus for this development came from the departments themselves who saw it as
a way of exerting more effective political pressure.
In fact lobbying was often the major activity of the
associations. Most had little in the way of an institutionalized structure. Furthermore, every time a governor was replaced, his or her successor had to be con-
vinced to join. As might be expected, the departmental
associations were plagued by internal disputes among
the member departments. The governors' dual role as
members of the association and head of their departmental governments was a major contributing factor.
Finally, the ad hoc nature of the association process,
which often joined departments with little in common,
was a problem. Where the association was large and
grouped several departments it was often difficult to
find a common perspective on needs.

The view from the planning office, which was active in the formation of only two of the associations, was critical, but its staff generally welcomed the experience as a learning process. The feeling was that this could serve as the basis for future efforts in which the DNP would take a more active role, having learned from the mistakes and problems of the departments' own efforts. In such a future experiment it was also clear that the planners intended to be more actively involved in the association process itself, incorporating a planning function as well as their more particular interest in still another decentralizing strategy, the introduction of regional units.

Regionalization[52]

Regionalization and the formation of regional governments was the DNP's own contribution to the administrative reform discussion. This theme was introduced late, with the emphasis on planning in the 1968 reforms, and got its initial impetus from the planners' education in French planning techniques. From the start the emphasis was on development poles and related concepts and it was only later that other influences crept in. The first regionalization scheme, formulated in 1970, but never officially released showed this early influence, but its highly theoretical bent prevented its acceptance. In attempting to work out economically and administratively viable regions, the planners ignored the old departmental boundaries and so lost any chance of political support. A second scheme, drawn up under the Lopez administration, but once again not released, presented two alternatives, one preserving the departments and the other ignoring their boundaries. The planners' own preference was for the second alternative as more economically sound. However, they were willing to recognize the departments as a historical and traditional factor and thus to back the first choice as the politically wiser one.

A second obstacle and one not considered in the development of their model was the existing distribution of ministerial offices. The planners' explanation was that this distribution had no technical base and no uniformity among ministries and hence did not need to be considered. Whatever the truth in this criticism, it ignored the need for cooperation from the ministries, as well as what the Venezuelan planners termed the "administrative rationale"--the differing organizational and administrative requirements of the various ministries. The regionalization proposed was thus strictly an economic planner's regionalization. The question of administrative organization within the units, whether municipal, departmental, or regional,

also continued to plague the planners. Their models
offered no solution to the coordination of the thirty
or so entities working in a single territorial unit.
So long as regionalization remains the province of the
economic planner and so long as the existing division
of functions among the various reform agencies prevails
leaving administrative planning to the other three, it
seems unlikely that this problem will be directly
addressed.

Although the planners' preferred outcome was a
regionalization scheme based on a regional planning
system they have also found themselves involved in a
number of other decentralization projects none of which
is necessarily compatible with this first objective.
Two of these, the associations of municipalities and of
departments have already been mentioned. Others include the development of industrial parks and other
industrial decentralization projects, the management of
the urban development enterprises (empresas de desarrollo urbano) a product of the Pastrana administration
subsequently deemphasized by Lopez, and the regional
development corporations of which eight were in operation by 1978. The latter were transferred to the
planning agency's supervision in 1975 at their own
request. According to the planners, two motives were
instrumental here: the corporation members' desire for
technical aid in planning, and, probably more importantly, the desire to have direct access to planning's
investment budget. As of late 1978, the DNP also had
requests from outside groups for the formation of four
more such corporations. Although the final decision on
these requests would be made by the Congress, the prior
approval of planning was required.

DNP's regional development office remained ambiv-
alent about all these projects, and about the regional
development corporations in particular (as the most recent and most popular form) because of their questionable compatibility with its other efforts. While two
of the existing corporations included two or more departments,[53] most were subdepartmental. Thus despite
their formation around the development of some resource, they still were not seen as an improvement over
the departments themselves as a basis for planning.
Here as in the other cases, the office's ability to
discourage what it saw as unadvisable remained limited.
Most of these projects had strong backers so that opposition could be politically costly to the office.
Equally important was the fact that even programs which
did not meet the office's criteria still might be used
to build up visibility and positive feelings elsewhere
and particularly among local level institutions it
wished to draw into other projects. As members of the
office often suggested in discussing specific programs,

one of the key motives for departmental or municipal participation was access to funds. So long as it was apparent that the office had funding, it could increase the chances of cooperation with its programs.

Although all this activity produced some interesting experimental programs, the long-run value of the experiments hinged on their input to the strategy eventually selected. It was clear that many of these experiments were the product of political opportunism rather than an effort to explore alternatives. For this reason their eventual contribution, despite the planning office's optimism, remained in doubt. Thus, if the Venezuelan and Peruvian regionalization schemes most often ran into trouble because of their formulators' unwillingness to compromise their theories, the empiricism of the Colombian planners had other disadvantages. By mid 1978, the picture in Colombia was one of a number of often conflicting decentralization programs, many of which may be hard to eradicate at a later point. None of them had succeeded in incorporating the rest of the bureaucracy or in affecting the latter's decentralization. Indeed not much effort had been made in this direction. Meanwhile complaints remained widespread about the quality of local level services, the inadequacy of departmental and municipal finances, and the centralized character of the bureaucracy.[54] The nature of the national political system, with its dispersed power and cluster of vested interests, makes it much harder to attack these problems head on than to indulge in experimentation with what remaining funds can be found. So long as none of these programs becomes more than a partial solution, however, it is unlikely that the situation will improve.

SUMMARY

As contrasted with the Venezuelan and Peruvian cases, the Colombian experience provides some interesting further insights into the complexities of the reform process, raising questions not only about how reforms might best be implemented, but also about the origins of their objectives and their relationship to other political values and issues. These themes will be treated in more detail in the next chapter. For the moment and in summarizing this section, we turn to another theme raised by the Colombian comparison, that of the relationship between the reform process and the wider political system.

As noted in the introduction to the section, a quick comparison of the three examples suggests very little relationship between type of political system and type or outcome of reform policies. However, a second and more selective examination does yield some generalizations couched in terms of a more specific and limited set of political variables. First, it suggests that two of the most critical of these political variables may be the levels of institutionalization and integration of the existing political system. The higher these are, the less chance there will be for domination of the reform movement by reform specialists. Especially under the post-1968 Peruvian military government, and, if to a lesser extent, in the civilian regimes in Venezuela and in pre-1968 Peru, the experts' power was enhanced by discontinuities in the political system and by the political leaders' lack of experience in administrative politics. Where political leadership has been directly involved in administration or at least has a long history of interaction with administrative agencies and actors, the mystique surrounding the experts' claims is dissipated just as is the politicians' willingness to let them control all aspects of change. We see a recent trend to this effect in contemporary Venezuela. Here the critical factor is not only a greater familiarity with administrative problems and a tendency to see them as less of a specialized problem for the experts; it is also the simple realization that many of the "technical" solutions are likely to have a broad impact on the power and resources of individuals and groups inside and outside the bureaucracy.

A second generalization can also be drawn from the three cases: the greater the diffusion of power within a political system, the less likely it is that comprehensive reforms will be attempted, and if attempted, implemented. Whereas in post-1968 Peru and in Venezuela, the existence of relatively more concentrated centers of power has encouraged reformers and politicians to think in terms of comprehensive reforms, the absence of these conditions in Colombia has discouraged such attempts. The relative diffusion or concentration of power is partly a matter of perception, and in this sense, related to the level of institutionalization of the system. It is likely in less institutionalized systems, as was apparently the case in post-1968 Peru, that actors will misperceive the extent of power concentration, exaggerating the strength and single-mindedness of the central government. Thus, in Colombia, it was not only the real level of diffusion but also the actors' greater experience with it and thus more accurate perceptions of their abilities that discouraged more ambitious reform programs.

Finally, although the Colombian case suggests that high levels of institutionalization, integration and diffused power will lessen the chances for attempts at comprehensive reform, it also indicates that these same

conditions raise the likelihood of incremental, piecemeal change. Two factors are at work here. The first
is simply the result of the more concentrated effort on
the second type of change. In the absence of more comprehensive programs, piecemeal reforms will get more
attention and so are more likely to be pushed through.
Furthermore, the lessened role for reform experts and
the correspondingly greater involvement of politicians
and bureaucrats means that even at the planning stage,
coalitions of supporters are being formed. Thus, contrary to the two-stage scenario of reform planning by a
specialized group, alliance formation among the interested parties is incorporated from the start and compromises with potential opposition can become a part of
the initial proposal.

NOTES

1. Jaime Vidal Perdomo, Derecho administrativo
(Cali: Biblioteca Banco Popular, 1977), p.166.
2. Roderick T. Groves, "The Colombian National
Front and Administrative Reform," Administration and
Society (November 1974), pp. 316-36.
3. Further background on contemporary Colombian
politics can be found in R. Albert Berry et al.(ed.),
Politics of Compromise (New Brunswick, New Jersey:
Transaction Books, 1980). A less up to date, but still
good overview is provided in Robert H. Dix, Colombia:
The Political Dimensions of Change (New Haven: Yale,
1967), and a more controversial interpretation is found
in James L. Payne, Patterns of Conflict in Colombia
(New Haven: Yale, 1968).
4. See the articles by Mauricio Solaun and
Harvey F. Kline in Berry et al., pp.1-58, 59-83.
5. Solaun, op. cit., p. 9.
6. See Kline, pp. 69-74 for a discussion of the
provisions.
7. See R. Albert Berry and Mauricio Solaun,
"Notes Toward an Interpretation of the National Front,"
in Berry et al., pp. 438-60 for a discussion of some of
the main issues. See also selected articles in Mario
Arrubla, et al., Colombia Hoy (Bogota: Siglo Vein-
tiuno, 1978).
8. One good summary in English does exist for the
period to 1973. See Groves, op. cit. There are a
number of Colombian summaries, most published through
one of the reform offices or an international agency.
The best early ones are Aryeh Attir, La reforma
administrativa en Colombia (United Nations, December
21, 1962) and Carlos Ramirez Cardona, "Esfuerzos
nacionales para la reforma administrativa: lecciones
de la experiencia" (Bogota: unpublished report to the
U.N. May 1, 1967).

9. Jaime Videl Perdomo, Derecho administrativo, p. 169.

10. These were the first Currie Mission in 1950 (under the IBRD and more generally oriented), the second Currie Mission (specifically on the administrative sector) in 1950-1, a U.N. technical assistance mission to do general studies on the administrative sector in 1954, and a French mission directed by Louis Joseph Lebret in 1957-8. The Lebret Mission like the first Currie Mission was oriented toward more general socioeconomic problems, but it also noted the urgent need for administrative reform in its findings. Ramirez, op. cit., pp. 1-10.

11. The influence is seen in the direct translation of some terms from the French and in the early hopes of turning ESAP into an institution like the French ENA.

12. In the Pact of Sitges establishing the Front this aim was clearly stated. In Groves translation one of the several relevant passages reads, "...a first limit (on Presidential power) must be the extremely urgent creation of a career civil service that will suppress the concept that the political victor has the right to the spoils of the vanquished... and to turn the public administration inside out, replacing all the employees with new favorites." Groves, p. 318.

13. Law 19 of 1958, Article one, as cited in Ramirez, p. 12.

14. Ramirez, p. 14.

15. Attir, p. 50.

16. Ramirez, p. 14.

17. Loc. cit .

18. Attir, p. 58.

19. Ramirez, p. 29.

20. Antioquia, Boyaca and Choco, respectively. Attir, p. 68.

21. Attir, p.37.

22. Ibid., p. 116.

23. Ibid., p. 38.

24. Interviews with actual and former members of the various reform agencies produced this observation.

25. A reading of any of the lists of decrees issued under the enabling laws (and particularly under the last four of them) as published in the Diario Oficial makes this characteristic very apparent.

26. Interviews, SOIAP, Bogota, 1978.

27. Interviews with members of SOIAP, DASC, and ESAP, Bogota, 1978.

28. A discussion of regional planning's history in Colombia is found in Alan Gilbert, "Urban and Regional Development Programs in Colombia since 1951," in Wayne Cornelius and Felicity Trueblood (eds), Latin

American Urban Research, V. (Berkeley: Sage, 1975) pp. 240-75.

29.   Summaries of these schemes are found in Colombia, DNP, Unidad de Desarrollo Regional y Urbano (URDU), "La politica de descentralizacion en el plan de desarrollo para 'cerrar la brecha'" (Bogota: May 1978).

30.   Planning and the civil service system are the two most important aspects of this reform because of their long term impact. Howver two other aspects worth mentioning are the restated reorganization model ("normas generales" as set forth in Decreto 1050 of 1968) and the effort to redefine the functions and status of the decentralized sector (Decreto 3130 of 1968).   The latter's major effect was to put all decentralized entities under some kind of at least formal ministerial supervision.

31.   Luis Carlos Galan, "La asamblea constitucional,: Nueva Frontera (Dec. 14-20, 1976) pp. 5-8.

32.   These emerged during interviews with members of SOIAP.   One of the most recent projects (at least as of mid 1978) was the publication of a five hundred page manual, complete with fold-out diagrams on the organization of the executive branch.   The exact purpose of this project was not entirely clear although it should keep visiting scholars happy for years to come.   Colombia, President, SOIAP, Manual de organizacion de la rama ejecutiva del poder publico, 1978.

33.   A discussion of the first fifteen months of operation of this office is found in Jaime Castro, Control sobre la moralidad y eficiencia administrativas (Bogota: DASC, 1976).

34.   Interviews, SOIAP and ESAP, Bogota, 1978.

35.   Interview, DASC, Bogota, 1978.

36.   Interviews, DASC, Bogota, 1978.

37.   Estimate by staff member, interview, DASC, 1978.

38.   Interviews, DASC, Bogota, 1978.

39.   Lopez's attitude toward public employees in general was marked by a certain measure of hostility, for example in his comments about "the war of the administration against the government" (la guerra de la administracion contra el gobierno), which was frequently cited by DASC staff who at least at the upper levels of that organization seemed to find it accurate.

40.   The DASC published a special issue of its bulletin, Carta Administrativa on the use of the state of siege and its effects.   See Jaime Castro, "Orden publico economico," Carta Administrativa (August 1976).

41.   These faculties took the form of another set of exceptional powers for the executive, Law 5 of 1978.

42. The DASC's structure and powers were officially changed to reflect this reorientation in 1976.
Decree 147, January 27, 1976.

43. These examples and the general analysis of
the situation come from interviews with DASC employees,
Bogota, 1978.

44. The account of the strike of 1978 and the
events leading up to it was provided by DASC members,
including two participants in the strike, both representative of DASC's internal union. The latter has a
rather difficult relationship with its parent entity,
and its members were generally no more sympathetic to
the 1978 reforms than were employees with no connection
at all with the personnel office.

45. It is important to note that the DASC view
(or at least that of its directors) is that larger increases would be most effective at the uppermost and
professional levels (who are normally not union members
in any case) where they could be used to attract and
hold high quality personnel. However, sufficiently
large increases for this group (making their salaries
comparable to those offered in the private sector)
would never be allowed by the Congress which views them
as inflationary. (Increases at the lower levels may be
equally inflationary, but they are also more politic).
Thus, the increases proposed in this sense contradicted
one set of objectives--they did however serve a second
set, the simplification of the entire salary schedule,
which it was believed could be done with the minimum
opposition by bringing up the lower levels. Unfortunately the DASC overlooked the possibility that the
unionized workers receiving the smallest increases (but
already having the largest salaries) would be able to
convince the lower levels to join their protest.

46. For a short but provocative discussion of
civil service unions in Colombia see Jonathan Hartlyn,
"Interest Associations and Political Conflict in Colombia" (Unpublished draft, Vanderbilt University, 1982).

47. Interviews with representatives of DASC's
employees' union.

48. Interviews, DNP, URDU, Bogota, 1978.

49. Some notions of the problems involved here,
although viewed from a different angle (that of the
traditional patronage functions of national bureaucracy
and the adjustments made under the National Front) is
found in Steffen W. Schmidt, "Bureaucrats as Modernizing Brokers?," Comparative Politics (April 1974), pp.
425-50. Some indication of the departmental, and local
roots of national politics and especially national parties is found in Gary Hoskins, "The Impact of the National Front on Congressional Behavior," in Berry et
al., pp. 105-30.

170

50.   Interviews, DASC, ESAP, SOIAP, Bogota, 1978.
51.   Information and opinions cited in this section are drawn largely from interviews in the regional
planning unit (URDU). A summary of the programs is
also found in DNP, URDU, "La politica de decentralizacion...."
52.   Information and opinions cited in this
section are drawn from interviews in the URDU. The
URDU publication cited in note 51 and the Gilbert
article are also relevant.
53.   These development corporations include the
CVC (Cauca Valley Corporation), the first of the line
and the most famous (in the United States as well as
Colombia, because it was patterned on the TVA). As is
often the case, its success and fame have made it more
popular as a model, than, in the purely technical eyes
of the planners, it really ought to be.
54.   There are some indications that centralization, especially in regard to the distribution of resources may be increasing rather than declining. See
Gilbert, op. cit.

Part III

Conclusion

7
Administrative Reform
and Administrative Development:
Possibilities and Constraints

The present chapter returns to the ideas and questions introduced in Part One, reexamining them in light of the case studies and pursuing some new themes suggested by the histories of the reform movements. Earlier chapters have stressed the similarities in the three programs, their conformity to a general Latin American model, and their and the latter's divergence from conventional ideas about how reform was attempted and how it failed. Here the emphasis is more explicitly on the positive lessons to be drawn and especially those that can be utilized by other kinds of administrative development programs. In this final chapter, the line of argument also shifts in response to another set of questions raised in the comparative analysis-- this time to a more speculative theme, the significance of administrative reform as a type of administrative development policy and what in fact reformers can realistically atttempt to achieve.

The chapter is developed in three sections. The first draws on the case studies to derive some generalizations about implementing administrative reform and by extension all directed administrative change. The second specifically applies the reform experience and its lessons for the new approaches to improving administrative performance. The last section looks at the wider significance of reform, at the purposes it can serve, and at its relationship to administrative development policy as a whole.

IMPLEMENTING ADMINISTRATIVE CHANGE:
PROCESS AND PROGRAMS

As the cases demonstrate, we are dealing with two levels of program failure: nonimplementation and failure to achieve the desired impact. Although much of the criticism of administrative reform involves the second type, the programs examined here rarely made it

that far. Their immediate failure was implementation.
Ironically, while public and development administration
have recently discovered implementation as the "missing
link"[1] in other program areas, they have been far less
concerned with its importance in producing administrative change. Thus, before proceeding to an examination
of impact failure we first examine what the reform experience demonstrates about the neglected topic of implementing administrative change.

The Policy Process

Implementation can be addressed at either of two
levels--that of the policy process or of individual
programs. The two are closely related, in some sense
either side of the same coin, but the emphasis in each
is slightly different. Furthermore, although they are
tightly enough linked so that changes in one level produce or reflect changes in the other, they represent
alternative ways of approaching implementation. Thus
there is a practical value in retaining the distinction
between them.

At the process level, the central concern is to
shape the policy making system so as to encourage the
production of implementable policy. In more concrete
terms this means encouraging planners to recognize and
work within existing constraints or to attempt to influence external conditions and so extend the limits of
what can be done. In the case of reform, the planners'
isolation made both tactics appear unnecessary. Thus,
higher rates of implementation may be structured into
the system through measures that reduce the experts'
isolation, integrate planning and implementation, and
draw the entire policy making process into a closer
relationship with other kinds of policy and other political values.

There are certain general characteristics of technical policy making which already encourage these
trends. The most important is the experts' dependence
on other actors to recognize their expertise and define
it as applicable to the problem at hand. Unfortunately, as the cases demonstrate, this dependence is frequently overridden by other factors and especially by
the effects of external assistance. From this stems an
interest in identifying variables which work in the
other direction and which can be manipulated or at
least utilized more effectively.

One of the most powerful, but least predictable of
these variables is the level of interest in reform or
reform related programs among politically important
groups and individual leaders. Over the short run, the
presence of a political leader with a strong personal
and often spontaneous interest in reform may force the

integration of reform planning into the wider political
process. While the cases do not indicate how such an
interest may be created or the nature of its "spontaneous" origins, they do suggest that it is more likely
among leaders with administrative background. It follows that those interested in promoting reform may want
to cultivate these leaders (although with the understanding that anyone interested in administrative
change is already likely to have ideas about its purpose and content).

Support for administrative change can come from
groups as well as from individuals. Group support is
not likely to be as erratic, but neither will it push a
program as far as can a single well-placed leader. A
group's lack of efficacy in pushing the program in directions it desires may also lead to a declining interest in reform and withdrawal of support, or to actual
efforts to establish alternative reforms. The apolitical self image of planners may also make them reluctant
to cultivate interested groups as opposed to individuals because of the more visible need for politicking in
dealing with the former.

Whatever kind of support is involved, the presence
or absence of other high priority programs is important. The cases suggest that administrative development programs are competitive with more substantive
policy and that a government deeply involved in the
latter is unlikely to have time for managing administrative planning. It may, however, promote administrative change in conjunction with other programs.
Those interested in administrative programs of a more
general nature can utilize these developments just as
they can incorporate high priority nonadministrative
issues in their own planning.

There are a number of other political and process
variables which shape policy making; the Colombian case
suggests one which seems uniquely important to administrative policy. The differences in the Colombian reform process did not reflect its political "distance"
from the other countries in the usual terms of regime
type or decision making style. They did reflect that
country's more institutionalized and integrated political system and the political leadership's greater
familiarity with administrative politics. Because of
their experience, political leaders were reluctant to
turn over reform planning to an independent expert
group and so kept a tighter watch on the latter, pre-
ferring to plan their reforms directly with groups
within the bureaucracy and holding the reformers to a
subordinate role. The effect on implementation was
like that of personalized leadership, but since it
emerged from systemic rather than individual traits it

was a permanent aspect of the reform process. Furthermore, as the Colombian example demonstrates, the two
types of control may occur simultaneously--the generalized political direction combined with a more active if
less constant intervention by individual leaders or
more narrowly defined groups.

Although, like experience and institutionalization, culturally based attitudes are not readily
subject to manipulation, their impact, if recognized,
can be used to advantage. In this sense, the cases
present largely negative examples since planners in all
three countries seemed oblivious to the possibility.
One attitude with potential importance is that toward
technical expertise[2]--the tendency to believe in and
trust it, or to see it as suspicious and running counter to important values. Both views were themes in
post-1968 Peru. Despite the military's presumed commitment to popular participation and their distrust of
outside influence, their faith in the technocrats pre-
vailed. Thus, they were willing to overlook the un-
revolutionary perspectives of the reform experts, although in the long run this worked against program
implementation.

A related attitude, the value put on wider participation in decision making, appeared not to function
to a great extent in any of these cases. In areas
where it does operate, two further considerations may
also play a part: one, a notion that participatory
decision making will encourage acceptance or acquies-
cence once a policy is announced,[3] and the other, a
belief in the value of practical experience.

The presence of a commitment to planning as opposed to pluralistic bargaining was also less influential than might be expected, perhaps because administrative reform is viewed as sufficiently specialized
to be subject to separate rules. The essential distinction was not between planning and bargaining, but
rather who would do the initial planning and how much
their plans would be compromised by later negotia-
tions. For all the Peruvian government's presumed
commitment to planning it was unusually sensitive to
outside pressures on administrative reform proposals.
One factor complicating the situation there and elsewhere was the rivalry between administrative and economic planners. A decision between planning and bargaining in a wider context still left this conflict
unresolved.

Most of the variables shaping the policy process
and modifying its isolation came close to being
"given". Attitudes and leadership are present or absent and one can at best hope to accentuate or minimize
their impact. The last factor--external assistance--is
thus doubly important, not only because of the strength

of its influence, but because its impact can be modified by manipulating the form or the nature of its delivery. Although it has been argued that external assistance aggravates the isolation and thus the impotence of reform planning, the effect is seemingly not inevitable.

One modifying influence, although itself somewhat of a given is the attitude initially taken toward the assistance and the advice it includes. While the three case studies don't vary greatly, Braibanti[4] in an earlier study of the Indian Civil Service reforms argues that the presence of a strong self-conscious civil service (the Indian Civil Service, later Indian Administrative Service) may have worked against the unquestioning acceptance of foreign aid and kept the bureaucrats in charge of early reform programs. Although he interprets the lesser foreign influence as an achievement in itself, he also argues that the higher level of internal control made for a more successful reform with a more decisive impact.[5] A comparison with the Colombian case suggests a related development taking the form of tighter political control of the process. The emergence of political as opposed to administrative control also gave the resulting program a different thrust.

The location or form of foreign input also conditions its impact. One speculative conclusion suggested by the cases involves the role of training institutes as channels of external assistance.[6] Whatever its more direct impact (which admittedly may be limited), aid channeled through training institutes rather than through specialized reform bodies may be less disruptive and its effects, if less dramatic, more permanent.

Training institutes along the lines of Peru's ESAP, Colombia's ESAP, or Venezuela's ENAP have not been notoriously successful in performing their manifest function--usually envisioned as a significant upgrading of administrative and other skills among new recruits and middle level bureaucrats. There are several reasons for that failure, not the least of which is the size of the undertaking. In addition, they have often become dumping grounds for problem cases--people who don't fit into their jobs but who could be dismissed only with difficulty. Here the schools suffer from their location at the center of a vicious circle--public administration is not understood or highly regarded, hence those seeking training in it are unlikely to be the most ambitious or best qualified, keeping its prestige low.

Still, if not plagued by political problems or overshadowed by their own reform commissions (as has been the case in Peru and Venezuela)[7] such institutes

can become centers of applied research and related
activities while performing their primary training
functions. Despite the general lack of enthusiasm for
these institutes, if not pushed too far or too fast
they have a potential for encouraging change and introducing externally generated technology. However low
key their contributions to administrative development,
their negative ones--in terms of reducing the credibility of efforts or stirring up opposition--is likely
to be far less than that of the reform commissions.
Training institutes may also have advantages in producing more innovative and realistic policy, as discussed in later sections.

Making Implementable Policy

At the process level, implementation is encouraged
through efforts to decrease the isolation of the reform
planner from other political actors, encourage planners
to consider the political aspects of their task, and
increase the overall support for reform. One substantive result should be the planners' heightened concern
with designing proposals for implementation. A new set
of variables--policy, political, and organizational or
process--enters here as they relate to the implementability of individual reforms.

Policy Variables The first group, policy variables,
refers specifically to characteristics of policy content. They resemble variables discussed in more general literature on implementation.[8] The case studies
bear out what the literature suggests: more complex
policies are more difficult to implement than less
complex ones. Policies that are partial as opposed to
comprehensive or unidimensional as opposed to multi-
dimensional have a higher chance of implementation (all
else held equal).
Looking at conventional policy types--reorganiza-
tions, personnel reforms, decentralizations--we would
expect that they would be more rather than less difficult to implement owing to their generally comprehensive nature and frequently multidimensional focus.
However, some, like reorganization and several aspects
of personnel reform (especially those relating to the
introduction of new basic procedures) have had noticeably fewer difficulties. These programs even where
implemented comprehensively tend to focus on one kind
of change rather than a more complex formula. In addition, there is a related factor, an aspect of uni-
dimensionality. This is the amount of cooperative
action or behavior change required from actors outside
the planning group. Although not necessarily more effective in producing secondary changes (this point is

discussed below), reorganizations and many aspects of
personnel reforms are more easily accomplished because
they either require very limited changes in behavior,
or because the more complicated work can be done by the
reform experts themselves. They are also in some sense
one-step programs, done once and they are over. While
they are reversible, reversal usually requires a positive action rather than (as in the case of decentralization) a simple failure to comply.

The passing suggestion about the limited impact of
less complex policies demonstrates one problem with the
notion of "implementability" as a guide for selecting
policy. The most easily implemented policies may not
be, in fact often are not, the more desirable ones.
Still, difficult policies can be restructured so as to
be more easily carried out.[9] For example, complex
policies like decentralization may be more effective if
done piecemeal rather than comprehensively, or if
slightly modified so as to attract more specific support. Such solutions may of course pose other problems. We have seen in the case of a number of regionalization schemes that the use of pilot projects does
not automatically lead anywhere else. However successful the projects were, they did not provide models for
wider adoption. Still one effect of such experiments
can be the creation of preconditions for future change.
To the extent that a nation can afford experimentation
and a delayed return on its investments, a strategy of
piecemeal, staged reform may be a way of breaking up
bottlenecks or better identifying them. When compared
with the alternatives, the delay appears much less
costly.

Political Variables Among the political variables
suggested by the case studies the most important is the
nature and level of support for individual proposals.
As in the case of the reform process as a whole, proposals that incorporated some specific interest of
political leaders or groups were more likely to be
implemented than those that did not. This was true
even where the interest was a relatively narrow one or
the group supporting it not generally powerful; in
fact, a highly specific change with a narrow target and
base of support is one of the best candidates for implementation.[10] The effect of support may have a wider
impact. Especially where backing comes from relatively
powerful groups a number of other proposals are likely
to be swept along with it. Thus Peru's 1969 reorganization introduced a number of changes not envisioned
by the government, the latter having ordered only the
creation of certain ministries. Because those ministries were urgently needed, a more comprehensive set
of changes was made possible. Another example is the

1970 passage of the civil service law in Venezuela,
accomplished because of its anticipated effect on
patronage appointments. In neither case did the reformers seem particularly aware of what was happening,
but the lesson--that support for one proposal may sweep
along others--is nonetheless valid.

A possible corrollary is that strong opposition to
a proposal, although less of an asset than support may
still be more advantageous than indifference. In the
instances where intense opposition was stirred up, although the immediate reaction was usually retraction of
the proposal, this was often followed by its passage
and implementation in a modified form.[11] Even where
this did not occur, it appears that at the very least,
a violent reaction may keep a proposal and problem
under consideration rather than permitting interest to
fade away. Although the pattern is not strong enough
for drawing the extreme conclusion that planners should
seek out opposition if they can't find support, it does
demonstrate the utility of dealing with concrete interests head on.

Organizational Variables A final set of variables
affecting individual programs includes the characteristics of organizations and processes producing them.
The discussion on the policy process focused some attention here; in this section, the emphasis is on how
these traits shape specific proposals rather than how
they attract support for the program as a whole. The
conclusions, however, are complementary.

Many of the problems of individual policies as
well as for the entire process originate in the channeling of reform through specialized central agencies.
These agencies, staffed by reform experts as opposed to
those with substantive program expertise, usually remained isolated from the rest of the bureaucracy, a
trait which affected the quality of their planning, the
level of support for proposals, and their influence on
implementation. In the case of the personnel programs
both the isolation and the resulting weaknesses were
minimized because unlike the other programs, personnel
functions had to be done anyway. In addition, the ministerial personnel offices already had a recognized
role. To the extent that the central office could provide resources or other aid, the entire system could be
held together. The resulting arrangement was not without flaws; evidence from all three cases suggests the
constant danger of the central office's assuming too
great a role and responsibilities, leading to its over-
burdening and a general disintegration of the system.

To depart from the centralized format, perhaps
relying on and building up effective ministerial work
groups, or simply as in Colombia, periodically giving

the ministries the chance to make their own reforms would greatly reduce the level of coordination, posing other problems. It would, however, facilitate implementation on at least two counts: first, by automatically breaking down reforms into smaller, piecemeal programs, and second, by guaranteeing the presence of specific support for proposals from those helping to design them. Decentralization may produce more implementable programs for other reasons. The central agency format encourages disembodied reforms with no base in the complaints and suggestions of clients, administrators, or political leaders. All of these, despite their biases, are ultimately the authentic judges of reform as well as the best sources of information on the problems to be solved. While reformers often express an interest in limiting consultation as a way of reducing political pressures on them[12] (and also of enhancing their own control of the process) such a step has two immediate costs. It reduces information on needs, interests, and priorities, and it eliminates an important source of concrete recommendations. Conventional reform doctrines with their emphasis on generalized reform do suggest that the additional information is unnecessary. Whatever the truth of that claim, it overlooks the other contributions of nonexperts to implementation.

Organizationally, isolation, centralization, and specialization (in reform as opposed to substantive policies) seem to be disadvantageous strategies from the standpoint of producing implementable programs and accurately assessing administrative conditions. They have nonetheless been actively encouraged because of their presumed advantage in generating coordinated, comprehensive planning incorporating the broadest and most disinterested views possible. On two of the three counts (coordination and comprehensiveness, but not a noticeably broader perspective) the cases do support this claim, but this raises still another question which is addressed in the last section--that of the ends or objectives of reform.

SOME PRACTICAL LESSONS FOR THE NEW REFORMERS

These lessons on planning and implementing administrative change although drawn from the reform experience are meant to have a wider relevance. The question remains as to whether they have anything to teach the proponents of the new development administration who claim to have remedied many of the old problems. A quick glance at the new approaches does suggest that some of the problems of reform have been circumvented. It also suggests that some very important ones remain.

The programs promoted under the title development administration or management development[13] are characterized by an emphasis on problem-and organization-specific change. Their proponents argue for this approach on both theoretical and practical grounds. Theoretically they reject the notion that administrative reform or improvement can be separated from the solution of substantive problems. These problems, defined as perceived deficiencies in adminstrative output, become the organizing concept for planning and implementing change. Practically, they are seen as a way of providing entree for those introducing change.[14] Their promised solution represents a potential visible benefit for those whose cooperation is needed and thus a way of generating support.

In light of the developments documented in the three country cases and the recommendations drawn from them, this approach should not seem novel. The second and third generation reformers, whatever their initial preference, have increasingly been forced to adopt similar tactics, focusing on organization-specific reform, emphasizing substantive improvements, and otherwise tailoring their efforts to the needs defined by their potential clients. It is evident that they often see this as a holding operation, a way of ensuring their survival or attracting more support in preparation for a later, more ambitious attack on the problem as initially defined. However, to the extent that they are successful in generating a demand for this kind of service, they may, like Colombia's ESAP, find themselves devoting a greater portion of their time to these activities and so move away from an emphasis on model building and reform on a grand scale.[15]

On the practical side, the experience of the reformers thus partially confirms the arguments behind the new approaches; change introduced at the agency level, linked to specific problems, and incorporating the view of members and possibly of clients of the target agency is more likely to be accepted. Whether it is also more likely to produce improvements in performance is unfortunately more difficult to determine. Logically, it appears that it should, but another shortcoming shared by the old and new approaches--the absence of standards and techniques for evaluation-- makes this a matter for speculation. Here too, there is a lesson to be derived from reform, the dangers and the long term negative consequences of simply attributing improvements without attempting to measure and document them.[16]

Aside from the questions of confirming impact, the new approaches face some less obvious problems whose solution may also benefit from the lessons of reform. The first of these stems from the effects of external

influence and externally induced change. Despite the
trends in the existing national programs, the most
systematic statements of the new doctrines have been
made by members of the international development community.[17] Thus, within Third World countries, these
approaches still constitute imported technologies. To
the extent they are incorporated as part of externally
or nationally sponsored efforts they are likely to encourage the outward focus associated with the older reforms. Over the short run this is less of an obstacle
because of the strategic and tactical advances--the emphasis on problem-oriented change, the rejection of
packaged solutions, and the involvement of a wide range
and number of participants in decision making. These
characteristics combined with the stress on beginning
with organizations where there is a perceived need for
interventions make it more likely that the initial programs will be implemented.

        After this first stage, the new approaches con-
front the same old problem of introducing technologies,
values, and perspectives that may effectively isolate
their converts from the rest of the administrative and
political systems. While this is hardly their aim,
they risk creating a new group of experts whose longer
range ability to introduce change may be no greater
than that of the reformers. Here as in the case of
reform the dilemma is that of any applied expertise,
aggravated by its foreign origins. The problem is to
convince the expert to deal with local perspectives and
priorities and to concentrate on the mundane, repeti-
tious applications of this knowledge as opposed to
pursuing it for its own sake (or for the sake of an
audience of other practitioners). While the new approach's emphasis on practical applications and participatory planning seems to define the problem away,
there are indications[18] that more active precautions
may be required.

        A second related problem has to do with the link-
ages established between the programs and the wider
political system. This is a cause for concern since at
one level the new approaches are more adamantly apolitical than their predecessors. The earlier reformers'
approach to the political sphere highlights the importance of two types of political linkages. The first
occurs as the generation and maintenance of high level
support for the program to guarantee it a place in the
political agenda and to provide some sort of institutionalized base through which resources and <u>demands</u> can
be channeled. The term "demands" is important because
for this high level linkage to be effective it must include not only diffuse support but also its translation
to specific requirements for program outputs and services. The first linkage is thus closely related to

the second type which occurs during the implementation
of individual projects and entails a series of measures
for eliciting cooperation at both higher and lower
levels. The early reformers' decision to leave implementation to the politicians meant that they did little
in terms of establishing the second set of linkages.
Their accomplishments in the first area extended only
to the securing of very general support and the establishment of an institutionalized base. Their assumption of the self-evident value of their efforts meant
that they rarely went further in building more specific
types of high level support.

The strategies adopted by the new approaches re-
verse these weaknesses without solving the overall
problem. They stress the linkages at the point of
implementation but show little concern for establishing
their programs at a general level or generating any
kind of institutional base. There seem to be two lines
of logic at work here: an effort to avoid the institutionalized isolation of the earlier movements and an
accompanying belief that they can build a more general
demand for and receptivity to change on the basis of a
series of successful interventions. The question remains as to what will sustain these programs until such
time as the requisite critical mass and demand are created.[19] Here the first type of political linkage and
the creation of an institutionalized base remain essential however unpalatable their earlier associations.
Such a base is important not only for channeling higher
level attention and resources to the program, but also
for guiding and coordinating the experts' efforts and
so maintaining their relevance to the wider political
system. Although guidance can also become the kind of
institutionalized irrelevance characteristic of the
earlier movements, the alternative extreme of a complete absence of coordination seems no more viable.

The argument thus leads back to a point raised
above, the desirability of experimenting with the
institutional base of programs aimed at introducing
administrative change. Variations in the organizational housing of such programs may prove one of the
most effective ways of reducing tendencies toward an
external focus while strengthening ties with the
national political system. That newer approaches have
learned from past failures is evident in their efforts
to improve implementation strategies at the point of
intervention and aim at relevant and realistic types of
change. However, in their dismissal of the older programs, the newcomers have overlooked their strengths as
well as some important lessons about attending to the
overall policy process.

THE SECOND MEANING OF FAILURE:
THE SIGNIFICANCE OF REFORM

The success or failure of reform or any administrative development policy is more than a question of
implementation. The ultimate goal of these programs
was presumably to produce changes in performance. The
initial set of structural or process changes even if
implemented might bring the whole program no closer to
success in this second sense. Such changes may even be
counterproductive, diminishing rather than increasing
the desired secondary effects, making the reformed unit
less rather than more efficient, less rather than more
responsive and so on There are many reasons why failures, defined as insufficient or inappropriate impact
on performance or other characteristics, might occur.
Assuming implementation, most of them are related to
the quality of reform planning. They include such
problems as insufficient contingency planning, insufficient control over a number of elements contributing
to or reinforcing undesirable behavior, or faulty analysis of causal relationships. This last factor has
been of most interest to critics of conventional reform
doctrines. It is related to another possible source of
failure: the likelihood that the sought after improvements are not improvements at all. Leaving for the
moment this second issue of whether the ends pursued
are desirable ones, we first address the question of
whether they can be attained through the proposed
reform measures.

In most of the examples used here we can only
speculate about the answer. Given the low level of
implementation and the numerous known and unknown intervening variables, it is difficult to say just what
the impact on performance has been or should be. There
are a few clear-cut failures--for example, the proliferation of ministries in the several Peruvian reorganizations which led to waste and confusion rather than
the sought after rationally coordinated policy. Other
examples include the programs in each country that had
to be temporarily abandoned because of the violent and
usually unanticipated reactions they provoked. However, even here there is a tendency to exaggerate the
disastrous consequences. In many cases, a longer term
evaluation might not have been so negative. Furthermore, it is rarely evident just how much of the failure
can be attributed to poor planning and how much must be
blamed on such unforeseeable developments as the dis-
tortion of programs by implementers, interaction with
other government programs and priorities, or a failure
of support at a critical moment (a problem with many of
the abandoned programs).

The difficulty in assessing impact can also be attributed to the reformers. Although they promised improvements, it was not evident that the planners had a clear idea of the linkages between their proposals and some future better state. In fact it was frequently hard to identify the effects they expected from specific changes. This was especially true as proposals became more comprehensive. The preferences for standardized organizational forms, for the adoption of centralized staff functions, or for regional governments and regionally based planning bodies often approached the arbitrariness of change for change's sake. Unfortunately, what began as an arbitrary decision sometimes became established doctrine.

To be fair, the choices were rarely entirely arbitrary, but were usually grounded in some general theory. Critics have charged, however, that this theoretical base was questionable and its empirical foundations often shaky. Thirty-five years ago Herbert Simon[20] demonstrated the internal contradictions of classical administrative principles. His criticisms are just as apt for the principles guiding many later reforms whether drawn from classical or more recent sources. Even such long accepted practices as the adoption of merit based civil service systems have been questioned.[21] There are many reasons for establishing such a system, it is argued, but the usual justification--more efficient performance--is not demonstrably one of them. This is more than an argument about cross-cultural transfers. The contention is that such practices may not be responsible for higher levels of efficiency and efficacy even where they have been successfully implanted. To the extent that modern bureaucracies have become better performers this may be the result of other unplanned factors (e.g., socioeconomic trends associated with modernization) and not of specific reform measures. There are even cases, it is suggested where reform failure (nonimplementation) may be a blessing because the most likely results are not the promised improvements but the creation of new problems and the further aggravation of existing ones.

The second criticism of reform suggests that efforts to identify impact on performance may well be pointless since this was never a serious goal of the planners. The real problem with reform, it argues, is that the experts' primary interest began and ended with structural and procedural change. The experts' priorities and vision of what needs to be done is based on a unique perspective and on a lack of contact with the day to day functions of the bureaucracy. One observer[22] has characterized this as the difference between the reformer's emphasis on "efficiency and institutional reform" and the regime's concern for "program implementation and efficacy." As he goes on to explain:

> While these two approaches are not contradictory, they do seem to be contrary. A preoccupation with efficacy will generally lead to inefficiency, or will at least not be overly concerned with existing inefficiencies, while a bureaucratic reformer may well lose sight of the output of the agency as he labors to rationalize its structure and personnel policies.[23]

A reform planner[24] in Venezuela expressed this more concretely as the reformers' interest in changing structures and processes and the public's interest in better service, with the one not necessarily connected to the other, or if so, only indirectly. The reformers have focused on smooth functioning within the bureaucracy, and occasionally, on strengthening the command relationship between political leaders and bureaucratic implementers. Other groups have been more interested in outputs and performance in the usual sense, that is, those delivered outside the administrative system. While it seems reasonable that change in one area would produce change in the other, the particular linkages implicit in the reforms are most often a matter of faith.

The absence of any effort to define performance in such a way that improvements could be identified and measured, and the lack of provisions for evaluating impact further reinforce the impression that this was really not the point. Programs like the Colombian "ombudsman" which began with a specific problem in output, in that case from the client's perspective, are rare. Those beginning with a specific verifiable and measurable complaint on the part of bureaucrats or political leaders were not much more common. While improved performance remained the ultimate justification for reform, it is hard to see it as having a concrete impact on most planning. Instead problems and objectives were defined in terms of organizational variables to which the planners alone were sensitive.

These two criticisms of reform--that it cannot produce the promised improvements in performance and, in some sense, was never intended to do so--are central to the rejection of the strategy and the demands for a new approach to administrative development. The examples of the three Latin American programs do nothing to reverse the arguments. They in fact suggest the greater efficacy of the decentralized, problem-led

approaches to improving administrative performance.
Whether on the basis of past experience or an assessment of the state of the art, administrative reform as
conventionally conceived (centrally planned, comprehensive, top-down change) does not seem likely to
achieve the performance goals used to justify it.

This does not mean that the new approaches are
without their own problems, and, as indicated, a good
deal to learn and occasionally borrow from reform. Nor
does it mean that reform serves no purpose, although to
identify that purpose requires a significant modification of our explicit and implicit understanding of its
focus. Lost in the confusion over its inability to
produce specific improvements in output is its immediate and possibly more legitimate end--within-system
change. To the extent that improved output was accepted as the primary objective of reform, within-system
change became a means, and a patently ineffective one.
Because it was not judged on its own merits, the reformers had still more freedom in programming it. This
in turn made it still less likely that within-system
change would incorporate the interests and perspectives
of other actors and so come to be recognized as a valuable end in itself. Thus out of this vicious circle,
what is arguably the original and most natural objective of reform has come to be ignored or rejected as
pointless.

The new approaches are of little help here since
they usually disregard the worth of general "improvements" in the internal operations and management of the
administrative system. To the extent that their sole
interest is output or performance this is a reasonable
position. Nonetheless, quite apart from any impact on
output, within-system operations (whether of the whole
or its subsystems) directly affect a large number of
values. To maintain that their only importance is
their impact at the boundaries of the system is to
overlook the intrinsic significance of activities oc-
cupying up to one-fifth of the work force and half of
the gross domestic product. Patterns and standards set
within the administrative sector affect the human,
material, and symbolic resources it employs and their
counterparts in the wider economy and policy. In effect, the repercussions are potentially so great that
decisions on change are best not left to the technical
experts. While its focus on structures and processes
makes reform the appropriate approach to designing or
coordinating within-system changes, the ends served by
those changes are political. Its design and implementation still require a closer integration of the reform
process with the rest of the political system as well
as with other administrative development policy.

Compared with that other policy, reform may remain
a secondary priority. Certainly, without the justification of improved output, investments in reform and
the extent of the changes attempted are likely to be
more carefully weighed. However, if expectations are
brought into line with what reform can accomplish both
generally and in specific circumstances, these decisions can be made realistically, and once made, have
more chance of being carried out. If reform is not the
universal solution to all administrative problems it
once seemed, it is an appropriate tool for solving certain problems and a necessary part of the repertoire of
those conducting administrative change. One of the interesting questions remaining for the current and future generations of administrative planners is how best
to coordinate the resources and objectives of the various kinds of change policy rather than attempting a
single choice among them.

NOTES

1. The attention to implementation as a special
theme first took hold in public administration, and
especially in studies of U.S. domestic policies in the
early 1970s. Representative works include Jeffrey L.
Pressman and Aaron B. Wildavsky, Implementation
(Berkeley: University of California Press, 1973);
Eugene Bardach, The Implementation Game (Cambridge,
Mass.: M.I.T. Press, 1977); Beryl A. Radin, Imple-
mentation, Change, and the Federal Bureaucracy (New
York: Teachers College Press, Columbia University,
1977); Robert T. Nakamura and Frank Smallwood, The
Politics of Implementation (New York: St. Martin's
Press, 1980); and Erwin C. Hargrove, The Missing Link
(Washington, D.C.: Urban Institute, July 1975).
Hargrove's piece is the source of the notion of the
"missing link."
The emphasis on implementation was picked up
slightly later by development administration, where it
has received even more attention, probably because at
one level it becomes a justification for the entire
field of study. Whereas public administration's treatment of the topic had put an equal stress on political
and administrative obstacles to implementation, development administration had concentrated almost exclusively on the latter. However, as noted, it paid less
attention to the implementation side of administrative
change policy. The bottom-up focus has encouraged attention to implementation tactics at the project level,
but there is little or no attention to program and
policy implementation, significantly the areas where
the political side of implementation becomes more
important. For a discussion of implementation in

development administration and a review of important
works, see Marcus D. Ingle, Implementing Development
Programs (Office of Rural Development and Development
Administration, Development Support Bureau, U.S. AID,
January 1979).

2. This might also include an attitude specifically directed at administrative expertise, as opposed
to other kinds, and often seen in the running battle
between economic and administrative planners. The literature on the politics of expertise in general has
some contributions on the popular view of experts. See
sources cited in note 20, Chapter 1.

3. Participation can of course be a value in its
own right with no need for further justification. It
appears this way in a number of arguments for participatory planning, especially those introduced by economic planners. Administrative planners generally don't
seem as sold on participation as an end in itself.
Generally, where, as in the Colombian civil service
reforms, they have included it, this is because of its
instrumental value, as a way of ensuring cooperation.
Occasionally, reformers have also acknowledged its
value as a source of information and recommendations,
but this is a less common view.

4. Ralph Braibanti, "Reflections on Bureaucratic
Reform in India" in Braibanti and Spengler (eds.) Ad-
ministrative and Economic Development in India (Durham:
Duke University Press, 1963), pp. 1-65.

5. Braibanti, Ibid.

6. This suggestion is made with the expectation
of a very skeptical reception. Institutes of public
administration have almost as bad a reputation as administrative reform among most development theorists
and practitioners. Like reform, they were a key element in the earlier institution building phase of development programs and like reform have for the most
part come to be regarded as irrelevant failures. While
there has recently been some interest shown (among the
community best described as "academic consultants") in
a more selective utilization of these institutes, this
still emphasizes the training function. This is in
contrast to the suggestion offered here: that while
training should continue, both it and other programs
would benefit from efforts to incorporate a larger
research and consulting component. For a discussion of
some recent thoughts on the role of training institutes, see Marcus Ingle and Irving Swerdlow (eds.),
Public Administration Training for Less Development
Countries (Syracuse, N.Y.: The Maxwell School, 1974);
and Laurence D. Stifel, Joseph E. Black, and James S.
Coleman (eds.) Education and Training for Public Sector
Management in Developing Countries (New York: The
Rockefeller Foundation, 1978).

There is another problem in the development of these institutions which is the frequent lack of continuity in their programs. This is often a function of their ties to a reform institute or commission which may radically change its view of their role over time. It is also a likely result of their inherently limited and much delayed impact which may provoke impatient government actors to tinker constantly with their programs. And finally, it may stem from the desire of directors, who recognize the insecurity of their tenure, to leave their mark on the institution through major changes in its programs. The end result in the case of the institutions surveyed here has been considerable instability in their focus, curriculum and target student body.

8. See sources listed in note 1, above.

9. An early argument to this effect is found in Clarence E. Thurber, "Islands of Development: A Political and Social Approach to Development Administration" in Clarence E. Thurber and Lawrence S. Graham (eds.), Development Administration in Latin America (Durham: Duke University Press, 1973).

10. The Colombian intraministerial reforms described in Chapter 5 are a good example. Here groups within the ministries came up with reform proposals based on specific changes they wanted made. Although they represented a narrow support base, the reforms were equally narrowly focused and thus their backing was sufficient for implementation.

11. Examples include the Peruvian regionalization scheme first issued in 1976 and the Colombian civil service reforms of 1978. In both cases, initial opposition produced an immediate setback, but the final resolution was the acceptance or passage of a modified proposal. Of course the less successful outcome of the Peruvian efforts at civil service reform demonstrates that opposition can also kill a program.

12. This view is hardly limited to these cases or to Latin America. Willis Hawley describing the Carter reorganization efforts recommends limiting consultation with outside groups because it stirs up unnecessary political controversies. He also suggests that too much preoccupation with politics will "drive out substance." One additional problem (also discussed by Hawley) faced in the United States is the likelihood that clientele groups will put pressure on reformers, often acting through Congress. While this could be a factor (as in pre-1968 Peru) it was not much of a problem in any of the three cases. Willis D. Hawley, "Even the Best Laid Plans.... Lessons in the Politics and Administration of Reorganization from the Carter Efforts." (Unpublished draft.)

13. For a list of representative works see note 18, Chapter 1. For a discussion of recent trends including the transition to a new title and new focus see Ferrel Heady, "Comparative Administration: A Sojourner's Outlook," Public Administration Review (July/August 1978), pp. 358-65.

14. The works included show perhaps their greatest variation in the value they ascribe to participation as an end in itself as opposed to a way of eliciting cooperation or better information. See for example the "people-centered approach" stressed by writers like David Korten as opposed to the more instrumental "action-training strategy". David Korten, "Community Organization and Rural Development: A Learning Process Approach, Public Administration Review (September/October 1980), pp. 480-512 and Morris J. Solomon, Fleeming Heegaard, and Kenneth Kornher, "An Action-Training Strategy for Project Management," International Development Review (XX, 1970), pp. 13-20.

15. In effect the consulting role had been a minor theme from the beginning. Foreign advisors worked to limit it, as one field report from the AID Mission in Lima noted early on. The notion was that this kept the ONRAP staff away from the more important work of planning a reform. This notion that provision of services to local agencies may dilute the thrust of the reform group is a concern even among proponents of its new development administration because of their interest in selecting interventions where the new approaches can be used and developed to the best advantage. See U.S. AID, "General Characteristics of Public Administration in Peru" (unpublished document, 1965), p. IV 8.

16. Procedures for evaluating administrative programs are the forgotten chapter of all stages of development administration. Even the new approaches with their emphasis on "problem-led" interventions have not come to grips with the question of establishing impact, and especially with the problem of defining normal and improved output and performance. What is needed is not sophisticated quantification, but simply some effort at the more precise specification of the objects and ranges of change.

17. In the case of reform the community of experts retaining an interest is quite truly international, many of them tied to international or regional organizations. For a representative sample of their thoughts and work see articles in A.F. Leemans (ed.) The Management of Change in Government (The Hague: Martinus Nijhoff, 1976).

18. The evidence for this judgment is impressionistic and rests on comments and informal assessments made by participants in such programs. Two types

of problems stand out. The first, and that most frequently mentioned, appears as a certain uneasiness about the discontinuities in the programs to date and the lack of any systematic follow-up on projects or interventions. The general feeling seems to be that without some such follow-up program, the changes produced in organizational and individual behavior and perspectives may simply fade away over time. A second concern, less frequently expressed but more directly relevant to the judgment, has to do with the difficulty of convincing national trainees to continue a focus on basic, rather low level change programs and techniques. One long-term consultant described this as his national team's preference for taking on more sophisticated applications which he seemed to see as less relevant to the types of problems with which they were likely to be dealing.

19. The recent emphasis in development theory on institutional development and "sustainability" is an example of this kind of concern. Once again, although these themes are stressed by those involved in development administration as one of the justifications for their work, there has been little if any attention to them as a characteristic of administrative change programs.

20. Herbert Simon, Administrative Behavior (New York: The Free Press, 1958), pp. 20-44.

21. Victor A. Thompson, "Administrative Objectives for Development Administration," Administrative Science Quarterly (June 1964), pp. 91-108.

22. William S. Stewart, "Public Administration" in John D. Martz and David J. Myers (eds.), Venezuela (New York: Praeger, 1977),. pp. 215-35.

23. Ibid., p. 228.

24. Interview, Caracas, 1978.

Selected Bibliography

Arrubla, Mario et. al., Colombia Hoy, Bogota: Siglo
    Veintiuno, 1978.
Andors, Steve, "Hobbes and Weber vs. Marx and Mao."
    Bulletin of Concerned Asian Scholars
    (September/October 1974): 19-34.
Argyris, Chris, Management and Organizational
    Development. New York: McGraw-Hill, 1971
Arnold, Peri E., "Reorganization and Politics: A
    Reflection on the Adequacy of Administrative
    Theory." Public Administration Review
    (May/June 1979): 205-11.
Attir, Aryeh, La reforma administrative en Colombia.
    United Nations, December 21, 1962.
Bacharach, Samuel B. and Edward J. Lawler, Power and
    Politics in Organizations. San Francisco:
    Jossey-Bass, 1981.
Backoff, Robert, "Operationalizing Administrative
    Reform for Improved Governmental Performance."
    Administration and Society (May 1974).
Bardach, Eugene, The Implementation Game. Cambridge:
    The MIT Press, 1977.
Benveniste, Guy, The Politics of Expertise. San
    Francisco: Boyd and Fraser, 1977.
    _____and Warren Ilchman, (eds.), Agents of
    Change: Professionals in Developing
    Countries. New York: Praeger, 1969.
Berger, M., Bureaucracy and Society in Egypt.
    Princeton: Princeton University Press, 1957.
Berry, R. Albert et. al., Politics of Compromise. New
    Brunswick, New Jersey: Transaction Books,
    1980.
Bigler, Gene E., "Regionalization of the Public
    Administration in Venezuela." Paper delivered
    at the 1975 Meetings of the American Political
    Science Association.
Bish, Frances Pennell. "The Limits of Organizational
    Reform." Paper delivered at 1976 Meetings of
    the Southern Political Science Association.
Braibanti, Ralph (ed.), Political and Administrative
    Development. Durham: Duke University Press,
    1969.
    _____and Joseph Spengler (eds.), Administrative
    and Economic Development in India. Durham:
    Duke University Press, 1963.
Brewer, Gary D., Politicians, Bureaucrats and the
    Consultant. New York: Basic Books, 1973.
Brewer-Carias, Allan, Introduccion al estudio de la
    organizacion administrativa venezolana
    Caracas: Editorial Juridica Venezolana, 1978.

196

_____, El estatuto del funcionario publico en
    la ley de carrera administrativa. Caracas:
    Comision de Administration Publica, 1971.
_____,"Reform Proposals for the Venezuelan
    Public Administracion (1972)." Journal of
    Administration Overseas (October 1974): 524-
    35.
_____ and Norma Izquierdo Corser (eds.) Estudios
    sobre la regionalizacion en Venezuela.
    Caracas: Universidad Central de Venezuela,
    1977.
Brown, David S., "'Reforming'the Bureaucracy: Some
    Suggestions for the New President." Public
    Administration Review (March/April 1977):
    163-9
Bryant, Coralie and Louise White, Managing Development
    in the Third World Boulder: Westview, 1982.
Caiden, Gerald, Administrative Reform. Chicago:
    Aldine Press, 1969.
_____(ed.), "Symposium on 'Public Policy and Admini-
    strative Reform.'" Policy Studies Journal
    (Special Issue, 1981).
Camp, Roderic A., "The Cabinet and the Tecnicos in
    Mexico and the United States." Journal of
    Comparative Administration (August 1971):
    188-214.
Candido, Norma de, "Further Thoughts on the Failure of
    Technical Assistance in Public Administration
    Abroad." Journal of Comparative Administra-
    tion (February 1971): 379-400.
Castro, Jaime, Control sobre la moralidad y eficiencia
    administrativas. Bogota: DASC, 1976.
Chambers, Robert, Managing Rural Development. New
    York: Holmes and Meier, 1974.
Chapman, Brian, The Profession of Government. London:
    Allen and Unwin, 1959.
Cleaves, Peter S. and Martin J. Scurrah, Agricultural
    Bureaucracy and Military Government in Peru.
    Berkeley: University of California Press,
    1982.
Colombia, Departamento Administrativo de Servicio Civil
    (DASC), Informe del jefe del departamento
    administrativo del servicio civil al Congreso
    nacional. August 1974-June 1976.
Colombia, Departamento Nacional de Planeacion, (DNP),
    Unidad de Desarrollo Regional y Urbano (URDU),
    "La Politica de descentralizacion en el plan
    de desarrollo para 'cerrar la brecha.'"
    Bogota: May 1978.
Colombia, Office of the President, SOIAP, Manual de
    organizacion de la rama ejecutiva del poder
    publico. Bogota: 1978.

Crawford, E. T. and A. D. Biderman, Social Scientists and International Affairs. New York: Wiley 1969.

Dalby, Michael T. (ed.), Bureaucracy in Historical Perspective. London: Scott, Foresman and Company, 1971.

Denton, Charles, "Bureaucracy in an Immobilist Society: The Case of Costa Rica." Administrative Science Quarterly (September 1969): 418-425.

Dix, Robert H., Colombia: The Political Dimensions of Change. New Haven: Yale, 1967.

Dwivedi, O. P. and J. Nej, "Crises and Continuities in Development Theory and Administration: First and Third World Perspectives." Public Administration and Development (II, 1982): 59-77.

Eisenstadt, S. N., The Political Systems of Empires. New York: Free Press, 1963.

Erlich, Howard J., "Anarchism and Formal Organization." Baltimore: Vacant Lot Press, n.d.

Esman, Milton J., Administration and Development in Malaysia: Institution Building in a Plural Society. Ithaca: Cornell University Press, 1972.

Figgins, Daniel W., Program Budgeting in Developing Nations: The Case of Peru, 1962-1966. Unpublished doctoral dissertation, Syracuse University, 1970.

Gable, Richard, "Development Administration: Background, Terms, Concepts, Theories, and a New Approach." Development Studies Program, U.S. Agency for International Development, unpublished manuscript, 1975.

Gilbert, Alan, "Urban and Regional Development Programs in Colombia since 1951" in Wayne Cornelius and Felicity Trueblood (eds.), Latin American Urban Research. Beverly Hills: Sage, 1975: 241-76.

Gillis, John R., The Prussian Bureaucracy in Crisis, 1840-1860. Stanford: Stanford University Press, 1971.

Gladden, E. N., A History of Public Administration. London: Frank Cass, 1972.

Golembiewski, Robert T., "A Third Mode of Coupling Democracy and Administration: Another Way of Making a Crucial Point." International Journal of Public Administration (II, 4, 1981): 423-53.

Gomez, Rudolph, The Peruvian Administrative System. Boulder: University of Colorado Press, 1969.

Goodman, Louis and Ralph Ngatata Love (eds.),
    Management of Development Projects: An
    International Case Study Approach. New
    York: Pergamon Press, 1979.
Gorman, Stephen M. (ed.), Post Revolutionary Peru: The
    Politics of Transformation. Boulder:
    Westview, 1982.
Graham, Lawrence S., Civil Service Reform in Brazil.
    Austin: University of Texas Press, 1968.
Grimes, C. E. and Charles Simmons, "Bureaucracy and
    Political Control in Mexico." Public
    Administration Review (January/February
    1969): 72-79.
Groves, Roderick T., "The Colombian National Front and
    Administrative Reform." Administration and
    Society (November 1979): 316-36.
Gulick, H. and L. Urwick, Papers on the Science of
    Administration. New York: New York Institute
    of Public Administration, 1937.
Hanson, Mark, "Decentralization and Regionalization in
    the Ministry of Education" International
    Review of Education (1976): 155-76.
Hargrove, Erwin C., The Missing Link. Washington:
    Urban Institute, 1975.
Hartlyn, Jonathan, "Interest Associations and Political
    Conflict in Colombia." Unpublished draft,
    Vanderbilt University, 1982.
Hawley, Willis D., "Even the Best Laid Plans...Lessons
    in the Politics and Administration of
    Reorganization from the Carter Efforts."
    Unpublished draft, 1980.
Hayward, Jack and Michael Watson, Planning Politics and
    Public Policy. Cambridge: Cambridge
    University Press, 1975.
Heady, Ferrel, "Comparative Administration: A
    Sojourner's Outlook." Public Administration
    Review (July/August 1978): 358-65.
    _____ and Sybil L. Stokes (eds.), Papers in Compar-
    ative Administration. Ann Arbor: Institute
    of Public Administration, University of
    Michigan, 1962.
Honadle, George and John Hannah, "Management Perform-
    ance for Rural Development: Local Empower-
    ment, Packaged Training, or Capacity
    Building?" Public Administration and
    Development (II, 1982): 295-307.
    _____ and Rudi Klaus (eds.), International
    Development Administration. New York:
    Praeger, 1979.
Honey, John C., Toward Strategies for Public
    Administration Development in Latin America.
    Syracuse: Syracuse University Press, 1968.

Hopkins, Jack W., _The Government Executive of Modern Peru_. Gainesville: University of Florida Press, 1967.

Horowitz, Irving Louis, "Social Science Mandarins: Policymaking as a Political Formula." _Policy Sciences_ (1970): 339-66.

Ilchman, Warren, _Comparative Public Administration and 'Conventional Wisdom.'_ (Sage Professional Papers in Comparative Politics II, 01-020) Beverly Hills: Sage, 1971.

Ingle, Marcus D., "Implementing Development Programs." Office of Rural Development and Development Administration, Development Support Bureau, U.S. AID, (January 1979).

Jimenez, Juan Ignacio, _Planificacion y administracion_. (Lima: ONRAP, November 1967).

Kilty, Daniel R., _Planning for Development in Peru_. New York: Praeger, 1967.

Kingsley, J. D., _Representative Bureaucracy_. Yellow Springs, Ohio: Antioch Press, 1944.

Kriesberg, Martin (ed.), _Public Administration in Developing Countries_. Washington: The Brookings Institution, 1965.

Korten, David, "Community Organization and Rural Development: A Learning Process Approach," _Public Administration Review_ (September/October 1980): 480-512.

_____ "The Management of Social Transformation." _Public Administration Review_ (November/December 1981): 609-18.

_____ and Felipe Alfonso (eds.), _Bureaucracy and the Poor: Closing the Gap_. Singapore: McGraw-Hill, 1981.

LaPalombara, Joseph (ed.), _Bureaucracy and Political Development_. Princeton: Princeton University Press, 1963.

Lawrence, P. and J. Lorsch, _Organization and Environment_. Homewood, Ill: Richard D. Irwin, 1969.

Leemans, A. F. (ed.), _The Management of Change in Government_. The Hague: Martinus Nijhoff, 1976.

Lindenberg, Marc and Benjamin Crosby, _Managing Development: The Political Dimension_. West Hartford, Conn.: Kumarian, 1981.

Lowenthal, Abraham (ed.), _The Peruvian Experiment_. Princeton: Princeton University Press, 1975.

Lynn, Laurence E. (ed.), _Knowledge and Policy: The Uncertain Connection_. Washington: National Academy of Sciences, 1978.

Marini, Frank (ed.), Toward a New Public Administra-
        tion: The Minnowbrook Perspective. New
        York: Chandler, 1974.
Martz, John D. and David J. Myers (eds.), Venezuela:
        The Democratic Experience. New York:
        Praeger, 1977.
Meltsner, Arnold, Policy Analysts in the Bureaucracy.
        Berkeley: University of California Press,
        1976.
Mickelwait, D., C. Sweet, and E. Morss, New Directions
        in Development: A Study of U.S. AID.
        Boulder: Westview, 1979.
Mosher, Frederick C., "The Public Service in the
        Temporary Society." Public Administration
        Review (January/February 1971).
Nakamura, Robert T. and Frank Smallwood, The Politics
        of Implementation. New York: St. Martin's
        Press, 1980.
Ouchi, William C., Theory Z. New York: Avon, 1981.
Palmer, David Scott, "Peru: Authoritarianism and
        Reform" in Howard J. Wiarda and Harvey F.
        Kline (eds.), Latin American Politics and
        Development. Boston: Houghton Mifflin Co.,
        1979.
Payne, James L., Patterns of Conflict in Colombia. New
        Haven: Yale, 1968.
Pena, Alfredo, Democracia y Reforma del Estado.
        Caracas: El Nacional, 1978.
Peru, Comision para la Evaluacion e Implementacion de
        la Reforma de la Administracion Publica,
        Informe Final. Lima: August 1973.
Peru, Instituto Nacional de Planificacion (INP)
        "Aspectos administrativos de la planificacion
        en el Peru." Lima: April 1971.
Peru, Instituto Nacional de Administracion Publica
        (INAP) Estudio de la Administracion publica.
        Lima: December 1974.
                Memoria Anual.
Peru, INAP, Direccion Ejecutiva del Plan de Reforma de
        la Administracion Publica (DEPRAP) Definicion
        y analisis de la problematica de la admini-
        stracion publica peruana. Lima: December
        1977.
_____, Estudio y propuesta de descentralizacion
        administrativa. Lima: December 1978.
_____, Modelos alternativos de gobiernos locales.
        Lima: c. 1978.
_____, Propuesta de reforma de ministerios. Lima: May,
        1977.
_____, Equipo A, Proyecto del plan general de la
        administracion publica a mediano plaza. Lima,
        1977.

Peru, INAP, Direccion Nacional de Racionalizacion
          (DNR), Diagnostico de la accion regional de
          los ministerios. Lima: 1975.
_____, "Exposicion a la Jefatura." Lima: January 1978.
_____, Problematica de la organizacion y el
          financiamiento de la administracion publica en
          el nivel regional. Lima: 1976.
Peru, Oficina Central de Informacion, La Revolucion
          Nacional Peruana. Lima, 1975.
Peru, Oficina Nacional de la Reforma de la
          Administracion Publica (ONRAP), Diagnostico
          preliminar de la administracion publica
          peruana y propuestas de reforma. Lima:
          December 1965.
_____, Guia del gobierno peruana. Lima: ONRAP, 1969.
Petras, James F., Political and Social Forces in
          Chilean Development. Berkeley: University of
          California Press, 1970.
Pressman, Jeffrey L. and Aaron B. Wildavsky,
          Implementation. Berkeley: University of
          California Press, 1973.
Rachadell, Manuel, "La reforma de la organizacion y el
          regimen del factor humano en la administracion
          publica venezolana." Caracas: n.d.
Radin, Beryl A., Implementation, Change, and the
          Federal Bureaucracy. New York: Teachers
          College Press, Columbia University, 1977.
Ramirez Cardona, Carlos, "Esfuerzos nacionales para la
          reforma administrativa: lecciones de la
          experiencia." Bogota: Unpublished report to
          United Nations, dated May 1, 1967.
Raphaeli, Nimrod (ed.), Readings in Comparative
          Administration. Boston: Allyn and Bacon,
          1967.
Riggs, Fred W., Administration in Developing
          Countries. Boston: Houghton Mifflin, 1964.
_____, Frontiers of Development Administration.
          Durham: Duke University Press, 1970.
_____, Thailand. Honolulu: East-West Center, 1966.
Rofman, Alejandro et. al., Administracion regional en
          America Latina. Buenos Aires: Sociedad
          Interamericana da Planificacion, 1976.
Rosenberg, H., Bureaucracy, Aristocracy, and Auto-
          cracy: The Prussian Experience. Cambridge:
          Harvard University Press, 1958.
Rothman, Jack et. al., Planning and Organizing for
          Social Change. New York: Columbia University
          Press, 1974.

202

Savage, Peter, "Optimism and Pessimism in Comparative
    Administration." Public Administration Review
    (January/February 1976): 415-23.
Schaffer, B. B., "Comparisons, Administration and
    Development." Political Studies (September
    1971): 327-37.
Schmidt, Steffen W., "Bureaucrats as Modernizing
    Brokers?" Comparative Politics (April
    1974): 425-50.
Seidman, Harold, Politics, Position and Power. New
    York: Oxford University Press, 1970.
Siegel, Gilbert B., The Vicissitudes of Governmental
    Reform: A Study of the DASP. Washington:
    University Press of America, 1978.
Siffin, William J., The Thai Bureaucracy. Honolulu:
    East-West Center, 1966.
_____ "Two Decades of Public Administration Research
    in Developing Countries." Public Administra-
    tion Review (January/February 1976): 61-71.
Simon, Herbert, Administrative Behavior. New York:
    The Free Press, 1957.
Smith, Peter, Labyrinths of Power. Princeton:
    Princeton University Press, 1979.
Solomon, Morris J., Fleeming Heegaard, and Kenneth
    Kornher, "An Action-Training Strategy for
    Project Management." International Devel-
    opment Review (XX, 1970): 13-20.
Stepan, Alfred, The State and Society: Peru in
    Comparative Perspective. Princeton:
    Princeton University Press, 1978.
Stewart, William S., Change and Bureaucracies. Chapel
    Hill: University of North Carolina, 1978.
Stifel, Lawrence D., Joseph E. Black and James S.
    Coleman (eds.), Education and Training for
    Public Sector Management in Developing
    Countries. New York: The Rockefeller
    Foundation, 1978.
Stout, Russel, Management or Control? Bloomington:
    Indiana University Press, 1980.
Sutton, Francis X., "American Foundations and Public
    Management in Developing Countries." Studies
    in Comparative International Development (XII,
    2).
Swerdlow, Irving and Marcus Ingle (eds.), Public
    Administration Training for the Less Developed
    Countries. Syracuse: The Maxwell School,
    1973.
Szanton, Peter (ed.), Federal Reorganization: What
    Have We Learned? Chatham, New Jersey:
    Chatham House Press, 1981.

Thomas, Theodore H. and Derick W. Brinkerhoff, "Devo-
        lutionary Strategies for Development Admini-
        stration." American Society for Public
        Administration, 1978.
Thompson, J. D., Organizations in Action. New York:
        McGraw-Hill, 1971.
Thompson, Victor A., "Administrative Objectives for
        Development Administration." Administrative
        Science Quarterly (June 1964): 91-108.
Thurber, Clarence E. and Lawrence S. Graham (eds.),
        Development Administration in Latin America.
        Durham: Duke University Press, 1973.
Tinoco, Pedro, El estado eficaz. Caracas:
        Italgrafico, 1972.
Toffler, Alan, Future Shock. New York: Bantam, 1971.
United Nations, Department of Economic and Social
        Affairs, A Handbook of Public Administration.
        New York: 1961.
United Nations, Department of Economic and Social
        Affairs, Public Administration in Venezuela.
        New York: 1961.
United Nations, Project VEN 44, "Reforma administrativa
        en Venezuela: Informe final del Proyecto."
        Caracas: 1977.
United Nations, Technical Assistance Administration,
        Standards and Techniques of Public Administra-
        tion with Special Reference to Technical
        Assistance for Underdeveloped Countries. New
        York: 1951.
United States Agency for International Development,
        Country Assistance Program, Peru. (1959,
        1962-68, annually).
_____, "Management Development Strategy Paper."
        (Unpublished draft, June 1981).
Venezuela, Comision de Administracion Publica, "El
        factor humano en la administracion publica:
        caso de Venezuela." Caracas, 1973.
_____, Informe sobre la reforma de la
        administracion publica nacional, Vol. I and
        II. Caracas, 1972.
_____, La reforma administrativa en Venezuela,
        1969-1971. Caracas, 1971.
Venezuela, CORDIPLAN, Plan de accion de la reforma
        administrativa 1976-1980. Caracas, 1977.
Venezuela, Office of the President, Programa de gobiero
        de Rafael Caldera, Presidente de Venezuela
        1969-1974. Caracas, 1971.
Vidal, Perdomo Jaime, Derecho administrativo. Cali:
        Biblioteca Banco Popular, 1977.
Villanueva, Victor, El CAEM y la revolucion de la
        fuerza armada. Lima: Instituto de Estudios
        Peruanos, 1972.

204

Waldo, Dwight, "Developments in Public Administration."
        The Annals of the American Academy of Politi-
        cal and Social Science (November 1972).
_____(ed.), Public Administration in a Time of
        Turbulence. Scranton, Penn: Chandler, 1971.
_____(ed.), "Symposium on Comparative and
        Development Administration." Public Admini-
        stration Review (November/December 1976).
White, Jr., Orin F., "The Dialectical Organization: An
        Alternative to Bureaucracy." Public Admini-
        stration Review (January/February 1969).
Wickwar, W. Hardy, The Modernization of Administration
        in the Near East. Beirut: Khayats, 1962.
Wynia, Gary, Politics and Planners. Madison: Univer-
        sity of Wisconsin Press, 1972.

Index